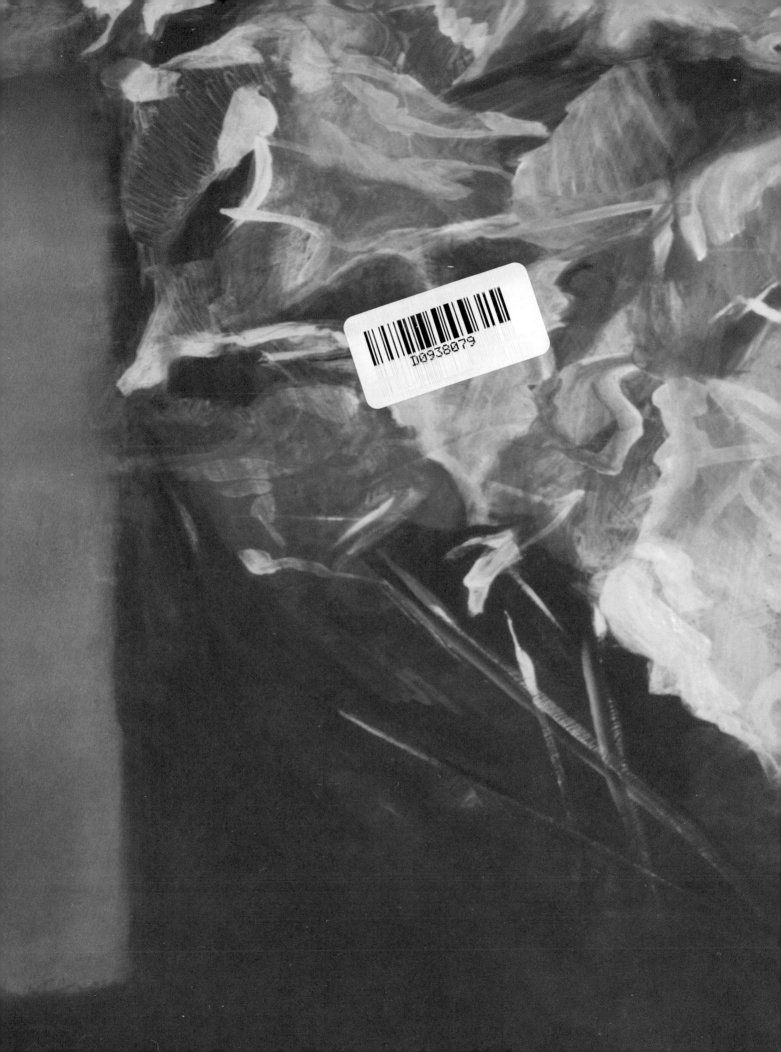

¡Concha!

Concha Ortiz y Pino

Matriarch of a 300-Year-Old New Mexico Legacy

By

Kathryn M. Córdova

¡Concha!

Concha Ortiz y Pino

Matriarch of a 300-Year-Old New Mexico Legacy

A *La Herencia* Publication

Editor/Publisher
Ana Pacheco

Editor
Richard McCord

Librarian
Theresa A. Strottman

Spanish Editor
A. Samuel Adelo

Art Director
Patrice Nightingale

Associate Editors
Walter K. López
Ree Strange Sheck
Nancy Zimmerman

Book Cover Design
Wes Fallon

Inside Front Cover Art by Jane Mahon
Inside Back Cover Photo of Galisteo Cemetery
Courtesy Concha Ortiz y Pino de Kleven

FIRST EDITION

ISBN 0-9743022-1-X
Library of Congress Control Number: 2004116055

Gran Via Incorporated
PO Box 22576
Santa Fe, NM 87502
www.herencia.com

¡Concha!

Concha Ortiz y Pino

Matriarch of a 300-Year-Old New Mexico Legacy

Dedicated to
Concha Ortiz y Pino de Kleven,
Ana Pacheco
and my family.
To Concha for providing such great material,
for without something to say, an author cannot complete a book;
to Ana for her confidence in me and for involving me in the project;
and to my family for living the book with me while I completed my work.

Concha Ortiz y Pino, age 14—courtesy Ron Ortiz Dinkel

¡Concha!

The Authorized Biography of Concha Ortiz y Pino de Kleven

Contents

Chapter 1: Her Name is Concha! 1

Chapter 2: Illustrious Ancestors 3

Chapter 3: Mamá Fita, Home Life, y *la Familia* 9

Chapter 4: A Village Grows 15

Chapter 5: Birth and Statehood 19

Chapter 6: Childhood in Galisteo 25

Chapter 7: Bluebelle 33

Chapter 8: Learning 41

Chapter 9: Political Roots 47

Chapter 10: The Depression and the FDR Caravan 53

Chapter 11: The Legislative Frontier 59

Chapter 12: The Man, Victor Kleven 65

Chapter 13: Agua Verde Ranch 77

Chapter 14: The Family 89

Chapter 15: Through the Lens of Robert H. Martin 107

Chapter 16: Choosing to Serve 135

Chapter 17: Sacred Moments 145

Chapter 18: Friends Along the Way 155

Chapter 19: Mixing and Mingling 161

Chapter 20: Honors Come 173

Epilogue: Into the Future 183

Acknowledgments

María Elena Álvarez

Adrián Bustamante

María Catanach

Center for Southwest Research, University of New Mexico (Albuquerque)

Center for Southwest Research of Northern New Mexico (Taos)

Arsenio Córdova

Theresa J. N. Córdova

Angélico Chávez History Library, Museum of New Mexico

José Antonio Esquibel

Judy Hasted

Robert H. Martin

Nita Murphy

Concha Ortiz y Pino de Kleven

Ron Ortiz Dinkel

Margo Ortiz y Davis Truscott

Jerry Ortiz y Pino

José Ortiz y Pino III

Loretta Ortiz y Pino

María Ortiz y Pino

Ana Pacheco, *La Herencia* Magazine

Gov. Bill Richardson

Rowena A. Rivera

Andrés Segura

Marc Simmons

University of New Mexico–Los Alamos Library

Susan Varela

Address Delivered by Gov. Bill Richardson July 16, 2004
On the Occasion of the Dedication of the Concha Ortiz y Pino Building
Reprinted by Permission of the Governor's Communication Office

I am honored to be with you today to pay tribute to *doña* Concha Ortiz y Pino, a true New Mexican, a pioneer, who has served her state and her community honorably for decades. As a legislator, educator, community activist and philanthropist, throughout her life she has worked to provide opportunities for her fellow citizens, she has fought for equality for women, and she has opened many doors that previously had been closed to her gender. From this day forward, this building will be known as the Concha Ortiz y Pino Building.

La historia de la familia Ortiz es una parte del entramado cultural de Nuevo México. Her family history is woven into the fabric of New Mexico. In fact, the Ortiz family has been a force in politics since even before New Mexico was a territory. In the early 1800s, *doña* Concha's great-grandfather, Pedro Bautista Pino, a rancher, was first elected mayor of Tomé, and ultimately was elected to represent the province of New Mexico to the Spanish Parliament. Public service is definitely in the Ortiz blood.

Concha Ortiz y Pino was born and raised in Galisteo. She attended Loretto Academy in Santa Fe, and after high school returned to Galisteo, where she founded the state's first vocational school. She taught the traditional arts and crafts of New Mexico, including woodworking and weaving. *Doña* Concha believes in celebrating and embracing one's culture and heritage, while at the same time pursuing education and advancement.

Eventually, *doña* Concha followed in her great-grandfather's footsteps, and was elected to the New Mexico State Legislature in 1936 at the tender age of 26. She was the first woman in the United States to be elected majority whip in a state legislature, and she was re-elected twice to the New Mexico Legislature.

It is fitting that this building, so connected to education, will bear the name of Concha Ortiz y Pino. She has always passionately fought to give *every* New Mexico child access to the best possible education. *Doña* Concha co-sponsored the first legislation to equalize funding in New Mexico schools. She understood the importance of being bilingual and passed a law to teach Spanish to seventh- and eighth-grade students. She served as chairwoman of the Institutions for Higher Learning. Ultimately, *doña* Concha earned a degree in Inter-American Affairs from the University of New Mexico, and later became dean of women, and taught at St. Joseph College.

Doña Concha's commitment to her community, and her country was recognized by several American presidents—President John F. Kennedy appointed her to the National Council of Upward Bound, President Lyndon Johnson named her to the National Commission on Architectural Barriers and President Gerald Ford appointed her to the National Endowment for the Humanities.

Doña Concha has never really "retired" from public service. She has always remained active, and dedicated to helping her fellow New Mexicans. She served on many boards and foundations including the Albuquerque Symphony Orchestra, the Board of Regents of the University of Albuquerque, the New Mexico Arts Commission, and the Albuquerque Hispanic Culture Foundation.

Doña Concha is a true New Mexican treasure. Her pioneering work as a legislator, advocate for her fellow women, educator, and community activist has improved the lives of countless New Mexicans, and has forever changed New Mexico for the better. For that, we say *gracias, doña* Concha.

I am proud to know her, and pleased she is with us today. I am honored to officially designate this the **Concha Ortiz y Pino Building**.

Foreword

Concha Ortiz y Pino

by Kathryn M. Córdova

When Ana Pacheco, publisher of *La Herencia* magazine, asked me to write a book about Concha Ortiz y Pino de Kleven, she stated her reason succinctly: "I find it astonishing that while countless newspaper and magazine writers have found Concha a marvelous subject for an article, no one has ever pulled her amazing life together into one book." In the pages that follow, that long-overdue omission has now been addressed.

Ana's assignment started out for me as a job—a piece of work. Although I, like most people in New Mexico, knew who Concha was, and even was familiar with her courtly appearance, I was not personally acquainted with her. But suddenly I had been tapped to tell her life story. I admit to some trepidation in approaching this legendary woman: *"La Grande Dame de Nuevo México."* I was fascinated by her 90-plus years, her history-making legislative service, her awards, her honors, her personal letters from governors and presidents and Spanish nobility, her incredible philanthropy aiding almost-countless causes. I felt somewhat inconsequential by comparison.

I needn't have worried. From our first meeting, Concha put me at ease. A few meetings later, I considered Concha a close friend. Right away, she and I discovered that we knew many people in common, some of them my relatives. More and more I began to look forward to our visits, and no two were ever the same. Always the perfect hostess, Concha would serve me coffee and cookies. *"Comadrita,"* she would say—a term of endearment, meaning co-mother, good friend— "come to the party." And then we'd get down to work.

Awaiting my arrival was a small table, with pen and paper and the files of material we would work on that day. Out came old scrapbooks with yellowing letters and articles. Plaques and awards lined her walls, and when Concha saw me attempting to write down the exact words, she helped by reading them aloud to me. Because she had donated many of her papers to the Southwest Research Center of the University of New Mexico, I sometimes went there instead of to her home. In that repository I marveled at photos of her with President John F. Kennedy or ventriloquist Edgar Bergen, or a handwritten note to her from movie legend Clark Gable. A special treat Concha provided for me one day was a tour of the assisted-living wing of the retirement home in Santa Fe, where she lives. "I want you to meet my friends and neighbors and all my boyfriends," Concha said, and introduced me to everyone there.

Perhaps the most magical days for me were the ones we spent in her photo albums. There Concha was, with politicians, an ambassador, the prince of Spain, members of the Ortiz y Pino family, her husband Victor. There she was in Egypt, London, Spain, Mexico, South America, with ethnic dancers, poor villagers, children, churches, castles, the pyramids. A few pages later, in dirt-streaked working clothes she stood among sheep at her ranch; or in crisp business attire she spoke into a microphone; or in a dark dress she sat reading quietly in a chair. In some pictures she was attired in a mantilla and fan, or a long fiesta skirt, or formal white gloves and hat.

Sometimes her hair was pulled into a bun, sometimes it was medium-length, sometimes short, sometimes fashioned into in the elaborate pompadour that became her trademark. In one picture a rose was in her hair. In another a little white poodle followed her around her kitchen. In flashy sunglasses she rowed a boat, in sturdy adventuring gear she stood beside a small "puddle-jumper" airplane. One picture showed her surrounded by friends and family at a long table, sucking in her breath to blow out the candles on a birthday cake. And one showed her with Santa Fe Archbishop Michael Sheehan. "You know what he was telling me in that picture?" Concha asked me with a laugh. "'You never do what I tell you!' And he was right."

Generous with her time, Concha told me the story of every picture. And before our work was done, she had told me the story of her life. The assignment that was a challenge at first had evolved into a privilege, a thrill, an honor. *The story of Concha's life!* With gratitude and respect, I now pass her story on to you.

Capítulo 1
Se llama Concha

Este tomo contiene la historia de una mujer. Su nombre completo, largo, y melodioso es Concepción María Ortiz y Pino de Kleven. Sin embargo, su verdadero nombre—el que usan miles de parientes y amigos, el nombre que más de 19 gobernadores de Nuevo México, seis presidentes de los Estados Unidos de Norteamérica han usado, igual que un sinnúmero de políticos del estado y de la nación, el nombre inscrito en docenas de premios y pergaminos, el nombre grabado en letras metálicas en el edificio de gobierno en Santa Fe y el nombre bajo el cual se convirtió en leyenda viva es su apodo "Concha."

Este libro es la historia de una familia y, por supuesto, la historia de la sucesión de muchas familias, la prole de familias de ascendencia hispánica y de ascendencia angloamericana en Nuevo México. Es la historia de los dos linajes familiares, hispánicos, angloamericanos de raza blanca y negra.

El enfoque de este libro es Concha, mujer de dos linajes ancestrales, el linaje hispánico y el linaje anglosajón que se distinguió en Nuevo México que ha vivido una vida buena y con entusiasmo. A través de la historia de Concha el lector logra ver indios y vaqueros, violencia y dedicación, la vida aldeana y la vida metropolitana, el poder legislativo del gobierno, y la vida de una persona dedicada a mejorar el nivel de vida de personas humildes, las bellas artes, la cultura hispánica, y la formación de la juventud.

Este tomo conserva para generaciones posteriores la exquisita historia de una distinguida mujer que ha vivido una vida benéfica y que personifica las cuatro virtudes: la fe, la esperanza, el amor, y la caridad.

Her Name is Concha!

This book is the story of a woman. Her long and melodious full name is María Concepción Ortiz y Pino de Kleven. But her real name—the one used by thousands of relatives and friends, the one used by 19 New Mexico governors, by at least six U. S. presidents, and by countless other state and national politicians, the one inscribed on dozens of award certificates, the one installed in timeless metal on a government building in Santa Fe, and the one under which she became a living legend—is her nickname: "Concha."

This book is the story of a family—or, of course, the story of many family streams that all flowed together in the endless river of time: the Pinos, the Ortizes, the Bacas, the Raels, the Senas, the Gómezes, the Bustamantes, the Gonzaleses, the Vigils; and on the Anglo side, the Davises, the Jacksons, the Dinkels, the Martins, the Hasteds, the Klevens. Some family members came to New Mexico from Spain in the 16th and 17th centuries, when the New World was young. Others came from Yankee or Rebel families that served with honor in the American Civil War. Many members were born and grew up in New Mexico. Others discovered New Mexico later in life, loved it, and never left.

This book is a story of history, beginning back in the mist, when native people lived, loved, and died in this land without leaving behind a written record, except for indelible images chiseled into rock. This is a story of bold Spanish *conquistadores*, succeeded by loyal but faraway subjects of Spain, then by proud *Mejicanos* staking claim to their own territory, then by the brash American nation, not yet 100 years old, on its inexorable march from the Atlantic Ocean to the Pacific. This is the story of a Southwestern land and its quest for a place as one of the United States of America, and then becoming and growing as one.

Concha Ortiz y Pino de Kleven—photo by Robert H. Martin

This is the story of races, of bloodlines—Native American, Hispanic, Anglo, African American. It is a story of Indians and cowboys, violence and dedication, wagon trains and atomic bombs, politics and compassion, very long lives and tragic young deaths, voting rights for women, the Great Depression, village fiestas and spectacular occasions, pride and humility, religious devotion, travel to many lands, accolades at high levels, funerals in tiny cemeteries.

This book is the story of a woman. Her name is Concha Ortiz y Pino de Kleven. She was born in 1910. In 2004 she reached her 94th birthday. As a child she spoke only Spanish, and did not learn English until she was 10 years old—and even then, most unwillingly. Along the lengthy track of her life, Concha became a college student in Washington, D.C., a state legislator in New Mexico, a faculty wife at the University of New Mexico, the boss-lady of a 100,000-acre ranch, a widow, a board member of 60 or more organizations working to make the world a better place, a champion for women and the handicapped and Hispanic culture and the arts and the poor. She has been inducted into halls of fame, has posed for official busts and portraits, has been honored on both sides of the Atlantic Ocean. She has officially been declared a treasure in Santa Fe, in Albuquerque, and by the state of New Mexico. And countless individual people, big and small, treasure her personally, as their friend.

This book is the story of a woman, and of a life well-lived, with passion and with love. This is the story of ¡Concha!

Capítulo 2
Ilustres antepasados

Pedro Bautista, tataranieto de uno de los capitanes que acompañó a Diego de Vargas en la Reconquista de Santa Fe en 1692 fue uno de los ascendientes de Concha Ortiz y Pino de Kleven.

Don Pedro nació y se crió en Nuevo México y falleció en 1829. Fue uno de los ciudadanos más acaudalados de su época. Según cuenta Concha, la vida de la familia Pino era formal, sociable, de graciosidad, y afectuosa al más humilde de sus vecinos." Los descendientes de don Pedro se distinguen por su idealismo político, su sentido de obligación a la comunidad, y fervor a su religión.

Con respecto a la Provincia de Nuevo México, la fidelidad y el patriotismo saltan a la vista en la exposición sucinta y sencilla que Pedro Bautista Pino, como diputado, presentó a las Cortes de Cádiz en 1812. Esa exposición manifiesta que don Pedro era un hombre de formación bien arraigada y cuidadoso observador que estaba bien enterado respecto a la geografía, historia, recursos, y grupos sociales de la provincia del Nuevo México. Bien redactado, el informe de don Pedro estaba repleto de "verdades desnudas y descubiertas por la práctica." En el informe acertado, don Pedro critica al gobierno español porque se había descuidado del bienestar de los habitantes de Nuevo México. El afecto y compasión que sentía don Pedro por la población de Nuevo México se refleja en su informe.

Illustrious Ancestors

Many proud New Mexico families trace their lineage to the early colonists who came from Spain to settle this harsh land and wrest it from the native inhabitants. The Ortiz y Pino family is one. Its first notable ancestor directly linked to this distant New World frontier has the peculiar distinction of being honored with the title of "Thief," directly from the King of Spain. His name was Nicolás Ortiz, and his full title was Nicolás Ortiz Niño Ladrón de Guevara—which translates, roughly, into: "Nicolás Ortiz, Boy Thief of Guevara." He lived from 1653 until 1742.

The story behind the title goes like this: At the age of 15 Nicolás left his boyhood pastimes to join the Spanish army in its last campaign against the Moors. When his captain was killed in battle, the youthful Nicolás took command of the forces and gained the last stronghold of the Moors, in Guevara. For this victory the King bestowed upon his family the somewhat ironic name "Ladrón," which means "Thief." To the family coat of arms was then added a bear's paw and a torch.

With his love of adventure still burning as he neared the age of 40, Nicolás joined Gen. *don* Diego de Vargas as a captain in the 1692 campaign to regain control of the colony of New Mexico, which had been lost to the Spanish in the 1680 Pueblo Revolt. After the Reconquest, Nicolás and his wife settled in Santa Fe, and raised six children. A great-grandson of Nicolás was *don* Pedro Bautista Pino, another

A composite drawing of Don Pedro Bautista Pino, Concha's great-great-grandfather by Ramor Baumann Ortiz—courtesy Concha Ortiz y Pino de Kleven

illustrious ancestor of today's Ortiz y Pino descendants, and one still remembered keenly. One of the first phrases likely to be heard by anyone meeting Concha Ortiz y Pino de Kleven is her proud proclamation: *"Pedro Bautista Pino was my great-great-grandfather."*

The reason why this declaration is so emphatic is found in the life story of *don* Pedro, who was born and died in New Mexico, and lived from 1752 until the late 1830s or early 1840s. He was one of seven sons of Mateo José and María (Sánchez) Pino, who raised their family in the vicinity of Isleta Pueblo and Rancho de San Clemente. Both Mateo José and his father before him, Juan Bautista, made their living as merchants traveling to and from Mexico City. In 1768 the young Pedro moved from San Clemente to Santa Fe, which remained his home until he died. Church burial records from that time have been lost, but his family states with certainty that he was laid to rest in Santa Fe.

Accounts of Spanish Colonial life of the time reveal a society of mixed blood, native and European. Much of the population consisted of farmers and artisans, some of whom, including *don* Pedro, were educated and others of whom were illiterate and superstitious. With fierce and unpredictable weather, Indian attacks, and isolation and lack of attention from a weakening and uncaring government in Spain, conditions were difficult for everyone. Yet some prospered while others struggled, and *don* Pedro emerged as one of the colony's wealthiest citizens. He owned much land and many herds of sheep, employed many villagers, and was regarded as a wise, fair *patrón*.

The HISTORICAL SOCIETY of NEW MEXICO

invites you to participate in a

HISTORICAL EVENT,

honoring NEW MEXICO'S ONLY DELEGATE to

The CORTES in CÁDIZ, SPAIN, in 1810

DON PEDRO BAUTISTA PINO

October 19, 1975   3 p.m.

Palace of the Governors

Santa Fe   New Mexico

"While residing in Spain, he (Pino) made and published a report descriptive of New Mexico, its people and government, which is one of the most valuable documents connected with New Mexico history."

L. Bradford Prince

Don Pedro Bautista Pino's report to the Cortes (Parliament) was published in Cádiz, Spain in 1812 under the title of "LA EXPOSICIÓN SUCINTA Y SENCILLA DE LA PROVINCIA DEL NUEVO MÉXICO."

As Concha tells it, the Pino family lived a life of formality, sociability, graciousness and kindness, "to the least of their neighbors." It was a life—passed down to descendants—of political idealism, social obligation, and religious fervor. *Don* Pedro's credo, Concha says, was "My Country (he served with distinction under both the Spanish and Mexican governments), My Religion (with honor to God and charity to man), and My Family (which encompassed his immediate family, his relatives, and all 22 people living in his household, whether or not connected to him by blood)."

In this frontier society *don* Pedro assumed roles of leadership. In the early 1800s he was chosen as a municipal councilman. The governor also asked Pino to act as his agent to review documents and land claims. In addition, he gained a singular distinction when New Mexico's mayors designated him the colony's lone delegate to a special convening of the *Cortes*, Spain's highest governing body, called by the king in 1810 to fortify the Spanish empire against the rising threat of Napoleon in France. Even little New Mexico was asked to send one man to help in this emergency.

Don Pedro took this obligation most seriously—so much so that he set out in 1811, at his own expense, to travel all the way to Spain and actually take his seat in the *Cortes*. Beyond helping with the Napoleonic crisis, however, he decided to also state the harsh conditions of life in faraway Nuevo México, and to request help and funding from the colony's distant rulers. In high hopes for the success of his mission, *don* Pedro's fellow New Mexicans gathered about $9,000 in the currency of the time as a contribution to the Spanish cause. Raising this sum was not easy. Some contributors went so deeply into debt, it was said, that they "sacrificed the liberty of their sons."

Don Pedro's journey began in October, 1811. By land he traveled to the Mexican port city of Veracruz, some "900 leagues" (2,700 miles) from Santa Fe by his own reckoning, and then by sea he continued another "1,900 leagues" (5,700 miles) to Spain. When he set foot on Spanish soil, he became the first person born in New Mexico ever to visit the mother country. Yet by the time he reached the city of Cádiz, the seat of the *Cortes*, the assembly was no longer in session, and he was too late to claim his seat that year—a major disappointment.

Quickly making the most of the situation, however, Pino made contact with important officials and a journalist, and in 1812 the report he had planned to make to the *Cortes* was published, under the title *La Exposición sucinta y sencilla de la provincia del Nuevo México* ("The brief and simple exposition of the province of New Mexico"). Then he also delivered his report in person to the 1812 session of the *Cortes*.

For many Spanish leaders, his account was the first detailed account of New Mexico they had seen, and it told them things they had not known. It proclaimed some two centuries of loyalty to Spain, from poor citizens living in an almost-lawless territory under the constant threat of warfare with marauding Indians. Pino reported that military needs of New Mexico received no funding from the Crown, that citizens themselves paid for supplies and ammunition. He recommended establishing five *presidios*, or forts, at strategic points around the province, instead of having just one, in Santa Fe. He urged Spain to establish a military academy in New Mexico to train professional soldiers, and to sell the main military building in Santa Fe. He suggested that citizens pressed into militia duty be paid for their services. He also sounded an early warning about the expansionist ambitions of the young American nation to the east, whose agents were slipping around telling the Indians that the Spanish were not invincible.

Don Pedro's report had many other requests of the king, which in sum he called "this most urgent aid for the relief of the province in order that it may begin to enjoy its legitimate prosperity." He asked that a bishopric be established in Santa Fe, and noted that the province had not seen a bishop for 50 years. He sought a seminary college of higher learning in Santa Fe, and public schools for the instruction of youth. He pleaded for a civil and criminal *audiencia* (court) for New Mexico to be established in Chihuahua, Mexico, instead of far-distant Guadalajara. "Is there any other province six hundred leagues from the seat of the administration of justice?" he asked. "There is no such province, no matter how miserably poor it may be."

Narciso Pino, Concha's great-uncle. Photo by W. Henry Brown—courtesy Museum of New Mexico, negative no. 10335

Pino went on to describe life in the peaceful Indian pueblos of New Mexico. The residents there were for the most part honest and truthful, he reported, and they possessed critical thinking skills. They also had the impressive foresight to protect and conserve their food supply, he noted. The Spanish friars among the Indians contributed greatly, Pino said, teaching the natives to read and write in Spanish, and to worship God. Still, he predicted the coming end of the ancient native way of life.

In the courtly language of the day, he beseeched King Ferdinand VII: "I have the honor of counting myself among those who constitute this sovereign congress in Spain, and the further honor personally to request of your majesty a remedy for the unfortunate condition of (my) province....In spite of the fact that I, disregarding my old age and infirmities, had to leave my family, composed of 22 persons, and notwithstanding all the hardships which I have had to endure, I shall consider these labors well spent if they contribute to remedy those misfortunes which afflict my fellow countrymen."

After delivering the report on his home province, *don* Pedro remained in Cádiz until 1814 and attended sessions of the *Cortes* subsequent to the one he missed. He became something of a celebrity among his colleagues, who called him the "Abraham of New Mexico," in a reference to the patriarch of Israel in the Bible's Old Testament. His recommendations were even formally adopted by the *Cortes*—but unfortunately, continuing European troubles and revolutions in the New World prevented Spain from actually doing anything to improve conditions on the ground in New Mexico.

The *Cortes* were dissolved in 1814, and Pino left Spain to return home. Along the way, he made stops in Paris and in London, where he acquired a splendid covered carriage, called a landau, which accompanied him on his journey. Eventually he arrived back in Santa Fe, where eager citizens awaited word of the results of his mission. He reported that his appeals had been approved; but as time went by with no visible changes, cynical New Mexicans came up with a terse phrase to sum up his epic: *"Don Pedro Pino fue, don Pedro Pino vino."*—*"Don* Pedro went away, *don* Pedro came back." The harsh implication was that nothing had happened as a result. Even so, when the next *Cortes* were convened, in 1820, *don* Pedro was again chosen to be New Mexico's representative. Once more he set out for Spain, but this time his travel funds ran out in Veracruz, and he never sailed again across the sea.

Despite the "old age and infirmities" that *don* Pedro cited in his 1812 appeal to the king, he was married four years later, in 1816, to Ana María Baca, a descendant of Captain Nicolás Ortiz, Ladrón de Guevarra. (Pino's earlier wives had died.) Their union produced five children, Hermán, Guadalupe de la Trinidad, Miguel Estanislao, José Facundo, and Nicolás de Jesús, who became Concha's great-grandfather.

To his contemporary fellow citizens, perhaps the most tangible evidence of *don* Pedro's long journey was his fine landau carriage, which he continued to use for many years, frequently inviting friends, rich and poor alike, to share with him. In the eyes of historians, however, Pino's contribution proved invaluable, for his *Exposición* set down on paper a detailed and accurate account of life in New Mexico at the time when Spain's rule would soon be supplanted by the rule of Mexico. In the words of the eminent New Mexico historian Ralph Emerson Twitchell: "To this work we are indebted for almost all the information of this period."

Also now officially indebted to *don* Pedro Bautista Pino are the country of Spain, which honored him in a 1975 ceremony in Cádiz; and the New Mexico Legislature and the U.S. Congress, which followed with tributes to him that same year.

Such honors notwithstanding, the words of Concha Ortiz y Pino de Kleven are sharp even now, almost 200 years later, and still a little bitter when she reflects upon her dedicated ancestor and his efforts on behalf of his native New Mexico: "Spain let us down," she says. "Some family members never got over the fact that *don* Pedro was ignored. So were the people in the colonies. My grandmother Josefa never forgave Spain for what happened. She was so hurt that she vowed to marry a true-blue American, not a Hispanic man."

Mamá Fita, la vida en el hogar, y la familia

Josefa Ortiz, nieta de Pedro Bautista Ortiz, desilusionada por el descuido de España de los habitantes de la Provincia de Nuevo México, eligió casarse con un hombre que no era de ascendencia española. Así fue que Josefa eligió a Sylvester Davis que fuera su esposo. Davis había venido de Massachusetts a Nuevo México después de la Guerra Civil en los Estados Unidos. La actitud de Josefa reflejaba la desilusión de su familia respecto a España.

Matriarca de la familia Ortiz y Davis, Mamá Fita, además de criar a la familia, recibía en su hogar a huéspedes de categoría: generales, arzobispos, gobernadores, ex-soldados de ambos ejércitos de la Guerra Civil, y a mucha gente pobre que necesitaba un lugar donde reposar. Además de ser anfitriona por excelencia, doña Josefa era la curandera del pueblo. Según cuenta doña Concha, "Mi abuelita hablaba inglés y español y era la patrona de Galisteo." Doña Concha articuladamente recuerda a sus tíos Sylvester, George, Juan, y Frank, a sus tías Victoria y Josefita, y a su mamá Pablita quien le ayudaba a doña Josefa con las tareas del inmenso hogar, eje de la comunidad de Galisteo.

En junio de 1897, José Ortiz y Pino se casó con su prima Pablita.

Mamá Fita, Home Life y la Familia

3

True to her vow, Josefa Ortiz, the proud granddaughter of *don* Pedro Bautista Pino, did not seek a husband among the young Hispanic men of New Mexico. Bitter because of Spain's failure to deliver on the promises it gave *don* Pedro during his epic voyage to the Spanish *Cortes* in 1811–14 as an emissary of the remote Nuevo México colony, she held to her rash statement that she would marry only a "true-blue American." And that is what she did, choosing a man named Sylvester Davis from Massachusetts, who visited the area with friends after his service with the Union Army in the Civil War.

In Concha's memory, the exact words spoken by her grandmother were: "*Mis hijos no se crearán aquí. Quiero que se pasen como americanos.*" ("My sons will not be raised here. I want them to be known as Americans.") New Mexico had become an American possession, and Josefa, who was born in 1853 and grew up in a land that was part of the United States, often said, "This won't be Spain, but Spanish New Mexico." Her attitude reflected not only her family's sense of disappointment with Spain for its treatment of *don* Pedro, but also the widespread wishes of citizens in the young territory to blend in with the American occupants. Many marriages between American newcomers and Spanish and other residents marked life in New Mexico at that time.

Capt. Sylvester Davis with his wife Josefa Ortiz y Ortiz, Pablita's mother, and their first son, George—courtesy Concha Ortiz y Pino de Kleven

Sylvester Davis was a proper Bostonian—a "blue-blood" as they were called, in keeping with Josefa's "true-blue" vow. In the notes of a later son-in-law, José Ortiz y Pino of Galisteo, "Captain Sylvester Davis was descendant from the Davis family in England who founded the pearl button business, and the family has the gold-tipped cane that the Davis family was given by Queen Victoria of England on founding that industry. Captain Sylvester Davis's Daily Diary, which he kept when he left Massachusetts to come to New Mexico, has been of great value to the Archives of New Mexico."

Sylvester was a geologist by training, but after his marriage he remained in New Mexico, learned Spanish, and became a rancher. He settled in the village of Galisteo, about 20 miles south of Santa Fe, the longtime home of his wife's family. But taking advantage of American homesteading laws, he also established a ranch in neighboring Torrance County, south of Santa Fe and east of Albuquerque.

When Sylvester Davis arrived in Galisteo, *don* Nicolás Pino, Concha's great-grandfather, was the *patrón* and dominant force in Galisteo. Son of *don* Pedro Bautista Pino, Nicolás controlled the vast grazing lands of the entire Galisteo basin. Juan Ortiz, Concha's grandfather, succeeded Nicolás as *patrón*. When Juan Ortiz married Concepción Pino, they joined their names and passed along to their children the Ortiz y Pino surname. While the Davis holdings were substantial, it was the Ortiz y Pino hacienda and mercantile store that

Pedro, Pablita, and Manuela—
courtesy Concha Ortiz y Pino
de Kleven

Davis holdings were substantial, it was the Ortiz y Pino hacienda and mercantile store that were the social and business center of Galisteo.

America's concept of Manifest Destiny, a phrase coined in the 1840s, called for constant westward expansion, because—so the doctrine held—the United States was divinely ordained to occupy the North American continent from the Atlantic Ocean to the Pacific. This quasi-theological quest was driven in large part by programs to make cheap or free land available to Americans moving west. The Pre-Emption Act of 1841 gave citizens the option of buying land for $1.25 an acre or acquiring it without cost by living on it for five years. Then in the midst of the Civil War, the Homestead Act of 1862 provided tracts of western land from the public domain, not to exceed 160 acres, for citizens who were head of a family, 21 years old, or a veteran of at least 14 days of service in the U.S. armed forces. To acquire the land, the homesteader was obliged to settle on the land or cultivate it for five years. From 1863 to 1900, about 5 million families acquired land in this manner. One of them was the Davis family, which claimed 160 acres for its Torrance County ranch.

Much of the development of the ranch was turned over to the four sons of Josefa and Sylvester. Concha has sharp thumbnail memories of all her mother's brothers. "Uncle Sylvester, named after Grandpa, was a very smart individual," she says. "Uncle George was a devil, harmless and full of fun. He was a very gentle, tall, kind, drinking man. Uncle John was a sweet, sweet man. He was gentle, saintly and very kind. He loved to do *maromas* (cartwheels) in the pool hall. Uncle Frank was a businessman who worked hard and became rich. Grandpa was quite a rancher. He taught his sons to work with the cattle. They became leading ranchers in Torrance County."

While the Davis boys were doing well in the early 1900s, however, many of the neighboring homesteaders dwelled in far more basic circumstances. Their flimsy homes, referred to as "Texas houses," consisted of two or four rooms framed with 2x4s and sided with 1x12 planks. Tar paper covered the outside surface of the frame, with 1x4 strips of wood nailed in place as a final layer of protection against the elements. Residents of these houses could hear the noise of rain or hail falling on the corrugated iron roofs. To soften the interiors, women lined the walls with cheesecloth sewn together and tacked on. In winter the residents kept warm with wood stoves, but the summer weather proved quite uncomfortable, with the relentless sun causing inescapable discomfort. The spring winds and sandstorms maddeningly pushed dirt and dust in between the cracks in the houses.

Torrance County was a bustling area for the railroad, which served many points along the tracks. Willard, a booming town in the south-central part of the county, included three hotels, two restaurants, two general stores, a newspaper, a drugstore, a bakery, a blacksmith shop, a livery stable, two grocery stores, several real estate firms, two dance halls, and three saloons. The dance halls did not allow liquor, serving mainly as meeting halls, a place for public and fiesta dances, weddings and engagement parties, attended by both adults and children. A small building doubled as a schoolhouse and a church. In the one-room schoolhouse students were taught for seven months of the year and went through eighth grade. Its graduates could get state certification to become teachers if they so desired. Though the building was called Union Church, all denominations shared the premises. Most of the county's farms really needed deep wells for agricultural activities, but few of the farmers could afford the cost. Therefore frequent digging for shallow wells remained commonplace.

Although the Torrance County ranch was prospering, Galisteo remained the Davis family's primary residence, and they were leading citizens of the village. Presiding over Galisteo's most prominent and generous family, Sylvester and Josefa were accorded the courtesy titles of "*don*" and "*doña*," which derive from the Spanish phrase "*de origen noble,*" or "of noble origin." Under Spanish tradition this sign of respect is used for people whose actions and stature in the community warrant it. The large Davis house, surrounded by high walls and huge barred gates, included a *placita* (a courtyard situated in or near the center of a large family dwelling), as well as a blacksmith shop, storehouses, and spacious gardens, all of which provided functional beauty to the premises. But when Indian raids came along from time to time, the home became a refuge for neighbors.

Beyond her many duties as matriarch there, Josefa also played several other roles in the community. A constant stream of guests flowed through her large hacienda, where she served as hostess extraordinaire. About 18 people—family and staff—lived there full-time, and visitors included generals, archbishops, governors, former soldiers of both the Confederate and Union armies, and many a poor person who needed a place to stay. People called it "*Doña* Josefita's Inn."

Josefa was also the village *curandera*, or healer. "She knew all about herbs, and helped deliver babies and bury the dead," Concha remembers. "Sometimes she was assisted by Doctor Friend Palmer, a good friend of the family. But he lived in the nearby village of Kennedy, and transportation was much slower than it is now, so residents could not easily receive medical help in emergencies. Besides, the physician's main duty was to care for people associated with the railroad, which paid his salary. So he taught her how to work on broken bones in addition to the other things she had learned.

"There were many facets to Grandma— Mamá Fita, as I called her," Concha says with pride. "She was the heart and brains of the community. Grandma was the complete boss of Galisteo. She really loved her people. Some said she was the memory of the village. She remembered all the important dates, who people were, when they were baptized, and by whom. When the politicians came calling, it wasn't the men—including my grandfather—they went to talk with first. It was Grandma. They valued her advice and her wisdom. The people valued her sense of judgment. She always ruled through gentleness." For fun, Mamá Fita enjoyed Spanish riddles, called *adivinanzas*.

Don Gaspar Ortiz y Alarid, Juan Ortiz' first cousin; drawing by Charles Batchelor—courtesy Museum of New Mexico, negative no. 50613

Doña Josefa was fluent in both English and Spanish, which remained her primary language. Her husband learned Spanish, and loved his Hispanic neighbors. But Josefa insisted that her sons concentrate on English, which she saw as the language of their future. They were educated in English by the Christian Brothers in Santa Fe. Their sisters got along in both languages, for their foremost training consisted of learning how to run a successful household. The times called for defined roles, in which the men were groomed to run a business, while women were expected to raise a family. Thus the three Davis daughters—Victoria, Josefita, and Concha's future mother, Pablita—learned how to help *doña* Josefa manage the huge and sprawling household, the hub of the community.

* * *

Mamá Fita, Home Life, y la Familia

Pablita Ortiz y Davis wearing the first gold necklace from the Ortiz Mountains mine—courtesy Concha Ortiz y Pino de Kleven

José Ortiz y Pino—courtesy Concha Ortiz y Pino de Kleven

Concha's future father, José Ortiz y Pino, was one of Josefa's nephews, a son of her brother Juan. He was born in 1874 and grew up in Galisteo. As a young man he started out with a parcel of land in the center of the village. He built a house there and owned many sheep that he fattened, butchered, and sold for profit. He had a lively mind and loved stories and riddles, but above all he worked constantly to acquire more land, and more money. He made arrangements with homesteaders at Agua Verde, a huge ranch tract near Las Vegas, N.M., to live on the land, cultivate it, and raise animals with José's financial support, then share with him the profits from selling the livestock.

For practical purposes, José seemed to have all that a young man could desire, except for a wife and family. Then the vivacious Pablita Davis stirred his romantic attentions. But the young man and woman lived in an age of rigid courtship rules. If both sets of parents did not approve, they could not call upon each other. Even then, they could never be together without a chaperone. The guidelines were strict, but because José's feelings for Pablita were ardent, he obeyed all the rules, won her hand, and wed her in June of 1897. "My mother and father were first cousins, but they married anyway," Concha says. "It turned out to be a good marriage. They celebrated their 50th wedding anniversary in the same church in Galisteo where they were married. The same priest who performed the original ceremony remarried them."

The long, strong union of these two spirits would produce, among their other children, the indomitable Concha Ortiz y Pino, in a family that continued to shape the village of Galisteo, just as much as it shaped them.

CAPITULO 4
Una aldea crece

La vida en Galisteo afectó muchísimo la formación de Concha. Galisteo es una aldea que está a 22 millas al sur de Santa Fe y 70 millas al nordeste de Albuquerque. Cuando llegó el explorador Coronado a la zona de Galisteo en 1540, esa aldea tenía el nombre Ximena y estaba rodeada de cinco pueblos indígenas.

En 1617, cuando Nuevo México era colonia española, se funda la Misión de San Cristóbal en Galisteo. Ese mismo año, Oñate le dio a uno de sus soldados una encomienda de tierra que incluyó a Galisteo. El encomendero recibió el derecho de utilizar la mano de obra de los habitantes indígenas del pueblo.

La revolución de los indígenas en 1680 resultó en la muerte de muchos españoles y otros se escaparon de la zona y se exiliaron en la zona que hoy día se llama El Paso. A mediados del siglo dieciocho, Galisteo contaba con 350 residentes.

En 1848, empiezó la época norteamericana. La ley norteamericana que regía la adquisición de tierras existía lado a lado con la ley de concesión de tierras que remonta a la época española. La Concesión de la familia Ortiz, una de las más grandes en la Cuenca del Río de Galisteo, tenía ricos depósitos de minerales incluso oro, todo lo cual ponía a los descendientes de la familia Ortiz en excelente situación para que lograra ser una familia próspera. Además, el ferrocarril que introdujeron los norteamericanos y el punto geográfico de Galisteo ponía a la familia Ortiz en excelente situación para que lograra prosperar aun más. Don José Ortiz, heredero de esa familia y padre de Concha, recibió 50,000 acres de tierra que, con la mina de oro ponía a la familia Ortiz entre las más ricas de la comarca.

Las diversiones de la zona eran las corridas de toros, los rodeos, carreras de caballos, y los bailes. A grandes rasgos, esos son los antecedentes históricos de la aldea de Galisteo donde en 1910 nació Concha Ortiz y Pino.

A Village Grows

Photo by J. R. Riddle   Museum of New Mexico   Neg. No. 76053

Life in Galisteo greatly affected and shaped Concha. Her birth and early years there prepared her for the future. When weighing this statement, however, one must know about Galisteo to understand why it provided such a profound background for her life.

The village, 22 miles south of Santa Fe and 70 miles northeast of Albuquerque, lies along a seasonal stream called Galisteo Creek. The earliest recorded descriptions place the town in the middle of five Indian pueblos: San Cristóbal, Chee, San Lázaro, San Marcos and Pueblo Galisteo. The explorer and conquistador Coronado visited the area in 1541, but he actually stopped in Ximena, a precursor of Galisteo, two miles north of the present village. Coronado noted that about 30 Indian houses occupied the site. The area grew a great deal in the next century.

In 1617, near the future village of Galisteo, the Indian Mission of San Cristóbal was founded. In the same year, Spanish authorities awarded an *encomienda*, a grant of tribute that encompassed Galisteo, to one of Oñate's soldiers. The *encomendero* and Spanish government officials took a portion of the produce from those who worked the land.

Encomiendas worked in favor of the Spanish elite, but very much against the native inhabitants. Prior to Spanish rule, residents enjoyed an agricultural situation in which sufficient water, grazing land, and feed existed. When the colonists brought their horses and increased the demand for more crops, overgrazing and soil erosion followed. Conflict between the government, the church and the Indians created growing tension.

By 1680, San Cristóbal was an important mission, counting 800 native converts. On the

Galisteo in 1884. Photo by J. R. Riddie—courtesy Museum of New Mexico, negative no. 76053.

Church in Galisteo in 1884,
photo by J.R. Riddle—courtesy
Museum of New Mexico,
negative no. 76052.

night of August 6, however, a convert named Juan Ye told Fray Fernando de Velasco of Pecos about a revolt planned against the Spaniards. Fray Velasco set out to warn the residents of Galisteo, but rebellious Indians killed him before he accomplished his goal. Another padre, Fray Manuel Tinoco of San Marcos, also went to warn the people of Galisteo, and met the same fate. The Pueblo Revolt of 1680 succeeded in killing many Spanish settlers and driving the others out of New Mexico. The Indians of Galisteo then left their village to take possession of the Spanish Palace in Santa Fe, which they converted into a pueblo.

In 1692, Gen. *don* Diego de Vargas retook Santa Fe from the Indians. Galisteo did not remain uninhabited for long. The former Tanoque Pueblo came back to life when Gov. Cuervo y Valdés re-established it with 90 Tano Indians in 1706. The governor called the village Nuestra Señora de los Remedios de Galisteo or Santa María de Galisteo, and its daily life mixing Spanish colonists and native inhabitants resumed.

In 1712, 110 people, mostly Indians, lived in the village. By 1749, 350 residents called Galisteo their home. By 1782, however, the numbers had dropped precipitously, to just 52, due to smallpox epidemics and Comanche raids. But again the community revived. Devoted Hispanic Catholics regarded religion as crucial to survival, and so in 1810 built the village a new church. Another church followed in 1856, early in the American era, and yet another was begun in 1880, a structure not completed until 1910.

The American era, which began in 1846, brought an age of prosperity to Galisteo. In New

A Village Grows

Mexico the U.S. Homestead Act existed side by side with the much earlier provisions of Spanish land grants dating all the way back to the conquistadors and the kings of Spain. The Treaty of Guadalupe Hidalgo, which spelled out the terms of New Mexico passing into American control, committed the U.S. government to honor those ancient grants, just as the Mexican government had previously done. One of the largest and wealthiest was the Ortiz Land Grant, which included all the land in the Galisteo River Basin, an area rich in deposits of gold and other minerals.

During the age of eager American expansionism in the late 1800s, descendants in the Ortiz family were well situated to prosper, with their extensive holdings from the land grant. Galisteo enjoyed an unusually beneficial location: near the capital city of Santa Fe, not very distant from Albuquerque, and alongside the new railroad pushing westward. The railroad played a key role in this golden age. As a sheep- and cattle-producing community, Galisteo took full advantage of the railroad for shipping. And when a spur was built into Santa Fe from the railroad's main line, that spur was established at a point adjacent to Galisteo, in the village now called Lamy. Residents of Galisteo gained quick and easy transportation to and from the capital, making the village even more attractive.

As an heir in the Ortiz family line, *don* José received 50,000 acres from the land grant, making him one of the region's major property owners. Contributing significantly to the family's wealth from the grant was the *don* Pedro Mine, a rich gold enterprise that—among other things—produced a pure gold necklace now worn by the statue of La Conquistadora in the St. Francis Cathedral in Santa Fe. (Recognized as the most important Hispanic religious relic in all of New Mexico, La Conquistadora accompanied the forces of *don* Diego de Vargas in his 1692 Reconquest of the territory.) By any measure, the Ortiz family was foremost in the community, and some latter-day observers have compared its stature to that enjoyed by the Kennedy family in Massachusetts.

Family notes kept by *don* José, however, indicate that on at least one high-spirited occasion, a large segment of the family wealth was placed in a precarious position. Like many other New Mexico towns, Galisteo enjoyed the pageantry and opportunities for gambling that cockfights provided. At one such event in 1876, Ambrocio Pino (Concha's great-uncle) reportedly gambled his entire fortune against that of one Santiago Baca of Pecos. On the day of the showdown, Baca's wife came to the cockfight with two maids to ensure that the hoops in her skirt stayed in place, and Pino arrived astride Captain Sylvester Davis' horse. Apparently Pino won the bet and increased his wealth—and *don* José's notes give insight into the life and sport of the day.

Other forms of entertainment in Galisteo included rodeos, rooster pulls (*corridos del gallo*), races, and *bailes* (dances). And many of the village's trademark celebrations were marked by a strong sense of religion and community. Feast days such as *Día de San Juan* (St. John's Day, June 24th) meant walking in procession and sharing food. Christmas traditions included *luminarias* (small wood bonfires), *farolitos* (candles lighted in paper bags), *Las Posadas* (a nine-day commemoration of Mary and Joseph's search for lodging prior to the birth of Christ), and the hanging of stockings for gift giving.

During World War I, many people left the area, to take industrial jobs supporting the American effort. Some of those who remained worked for *don* José as ranch hands, while others worked on the railroads or built roads, bridges, and fences for Santa Fe County, in the brand-new U.S. state of New Mexico, which joined the Union in 1912. With the manpower depleted, children helped with the work. The spirit of survival involved the entire community. Even so, Galisteo was in decline. World War II had an even greater negative impact upon the community, and Galisteo residents began to worry about the village's future. Today it is a small, quiet, and rustic community of about 260 residents and almost no commercial activity, with busy Santa Fe just minutes away. Galisteo's heyday has come and gone, but its storehouse of memories is rich and full.

Such is the village into which Concha Ortiz y Pino was born, in 1910, and in which she grew up and came of age. The saying "It takes a village to raise a child" was certainly true in her case—but then she, in turn, profoundly shaped the life of Galisteo.

1910 - Nace Concha y el Territorio de Nuevo México se convierte en estado de la nación norteamericana

El nacimiento de Concha en 1910 coincide con el año cuando se convocó la Convención Constitucional de Nuevo México, que redactó y adoptó el documento clave para que Nuevo México sea admitido como estado de los Estados Unidos de Norteamérica. En 1912, terminó la iniciativa que algunos residentes de Nuevo México lanzaron en 1850 para lograr que Nuevo México fuera admitido. Mientras tanto, la familia Davis Ortiz y Pino siguió trabajando para ganarse la vida y criar la prole en Galisteo.

Concha nació cuando el abuelo Sylvester Davis tenía 76 años de edad, su esposa Josefa tenía 56. La nieta Amelia vivía con los abuelos, así mismo los huéspedes John de 19 años, José de 76 años y Manuel de 56 años. Una muchacha, Felipa Lucero de 23 años, trabajaba en la casa y una niña mulata de 3 años de edad, Braulia Jackson (después conocida con el nombre Bluebelle), vivía en el hogar como niña adoptiva.

El 12 de junio 1912, José y su esposa Pablita se presentaron en la Iglesia de San Antonio en Pecos, N.M., para bautizar a la infanta Concha. Los padrinos Germán Pino y Cleofas Gonzales presentaron a la niña frente a la pila del bautismo al Reverendo Padre E. Paulhan, quien bautizó a Concha. Ese bautismo fue debidamente registrado por el Reverendo Vito C. de Baca.

Birth and Statehood 5

Concha's birth in 1910, concurrent with New Mexico's Constitutional Convention to draft the key document for becoming a new American state, could be seen as mere coincidence. People familiar with her life, however, might see the two events as bound together by fate. Though Concha the tiny baby did not participate directly in the Constitutional Convention or statehood two years later in 1912, her family roots definitely helped shape those events, and her life helped shape New Mexico's future.

To say that the 1910 Constitutional Convention alone gained statehood for New Mexico vastly oversimplifies the process. From start to finish, the push for national designation took 66 years, from the start of the Mexican-American War in 1846 until 1912, when statehood was officially bestowed. In the larger perspective of history, however, the saga stretches across at least five centuries, from the time early Spanish explorers landed in North America in the early 1500s. And for unrecorded eons before then, the land now called New Mexico was the province of native inhabitants.

From 1610 until 1821, however, New Mexico was a colony of Spain, and was governed through Mexico, an even earlier Spanish dominion. When Mexico won independence from Spain in 1821, part of the settlement included the New Mexico territory. For the next 25 years, Mexico's interest remained inadequate due to lack of financial resources, with an appointed governor running day-to-day affairs. During this time, trade routes with the United States flourished, along the Santa Fe Trail connecting New Mexico and Missouri.

In 1845 the United States annexed Texas, which was technically a part of Mexico but which in 1836 was declared an independent republic by American settlers living there. Mexico refused to accept either the United States' claim or Texas independence, and threatened war if Texas became an American state. Diplomatic relations between the two countries broke off. Driven by the concept of Manifest Destiny, which held that America was divinely ordained to expand to the Pacific Ocean, U.S. President James Polk was under pressure to annex not only Texas but all of the American Southwest, including New Mexico and California. Polk tried to settle the dispute by offering to buy New Mexico and California from Mexico, but Mexican authorities refused. With tensions rising daily, Polk sent General Zachary Taylor and his troops into the disputed area.

On April 23, 1846, Mexico declared war on the United States. On May 13, 1846, Congress reciprocated with its own declaration. The Mexican-American War had begun. After more than a year of fighting, the end of war was near, with the United States winning. On Sept. 14, 1847, U.S. General Winfield Scott took possession of Mexico City. Both countries could agree on only one issue at this point: End the war!

On Feb. 2, 1848, representatives of the United States and Mexico signed the Treaty of Guadalupe Hidalgo, which set the Río Grande as the boundary between the countries. Nevada, Utah, Wyoming, and most of New Mexico became American territories. The U.S. also paid Mexico $15 million and took responsibility for payment of Mexico's previous debt to United States citizens. This settlement paved the way for granting territorial status to New Mexico, but did not allow for statehood—which was a long time coming.

During this time, Congress established a territorial government for New Mexico. But then things bogged down. Lawmakers in Washington cited many concerns about New Mexico, including the Spanish language, the religious rights of the Catholic population, the welfare of the citizens, the undeveloped condition of the region, and its relative poverty

The original Our Lady of Angels and San Antonio church in Pecos, N. M., where Concha was baptized. Photo by Ben Wittick—courtesy Museum of New Mexico, negative no. 15807.

Baptismal Certificate

ST. ANTHONY CHURCH
PECOS, NEW MEXICO
NAME OF CHURCH

The Records of this Church certify, under date of _June 12_ 19_10_

to the Baptism of _Maria Conception Ortiz_ born _May 20_ 19_10_

of _Jose Ortiz y Pino_ and _Paula Davis_

Place of Birth _Galisteo, N.M._

Said Record is signed by Rev. _E. Paulhan_

with sponsors, _German Pino_ and _Cleofas Gonzales_

III

135:2.

Rev. _Vito C. de Baca_

Date _Jan 6, 1955_

THE A. J. EGGERS CO., CINCINNATI

A copy of Concha's baptismal certificate from San Antonio church—courtesy Center for Southwest Research, University of New Mexico

when compared with existing states. Slavery also played a part in these pre-Civil War deliberations—would the practice be allowed or prohibited? In both the 1848 and 1849 sessions, Congress took no action progressing toward statehood.

In 1850, New Mexico residents took the initiative. A constitutional convention met in Santa Fe and drafted a brief bilingual document, in Spanish and English. Modeled after the U.S. Constitution, it called for three branches of government and a bicameral legislature. It prohibited slavery. Citizens of the territory voted to accept the document and submitted it to Congress. Instead Congress approved a compromise measure, which did not grant statehood but at least established a full civil government in New Mexico, and provided for permanent post offices and monthly mail routes. A year later, in 1851, the new Territorial assembly made Santa Fe the official capital and established judicial districts. In 1852 the governing body established nine counties.

In 1860, another bid for statehood stirred in Congress the question of whether Hispanic residents would be loyal to the United States—with opponents of statehood suggesting that they would not. The Civil War then interrupted the statehood question. But even during the war, in 1863, the land mass of Arizona, which had comprised about half of the area called New Mexico, was carved out into its own territory. When peace returned, New Mexico officials again pressed their bid for statehood, now fearful that more land would be lost if Congress did not move quickly enough. But again the issue of loyalty, plus the menace of Indian unrest, arose as negative arguments. Another fear included expense. Would it cost more to run New Mexico as a territory or a state?

A positive development for New Mexico came in 1874, when the territory sent an official representative to Congress, Stephen B. Elkins. Many political observers viewed territorial representation as a sign of impending acceptance. Like *don* Pedro Bautista Pino long before

Birth and Statehood

him at the distant *Cortes* in Spain, Elkins pleaded eloquently for his homeland. New Mexico had sufficient population and capital for statehood, he said. A large share of the territory's taxes supported education, and taxes also had the capacity to improve transportation facilities. Residents had proved their loyalty to the Union during the Civil War. An excellent medical climate also added to New Mexico's suitability as a state. Yet when the topic of wars with nomadic Apaches arose, Congress lost interest. At the end of the session, Colorado received statehood but New Mexico did not.

In 1888 New Mexico tried again, with a bid that included the controversial proposal to change the territory's name to Montezuma. But New Mexico was dropped from an omnibus bill, which approved other territories, after a senator from Kansas presented a document titled "Protest of the Citizens of New Mexico Against the Admission of That Territory Into the Union of States." In it a number of prominent business people from Albuquerque argued that New Mexico was not ready for statehood. Heated counter-petitions followed, but Congress no longer was considering New Mexico.

As the statehood battle stretched over years and then decades, controversy roiled at home, with New Mexicans quick to blame one another. Disputes arose over growth of monopolies, religious freedom, legal debts of the territory, and even divorce laws. New proposed constitutions were presented to the voters, but earlier versions often were declared better. In 1889 voters rejected what was widely called "the land-grabber constitution," because it was seen as harmful to the claims of indigenous people.

In the 1890s New Mexico continued to grow in wealth—from gold, silver and other minerals, and from wheat, corn and cattle. It also made great progress in the areas of irrigation and education, and settlers continued to stream in from the East. Yet every time the question of statehood arose in Congress, the nagging question of English versus Spanish would rise. An even greater obstacle was partisan politics, for the admission of new states could upset the balance between Republicans and Democrats in Congress, and also the balance of national influence between the East and the West.

During this era the Senate Committee on Territories made a long western trip to assess the suitability of Arizona, Idaho, New Mexico, and Wyoming as states. Only Idaho and Wyoming were approved. An attempt in 1894 to admit New Mexico, Arizona, Utah and Oklahoma failed altogether. Efforts in 1898 and 1902 also were defeated. In 1905, however, after President Theodore Roosevelt delivered a message to Congress extolling his knowledge of the West and his sympathy for the people, Congress moved to admit Oklahoma and the Indian Territory as one state.

Bowing at last to unrelenting pressure from the West, the Enabling Act of 1910 allowed citizens in U.S. territories to hold a convention, prepare a constitution, and submit it to Congress for approval of self-government. In October of that year delegates from New Mexico's nine counties met in Santa Fe to achieve this momentous task. They eased the tension with parties, receptions, and buggy rides, and also invited President William Howard Taft to join them, but he did not attend. The Constitutional Convention completed the document in November 1910, and New Mexico voters approved it in January, 1911. A year later, on Jan. 15, 1912, the United States of America finally admitted New Mexico into the Union after a 66-year struggle.

While this long-drawn-out drama was unfolding, the Davis, Ortiz, and Pino families in Galisteo were busy earning a living and raising the young people in their community. The 14th Census of the United States of America, dated April 23, 1910, duly noted Concha's family, listing as the head of household José Ortiz y Pino, 35; his wife Pablita, 29; and two children, Josefita, 13, and Frank, 1. A 7-year-old *mulatta* (mixed breed, at least half black), Alma, or Alice, also lived in the household as a minor under the guardianship of the head of household.

Not quite born in time to be noted on the census form was little Concha (who was christened Mabel Concepción, who later disliked her first name and changed it to María). She entered the world on May 20, 1910, as New Mexico's Territorial leaders were making plans for the Constitutional Convention. Dr. Palmer from the nearby town of Kennedy, called "the railroad doctor" because the railroad sponsored his medical practice, delivered her. Unknown to her family at the time, the tiny being lying in her crib would conquer many barriers and make her mark on the world, just like her ancestors.

Across the street, the Davis household bustled with the news of the baby born that day. From the moment baby Concha and her grandmother Josefa Ortiz Davis—"Mamá Fita," as Concha would call her—met, and Josefa held the child in her arms, a bond existed—one that would influence the youngster forever.

According to the census, the Davis household consisted of eight members at the time. Grandfather Sylvester Davis was 76 years of age at the time of Concha's birth; his wife, Josefa, was 56. A granddaughter Amelia, 13, lived in the household. So did boarders named John, 19; José, 76; and Manuel, 65. A 23-year-old female named Felipa Lucero worked in the home, and a 3-year-old *mulatta* Braulia Jackson (later known as Bluebelle) lived there as an adopted daughter.

On June 12, 1910, José and Pablita, along with other family members and friends, went to St. Anthony's Church in Pecos for the baptism of infant Concha. Godparents Germán Pino and Cleofas Gonzales were also there. The baptism was presided over by Rev. E. Paulhan. The event was duly recorded by Rev. Vito C. de Baca.

Capítulo 6
La época de niñez de Concha

Pese a que los padres de Concha, José Ortiz, y Pablita Davis eran de familia acaudalada, era una pareja que estaba dedicada a trabajar. El caudal de José y Pablita consistía en una tienda, una oficina donde José llevaba a cabo el negocio de empresario, un almacén donde almacenaba lana para exportarla a Boston y a otros centros comerciales en el este de la nación norteamericana. Los vecinos de Galisteo, aparte de criar y cuidar sus rebaños de ovejas, se ganaban la vida cosechando alimentos en sus propios jardines y hortalizas e intercambiando mercancías y servicios entre sí. Mientras tanto Pablita confeccionaba la ropa de su familia o mandaba a pedir ropa fina de Santa Fe, y según cuenta doña Concha, sus familiares sentían que eran personas "especiales y ricas." "Mi mamá siempre andaba bien vestida." Como la abuela Josefa, doña Pablita no sólo era una mujer muy bella sino también se distinguía por su gentileza y generosidad.

De la pareja, nacieron siete hijos e hijas: Josefita, Frank, Margaret, Mela, Concha, Josecito, y Juanito. Dos murieron cuando eran niños. De los siete hermanos y hermanas, Concha es la única que vive. En particular, Mamá Fita, su abuelita, tuvo mucha influencia en la formación de la joven Concha. "Aprendí mucho debido a su actividad en la comunidad y sus obras de caridad, la compasión que sentía por el prójimo, y así mismo Mamá Fita desempeñó un papel importantísimo en mi formación." Inspirada por el ejemplo de su abuelita, Concha desde joven ingeniaba muchos planes sistemáticos para ayudar a las personas más necesitadas de la comarca.

Childhood in Galisteo

Although Concha's parents—José Ortiz y Pino and Pablita Davis—came from Galisteo's leading family, their marriage still involved a great deal of work for them both. In addition to running a ranch for cattle and sheep, José also owned the village's general store, in which he had a private office for conducting all manner of business deals. The store stocked most of the items needed for life in a small town like Galisteo: wheat flour, cornmeal, potatoes, onions, and other staples in big bins, plus candy, toys, clothing, and nails, tools, and equipment for ranching and other lines of work.

Along the railroad track José built a wool warehouse for export to Boston and other Eastern centers of commerce. Each winter his flocks had to be relocated from high mountain pastures to the ranch, and José provided work for many sheepherders. Some residents of the area had flocks of their own, while other local homesteaders carved out a hard agricultural existence by cattle ranching or growing crops. The homesteaders lived a difficult, seasonal economic life, different from that of residents in towns or cities. They basically received payment for their labor only once or twice a year, at harvest time. During the long months leading up to that payday, they charged the goods they needed at José's store. When they finally were paid, so was the storeowner.

Historians view the "company store" concept as a mixed blessing. While it did provide the necessities of life on an ongoing basis, it often led to backbreaking debt, particularly in years when the harvest was poor. The song "Sixteen Tons," by Tennessee Ernie Ford, emphasizes the refrain "I owe my soul to the company store." Though this song is about mining rather than ranching, its message is the same for both types of work: that in situations where the

In the back row, left to right: Manuelita Ortiz, Juanita Villanueva, Margarita Pino de Ortiz. In the front row: José Ortiz y Pino with child, Manuela Martínez, and Pedro Ortiz y Pino—courtesy Judy Hasted.

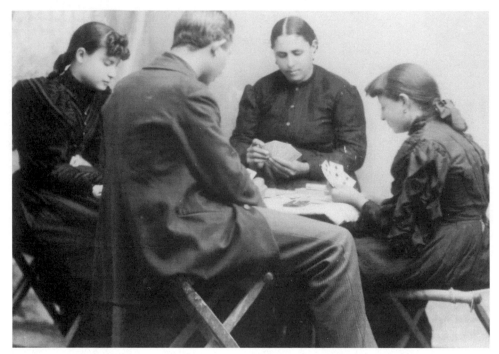

employer owns the store where employees shop, debtors sometimes never complete repaying the balance. Galisteo-area residents augmented their seasonal incomes by growing much of their own food in gardens and fruit trees, and by bartering goods and services with one another.

Meanwhile, on the Ortiz y Pino home front, Pablita presided over an eight-room house surrounded by several porches, or *portales*. The grounds included an orchard. The inside furnishings were an interesting blend of items acquired from places important to the family. Maple and oak furniture from New England, Spain, and Mexico mixed with Navajo and Río Grande tapestries and pottery. Chimayó rugs and linen shawls from Spain

José Ortiz y Pino, Concha's father; Manuelita, José's sister; Josefa Ortiz y Davis, facing camera, and Pablita Ortiz y Davis, Concha's mother— courtesy Concha Ortiz y Pino de Kleven

decorated almost every room, and for warmth each room had a fireplace.

Pablita made much of the family's clothing by hand, either the old-fashioned way with thread and needle, or by using a newfangled sewing machine, which Anglo friends taught her how to use. From time to time, she would also send to Santa Fe for fancy garments that made the wearers "feel special and rich," Concha remembers. Pablita enjoyed seeing her children look attractive, and she always—*always*—insisted on good grooming. "I guess that's why I feel looking one's best is so important," Concha says.

Concha at the front of wagon, with her brother Frank and first cousin Reynalda Ortiz y Pino de Dinkel—courtesy Concha Ortiz y Pino de Kleven.

Childhood in Galisteo

"Mother was never in a dirty dress, nightgown, or robe. She always had makeup on, with her hair combed and fully dressed, with stockings and complete underwear." Pablita also enjoyed wearing jewelry, and passed that love along to her children. Even the smallest Ortiz y Pino child wore toy baubles to play dress-up. To enhance her rings and bracelets, Pablita displayed perfectly manicured hands and nails. "Mother always spent a lot of time in the bathroom grooming herself," Concha laughs. She describes her mother as "always moving with grace, sincere, never scolding, a wonderful presence, fun, and a music lover." Like her mother *doña* Josefa before her, Pablita was not only beautiful but also kind and generous in her actions.

Music was very important to Pablita. Her favorite pastimes included playing the organ and listening to the guitar. And she loved being on the dance floor, where she and José cut grand and graceful figures at village *bailes* and fiestas. Pablita loved such events, and as they drew near, she made sure to include all the people of Galisteo in the fun. She sewed festive party clothing for village children, making no distinction between rich and poor. But Pablita had a hard side as well. "Everybody loved Mother, but she could be a tyrant when distinguishing between right and wrong. She just said exactly what she felt. I guess these were traits she learned from my grandmother."

Pablita had a fine sense of self-deprecating humor, and liked to joke about being seriously nearsighted. "As long as my nose is, I can't find it!" she would laugh. She suffered from other physical infirmities as well, especially what was called "female troubles" in those days. Of 22 pregnancies, only seven children were born. In birth order they were: Josefita, Frank, Margaret, Concha, Mela, Josecito, and Juanito. Sadly, Josecito and Juanito died in childhood. Coincidentally, Concha's uncle, Pedro Ortiz y Pino and his wife, Agueda, also had two sons named Josecito and Juanito who died at a very young age.

Looking back with sadness, Concha remembers her young siblings' deaths. "Margaret passed away as a child. Her death occurred suddenly," she says. With Concha's little brother Josecito, the story was different. "When he was a baby, the nurse fell down the stairs with him. That left him crippled. Even though he couldn't move on his own, he was so good-natured. Everyone loved him. They brought him toys, and there were so many things to play with in the house—a pile in every room, so many that we gave away some to the poor children." Josecito was smart, too— Concha marveled at his intellect, and looking back, calls him a "genius." But he also did not live to become an adult. Concha is now the last surviving Ortiz y Pino child of all seven siblings.

Almost as influential as her own parents in Concha's formative years was her grandmother Josefa—"Mamá Fita," as the young girl called her. The Davis family lived just across the street from Concha's family home, and she spent a great deal of time there, frequently spending the night as well. One of the reasons she loved being there was that she had an enormous appetite. "¡La Concha siempre tiene hambre!" ("Concha is always hungry!") Mamá Fita continually complained. Several times a day the girl would check the pots on the stove to find out what was cooking, and almost always something was—which she would sample. Concha loved having such a ready supply of tasty food. Not until years later did she realize why it was there: Mamá Fita wanted to be ever ready for guests, traveling strangers, lodgers in her house, and hungry villagers.

Concha emerged as Mamá Fita's favored granddaughter, and some

Concha, age 4, with her pet lamb Chiquito— courtesy Concha Ortiz y Pino de Kleven

Frank and Concha's First Holy Communion, circa 1917—courtesy Center for Southwest Research, University of New Mexico, negative no. 000-457-0005

The Ortiz y Pino general store in Galisteo—photo by Robert H. Martin

people in the village referred to her as a "pampered princess." Yet at *doña* Josefa's house the little girl did more than merely indulge her appetite. Her grandmother gave Concha many chores to tend. With her young black childhood friend Bluebelle, she was sent out through the village and surrounding countryside with pots of soup, fresh-baked bread, and clean diapers for families in need. Another chore was feeding leftover food or scraps unfit for human consumption to the pigs and chickens. A vivid childhood memory is walking a blind man around the village. In addition to guiding him, she kicked rocks out of the way so he would not stumble on them. "I learned so much from these works of charity—compassion, helping others," she says. "Mamá Fita shaped my future."

Mamá Fita also helped with grandmotherly advice. "Remember the people you grew up with—don't forget where you came from," she would say. Or, "María Santísima will always watch you." Or "Use good wisdom and it will serve you well." Or "As long as you're alive, the poor and needy people should be your friends. Even if you are pretty and rich, still help them." Or "Do things with a good heart for others, not for yourself."

Looking back over her grandmother's legacy, Concha sometimes wonders how Josefa managed to do everything she did. A big help was that an Ortiz cousin named Ambrosia and a Santo Domingo Pueblo woman named Felipa took charge of household duties to let Mamá Fita tend to other matters. "Grandma loved the Indians," Concha says. "She was one of the few people who did." It was a love that helped her in turn.

Childhood in Galisteo

Tiá Vicenta from Santa Domingo Pueblo, who worked in the Ortiz y Davis household with her African-American husband and their child—photo courtesy Ron Ortiz Dinkel

Josefita Ortiz y Davis was laid to rest in the Galisteo Cemetery—photo courtesy Concha Ortiz y Pino de Kleven

Although the Davis family was relatively well-off financially, it was not "terribly rich," Concha says. "They had many cattle, but after the rustlers were through stealing, there wasn't that much left. Yet there was always enough food for all." Helping to keep the supply plentiful was Josefa's beloved brother Juan, who ran a small store and let her maintain a generous charge account there.

Inspired by her grandmother's example, the young Concha came up with endless girlhood schemes to help the needy people around her. Sometimes all that was needed was an act of kindness. But when financial support was also necessary, she learned that she must go to her father. José often reached for his wallet, but after awhile, enough was enough. "At first my father would embrace my ideas with enthusiasm," she recalls. "Later he would tire of me and say, '*Concha, deja a la gente sola. Ya las aburriste.*'" ("Concha, leave the people alone. You've already annoyed them.")

Doña Josefa always remained a monumental figure for Concha. "I think down in my heart, I knew Mamá Fita was a perfect lady," she reflects. "I always wanted to be around her. The older I got, the more I realized how beautiful and intelligent she was. I believe she raised at least 25 children that she didn't give birth to. When she passed away, I mourned her terribly." Josefita Ortiz y Davis was buried in 1940, when Concha was 30, in the Galisteo Cemetery, on land donated by her family to be the community's final resting place. By her side was her husband, Sylvester, who died in 1920.

Juan Ortiz, far left, and José, to right of coffin, at a funeral in Galisteo—courtesy Jerry Ortiz y Pino

Pauline Gómez, Josefita's (Concha's older sister) daughter, who was born visually impaired and was totally blind by adulthood— courtesy Susan Varela.

Concha (bottom left) with her parents, José and Pablita, brother Frank, sisters Josefita (standing) and Mela (seated)—courtesy Judy Hasted

Childhood in Galisteo

Pablita, Concha, and Josefa amid their hollyhock garden in Galisteo, circa 1916—courtesy Judy Hasted

Family picnic, left to right: José Ortiz y Pino, Irene Irving, (maid), Frank Johnson (chauffeur), Pablita, Mela, and Franciscan Father Eric—courtesy Center for Southwest Research, University of New Mexico, negative no. 000-457-0053

Capítulo 7
Bluebelle

Una de las más íntimas amigas de Concha cuando era niña fue una niñita mulata de nombre Braulia Jackson, conocido con el apodo Bluebelle. Poco se sabe de su origen. A Bluebelle la halló el Capitán Sylvester Davis un día en 1907 cuando iba a la aldea Kennedy a caballo. Con Bluebelle estaba otra niña que tenía aproximadamente 5 años de edad. Después de que el Dr. Palmer les hizo la exploración física a las dos niñas, le dijo a Davis que estaban en buena salud y agregó, "Usted y doña Josefa siempre socorren a los necesitados y se las entrego para que Uds. las críen."

Concha y Bluebelle se criaron juntas. A la edad de 10 años, Concha se fue a estudiar a Santa Fe, pese a que no quería separarse de su amiguita Bluebelle. Las dos amiguitas se veían cuando Concha venía a Galisteo de visita.

Este capítulo de la bibliografía en inglés tiene un excelente resumen del papel que, en Nuevo México, desempeñaron las personas de la raza negra en la última mitad del siglo XIX. Bluebelle se enamoró de un tal Ramón Hurtado, que era pastor de ovejas. Mamá Fita les permitió que se quedaran con la familia en una casita de tres cuartos que quedaba en el mismo entorno de la familia.

Otros rasgos en este capítulo indican la generosidad de la familia Ortiz y Pino respecto a Alice, la hermana de Bluebelle. Cuando Bluebelle falleció, el sepelio tuvo lugar en el cementerio de Galisteo cerca de la tumba de su madre adoptiva, Mamá Fita.

Bluebelle

One of Concha's closest and dearest childhood friends was a little girl named Braulia Jackson, nicknamed Bluebelle. Three years older than Concha, Bluebelle lived in the Davis household as an adopted daughter. Not much was known about her origins. She came into the family as a foundling. Her father was never identified, and her mother was thought to be a prostitute, surnamed Jackson. Bluebelle was a *mulatta*—partly black.

While riding on horseback to the village of Kennedy one day in 1907, Capt. Sylvester Davis heard a baby's cry. Tracking down the unexpected sound, he discovered a female baby about 6 months old and an older girl about 5 years old, near the railroad tracks. He wrapped the infant in his jacket and took both children to Dr. Palmer, employed by the railroad as the area's only doctor. He examined the girls and declared them healthy, and instructed his nurse to bathe and feed them. Davis paid the doctor for his services, and the two men discussed a course of action.

"You and *doña* Josefa always help those in need," said the doctor. "I now give these little girls to you, to raise and take care of them." When the captain returned home that afternoon, he arrived with two new children who had just joined the household. Immediately his wife set about establishing the youngsters in the daily routine. The older girl, called Alma and also Alice, seemed at once to enjoy the attention and regular meals in the Davis home. Baby Bluebelle, too young to make comparisons with whatever life she had

Alice on left with her sister Bluebelle and Frank, Concha, and Reynalda in the wagon, circa 1913—courtesy Concha Ortiz y Pino de Kleven

The Buffalo Soldiers Troop L, 9th Calvary in Fort Wingate, N.M.—courtesy Museum of New Mexico, negative no. 98373

led before, just did what babies do. Inquiries revealed that the girls had lived with their mother, who proved incapable of caring for them and so abandoned them.

Black children, abandoned or otherwise, were not commonplace in New Mexico in those days. Although there was a discernible black segment of the population, it was quite small. In a historical oddity, a black man played a prominent role in one of the earliest interactions between the natives and the Spanish conquistadors. His name was Estevanico, or Esteban. In 1539 he accompanied Fray Marcos de Niza on an expedition into New Mexico in search of the fabled Seven Cities of Cíbola, rich with gold. As the party approached Zuni Pueblo in what is now northwestern New Mexico, Estevanico, an advance scout, entered the native village. Thus the first "European" seen by the Zunis was black. Presenting himself as a friend, he gained a wary welcome from the Indians. But he soon showed a great appetite for the tribe's turquoise and its women. This angered his hosts, who killed him—and then, fearing he was a sorcerer, cut his body into pieces.

After that gruesome first encounter, history records few black people in the early years of New Mexico. In the Spanish territories to the south and west, and also in the English-speaking areas to the east, most of the blacks who came were slaves, and were relegated to the bottom of the social scale. The American Civil War, from 1861 to 1865, was fought largely over the issue of slavery, with the North seeking to abolish it and the South fighting to keep it. More than 180,000 African-Americans served in the Union Army during the war, in special all-black units. When the North won, slavery was abolished, but black people still occupied the lower rungs of society.

Seeking to take the best advantage of the black military training during the war, Congress in 1866 established half a dozen regiments whose enlisted men were African-American. The mounted units were the 9th and 10th Cavalries, and for the most part they were sent west to quell hostile Indians, Mexican revolutionaries, bandits, and rustlers on the frontier. Their more famous adversaries included Geronimo, Sitting Bull, Victorio, Billy the Kid, and Pancho Villa. Because of their coiled black hair, which some Indians said resembled the mane of the bison, they were nicknamed the Buffalo Soldiers. Until the early 1890s these units comprised about 20 percent of all U.S. frontier cavalry forces.

When not engaged in hostilities, the Buffalo Soldiers explored and mapped vast areas of the Southwest, strung hundreds of miles of telegraph wires, built forts and outposts that later grew into cities, protected mail carriers and wagon trains of supplies and settlers, and also provided military support for the huge task of building railroads across the West. Their contribution to developing the region was invaluable, but because of lingering racism, they were given some of the worst assignments in the Army and faced prejudice in the frontier society. Their uniforms were often threadbare, their housing was often substandard, and their food and other supplies were often inferior. Black men could not dance with white women at on-post parties, and with very few black women available, the Buffalo Soldiers frequented houses of prostitution.

Black soldiers seldom were promoted to higher rank in the Army, but their feats of valor were officially recognized with decorations, and several were awarded the Congressional Medal of Honor. Late in 1881 all the black troops in New Mexico were relocated to posts in Kansas, where one of their major duties was to guard the Old Santa Fe Trail. As New Mexico continued to advance as a U.S. Territory, railroads supplanted wagon train routes and Indian hostilities steadily tapered off. But black units remained in the Army, and in the Spanish-American War in 1898, the 9th Cavalry rode ahead of Theodore Roosevelt's Rough Riders in the charge up San Juan Hill in Cuba. "Black heroes, every one of them," read an official report.

Though the Buffalo Soldiers were recollected fondly by many New Mexico settlers, few black people lived in the Territory at the end of the 19th century. Finding work was difficult for both men and women. But even so, the raw frontier displayed less prejudice than some more-established parts of the country, and African-Americans often found more opportunity out West than back East. The new public high school in Santa Fe, for example, included a young black woman in its first graduating class in 1905. And the fossilized remains of the prehistoric Folsom Man in far northeastern New Mexico were discovered by a black cowboy, also in the early 1900s.

Both of the little girls found by Capt. Davis on the railroad tracks were taken into his Galisteo home as members of the household family. By the time Concha was born in 1910, Bluebelle had celebrated her third birthday and Alice had turned 7. Bluebelle remained with Mamá Fita, whom she called "tía"—"Aunt"—and Alice moved into the home of Pablita and José. But with the two houses across the street from each other, it was all one household. Family photos picture all the children around a wagon, smiling. Newborn Concha, already emotionally attached to her grandmother, spent much time on a mattress in the kitchen, where Bluebelle hovered over her. As the girls grew, they shared many firsts: Concha's first words, her first steps. "Bluebelle was much smarter than me," Concha confides. "I was happy to follow in her steps and learn from her."

Some Galisteo residents said Mamá Fita spoiled the two little girls. But such a description was far from accurate, for Josefa assigned the young ladies many chores, to teach them to be caring members of the community. Their daily work included a trek around the village to feed the underprivileged. "We'd take soup, bread, beans, whatever was available," Concha recalls. By far, her most vivid memory is of the diapers they delivered to poor families and wet cloths with which to clean themselves. "The mothers, in turn, gave us the dirty diapers we had delivered clean the day before," she remembers. "Oooh, the smell! We hurried to get the diapers home so someone could wash them quickly. But then we had to do the same thing the next day."

As the girls made their rounds, Bluebelle remembered every detail of every household—and then passed it all along to anyone who would listen. "Everyone hated us," Concha chuckles. " They'd say, '*Ahí viene la negra y la nieta.*' ('Here come the black girl and the granddaughter.') With her fantastic memory, Bluebelle knew all the gossip in the community. She knew everything about everybody. She also had ideas of her own, and sometimes put them in. Bluebelle knew it all. No wonder they hated us!"

Doña Fita's role as Galisteo's "lady boss" extended to the church. "Grandma was a big shot with the priest, so she had her own pew," Concha says. "Bluebelle and I sat there with her. But later, my mother bought an organ for the church. I took singing and piano lessons, and I wanted to learn how to play the organ. But my feet wouldn't reach the pedals. So Castro, who worked for our family, would sit on the bench, and if I sat on his lap I could pump them. Sometimes I would sit on my brother Frank's lap or on his friend Ernest's, but I didn't like to do that, because people would say I had a boyfriend.

"Bluebelle and I decided to sing along with the hymns, so the priest let us go upstairs to the choir loft. I had a sweet singing voice, and members of the congregation were glad I was going to accompany the organ. But instead of singing, Bluebelle actually screeched. Everybody was hoping she would not join in. But she did, and that's how she was singing, until my dad motioned us to stop. Afterward my dad said, 'Poor priest!' and Mamá Fita told us to behave. Bluebelle and I got a spanking and a pinch, and we didn't do that again. Ah, she enjoyed herself, but no one else did."

Some more church mischief involved the tolling of the bell. In Spanish tradition, when a church bell tolls during nonservice hours, it signifies that someone has died, and the girls knew about that ritual. "Grandma had the key to the church. We helped her toll the bell when people passed away," Concha recalls. "One day, Bluebelle and I stole the key and unlocked the church. I asked her what we should do next. She said we should ring the bell. When we rang it by ourselves without Mamá Fita's help, we were so small that we went up with the rope. After we rang, everyone came to the church to find out who died. Then we spat at the people from the choir loft. I was really scared. When we got home, boy, we were really in trouble," Concha says. It brought another spanking.

At home, the girls—who called each other "*hermanita*," or "sister"—found a new use for one of the family outhouses. In the 1920s Galisteo did not have indoor plumbing. Later on, the Davis and Ortiz y Pino homes were among the first to install plumbing and electricity, but not during Concha's youth. Inside the outhouse next to the corral, the girls could peek out into the street. "We had a lot of fun," Concha says. "We sat on the toilet and watched cows, horses and people go by. We'd yell out *picardillas* (swear words) and names like '*feo*,' 'ugly,' and 'rascal.' Bluebelle and I thought it was great—until people complained to Grandma. She made the men take down the toilet, and the ranch hands were angry because they had to use one farther away. Mamá Fita had a new one built, facing the gates to our home, not the road. Bluebelle and I lost our favorite space."

Mamá Fita often sent Concha and Bluebelle to Uncle Juan's store with a list of items to buy. The girls viewed the storeowner as quite wealthy and not terribly generous. So they came up with their own shopping plan. "While I was buying the meat and other items on the list, Bluebelle was wandering around the store," says Concha. "We'd leave, and Bluebelle would produce some candy or a bag of popcorn from under her skirt or her pocket. She'd offer me some, and we'd always share the stolen merchandise." Only once, in Concha's memory, was Bluebelle caught. Her punishment was to return the items.

The young troublemakers never viewed themselves as "naughty girls." They considered their behavior normal and even desirable. So they became distraught one time when Mamá Fita got angry and punished them. "I guess we had been bad," Concha admits now with a wave of her hand. "But Bluebelle said, 'I know who likes us: the Indians at Santo Domingo. And I know the way to their pueblo.' So we got two bags of food and left. That day, we did not go help the sick. At 7 or 8 in the morning, we headed to the arroyo. Grandma noticed we were gone, and got worried. She asked Uncle Juan to find us. He said, 'I know where they went,' and headed down the arroyo on horseback."

When he caught up, he threatened to spank the girls. But they had already eaten their food, and when he grabbed Bluebelle's arm, all she said was, "*Tengo hambre.*" ("I'm hungry.")

Castro (a ranch worker), Concha with hand on Bluebelle's head, and Mela, circa 1918—photo courtesy Robert H. Martin

Bluebelle dancing with Antonio Chávez at a party in the Ortiz y Pino home in Santa Fe—courtesy Concha Ortiz y Pino de Kleven

Juan replied, *"Cállate."* ("Be quiet!") Back at Mamá Fita's house, Josefa showed her disapproval by saying sarcastically, *"Quieres ir—lava tu ropa."* ("If you want to leave, wash your clothes.") "Of course, by then we didn't want to leave," Concha tells. Mamá Fita washed and fed the runaways. "After the long walk, it felt good to soak our feet." The girls slept late the next day, and then proceeded to perform their chores, feeding the poor and sick as though nothing out of the ordinary had ever occurred.

From time to time, the family children left Galisteo to attend silent movies 22 miles away in Santa Fe. The fashion-conscious Concha reports that some women actually wore hats to the theater. During these outings, Concha and Bluebelle loved the entire scene—what happened both on and off the screen. They loved to watch the actors perform on the screen with stunning outfits, and they compared those with clothes in the audience. When boredom set in, they began talking to each other and people around them. "My brother Frank, who went with us, hated those moments," Concha confesses.

When Concha turned 10, the time came for her to separate from Bluebelle. Until then, the "sisters" had lived all aspects of life together. Mamá Fita had arranged for both to be taught at home by a series of teachers. However, *don* José felt that his children must be taught in Santa Fe if they were to succeed. "My father didn't have confidence that schooling in Galisteo was sufficient," Concha remembers. She then insisted that Bluebelle go with her. But the girl was deemed too valuable to the family in Galisteo, thus requiring her to remain. In protest, Concha staged scenes worthy of any "drama queen" today. "I wanted to take Bluebelle with me to Santa Fe. Why couldn't she go? After all, she was my sister." But

Concha lost the fight, as she did the battle to take her pets with her. "The animals—I didn't like it, but I could understand. It was losing Bluebelle that hurt the most," Concha recalls, still with a touch of emotion.

From time to time afterward, the girls saw one another when Concha visited Galisteo. But life for them would never be the same. While Concha studied in Santa Fe, Bluebelle fell in love. "She wanted to get married. Mamá Fita begged her not to do so. Grandma even tried to bribe her by offering her a little house of her own, and took her to Santa Fe to buy new clothes. But Bluebelle was adamant. Her exact words were, 'No, Ramón is everything I want.' She married a sheepherder named Ramón Hurtado. He wasn't from Galisteo, but he temporarily worked for my dad. I was the *madrina* (bridesmaid) at their wedding. To keep them around, Grandma let the Hurtados live in a little house with three rooms and furniture. During their brief stay, Bluebelle gave birth to a son, Frank. The child and Uncle Juan developed a strong bond. But the family soon moved on.

"Some while later, Bluebelle came to visit us in Santa Fe. She was all grownup and wore a hat, gloves and a new dress. My mother used to give her clothes, but this time Bluebelle wore her own. She told us, 'I'm here to visit and be served, not to serve anyone.' We promptly prepared tea and enjoyed a pleasant visit," Concha recalls. Years later, Bluebelle appeared again, this time as a young widow with two small children—a daughter, Clara, in addition to her son. She said that her husband had treated her well when he was alive, and she considered her marriage a happy one. The Ortiz y Pino family assisted Bluebelle in her widowhood, although Concha does not know to what extent.

As for Bluebelle's sister Alma, or Alice, she did not stay with the Davis family very long. After only a few years, her mother came to claim her older daughter, and the girl left the household. While living there, however, she had become very attached to one of Concha's sisters, Margaret Ortiz y Pino, a few years younger in age. When Alice left, she said she would always love and miss the child. "Alice spoiled Margaret so much that she'd sleep next to her bed. When Margaret cried, Alice wouldn't let anyone else tend to her," according to Concha. But a few years after Alice left, Margaret died young.

The morning after Margaret's death, Alice appeared at José's and Pablita's door. Concha opened it. "*¿Está Mamá aquí?*" ("Is Mother here?"), she asked, inquiring about Josefa. Before Concha could answer, Alice recognized her. "*Eres Concha.*" ("You're Concha.") Concha nodded. "I knew something happened, so I came from Colorado," Alice said. When she heard that Margaret had died, she fainted. When she regained consciousness, she screamed. Then, she said, "She's with the angels now. Don't worry. I'll take care of everything. I'll order the food and make the arrangements. You just wait for the people to come."

In those days, visitors who wished to pay respects to a family in mourning came to the house, not a funeral parlor. The body lay in state at home, and guests ate with the family. Custom also called for friends and neighbors to help by cooking and assisting with household routine. Alice assumed the role of chief organizer in this time of grief. After Margaret's burial, Alice introduced her husband and two children.

A grateful José Ortiz y Pino invited Alice's family to live in Galisteo. The *patrón* provided a small house and enrolled the children in public school. Alice assisted *doña* Pablita with household chores, while her husband served as a chauffeur and handyman. *Don* José called the youngsters "my grandchildren." The arrangement worked for two years, but after a serious domestic dispute between Alice and her husband, *don* José canceled it. He gave the family funds to relocate to another New Mexico town.

When Bluebelle's children Frank and Clara achieved adulthood, each paid separate visits to the Ortiz y Pino family. Concha says that Frank had served in the Army, and was "a genius." He shared tales about his mother and said from his heart, "Nobody had a world like I did." Clara came as a young well-mannered woman who worked at a hotel restaurant in Santa Fe. Concha recalls Clara as "quiet and reserved."

When Bluebelle died, she was buried at the Galisteo cemetery, not far from Mamá Fita, her *tía* and adopted mother. She rests in ground donated by her adopted father.

CAPÍTULO 8
La educación de Concha

La formación de Concha no empezó en escuela pública. Al principio, la familia le facilitó a Concha enseñanza de maestros particulares que venían a dictarle clases en su casa. Una de las personas que más le enseñó fue Mamá Fita. Los maestros vivían en el hogar y les dictaban clases en matemáticas elementales, lectura, y ortografía a Bluebelle, Concha, y sus dos hermanitos y hermanitas.

Cuando Concha cumplió 10 años, sus padres decidieron que se fuera a vivir en la casa que tenían en Santa Fe y que se matriculara en la Academia de Loretto. Su hermano mayor asistía a clases en el Colegio de San Miguel. Bluebelle se quedó en Galisteo donde asistía a clases en la escuela pública. Concha se quedó muy triste cuando tuvo que dejar a su Mamá Fita y a su íntima amiga Bluebelle en Galisteo mientras que ella asistía a clases en Santa Fe.

Concha no se sentía a gusto en la Academia de Loretto. Lo que más le interesaba a Concha era reunirse con su padre, don José, cuando éste estaba atendiendo a sus tareas de legislador en el Capitolio en Santa Fe. Después de las clases, don José permitía que su hija Concha lo acompañara mientras él desempeñaba el cargo de legislador. Hizo arreglos para que hombres de negocio y otros líderes se reunieran con Concha una vez por semana con el fin de explicarle las cuestiones del momento que acaloraban los ánimos. Por consiguiente, que la joven Concha estuviera expuesta a la legislatura y a sus mentores fue parte importante de su formación. Pensaba Concha: "¿Por qué los asuntos en la Legislatura son fáciles de comprender cuando las materias en las clases en Loretto no lo son?"

Este capítulo de la biografía de Concha contiene un excelente resumen de la situación respecto a la educación de la juventud cuando Nuevo México estuvo bajo los dominios de España, México, y como territorio de los Estados Unidos de Norteamérica. En la época territorial, las escuelas en Santa Fe donde asistieron los Ortiz y Pino eran escuelas particulares lo suficientemente adecuadas pese a que a Concha no le gustaban las clases en la Academia de Loretto. En 1928, Concha terminó su carrera académica en Loretto. Regresó a Galisteo donde no permaneció mucho tiempo. Su padre le recomendó que vaya a estudiar en la Universidad de George Washington en Washington, D.C. A Concha no le gustaron las clases en la universidad, sin embargo lo que sí era de mayor atractivo para ella eran los museos, los teatros, y la vida social en la capital de la nación. Cuando el padre se daba cuenta que a Concha no le gustaba asistir a clases, le mandó que regresara a su hogar en Galisteo.

Sigue la etapa cuando Concha fue elegida legisladora de Nuevo México. Cuando terminó esta etapa, se matriculó en la facultad de estudios Inter-Americanos en la Universidad de Nuevo México; facultad que ella ayudó a establecer cuando fue legisladora. Al terminar ese curso, recibió su licenciatura en estudios inter-Americanos y ciencias políticas. En 1950, Concha acepta el decanato de mujeres en el centro docente San José en Albuquerque.

En 1975 la Universidad de Albuquerque le otorgó el título de Doctorado Honorario. En el título está inscrito que esa universidad le otorgó a la Señora de Kleven el doctorado en humanidades. Textualmente en el título está inscrito: "Este título honorario se le otorga a una mujer que ha dedicado su vida a la comunidad, la iglesia, al estado, y particularmente al pueblo."

Learning

As a child, Concha did not begin her formal learning at public school. Her family believed that both males and females deserved an education, but they also felt that home tutoring would suffice at first. The Ortiz y Pino philosophy included the idea that "you don't just learn in the classroom," Concha says. "There are things to learn everywhere—in every facet of your life." Mamá Fita was one of the girl's most important mentors, showing her how to deal with individuals and objects around her. "I was interested in everything. I'd go for a walk with Grandma, and she'd identify all the rocks, plants, and herbs. These are the first things I learned." Tutors boarding at the Davis home in Galisteo taught Concha, Bluebelle, and other children elementary math, reading, and spelling.

When Concha turned 10, however, her parents decided to send her to live at the home they owned in Santa Fe, and to enroll her at the Loretto Academy for girls. Her older brother, Frank, was also attending school in Santa Fe, at St. Michael's College, but

Graduation picture from Loretto Academy shows Concha back row right, next to Our Lady of Guadalupe— courtesy Concha Ortiz y Pino de Kleven

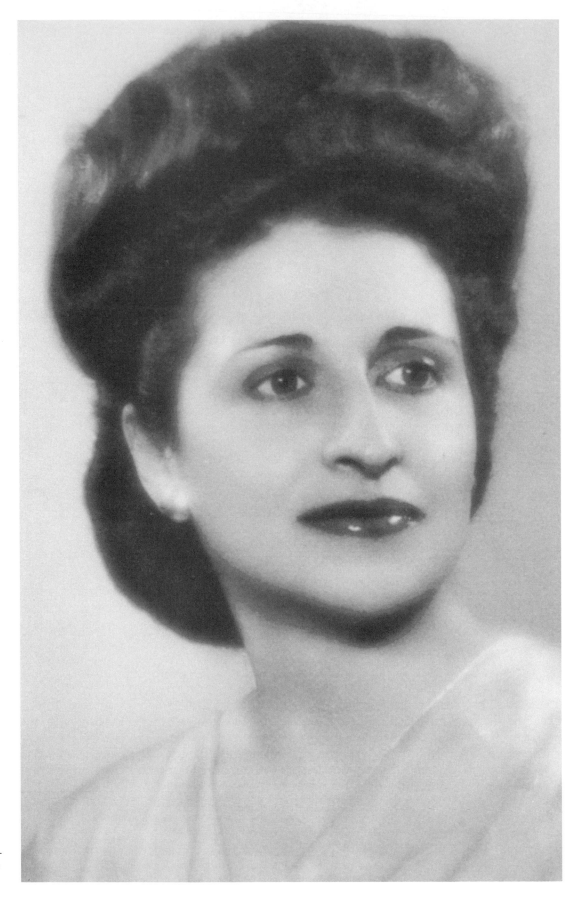

Concha as a college student—courtesy Concha Ortiz y Pino de Kleven

Learning

Bluebelle would remain in Galisteo, and go to public school. "How it broke my heart to leave Bluebelle and Mamá Fita!" Concha exclaims, even after the passage of over 80 years.

The family's in-town home was on Santa Fe Avenue, a few blocks south of the government complex in New Mexico's capital city. A man named Marcelino, who worked for the family, escorted the children to school each day. Frank was delivered first, then Concha and Marcelino continued on to her academy, near St. Francis Cathedral. The girl enjoyed talking with Marcelino, and always regretted when their walk ended—for she did not enjoy school very much. "The nuns didn't like me," she remembers. "I was a very shy child, although you can't tell that now. When I first went to Loretto to meet the sisters, one of them called me 'Cochinita,' because she said she couldn't pronounce my name. Well, that means 'little pig' in Spanish, so she didn't make a terribly great impression on me. Through all the years that's what the nuns continued to call me—'Cochinita'—even though I corrected them. I think they did it on purpose."

The Spanish language was indeed a point of friction between Concha and her Loretto Academy teachers. Only English was allowed to be spoken there, and when students were heard using Spanish, they were punished by being forced to sit behind a statue. Yet Concha spoke only Spanish when she first came. She remembers a day when one of the nuns seemed particularly hostile to her for one reason or another. "Sister was mad at me, and oh so mean," Concha says. "I really didn't want to be there." So she didn't stay. "I had ridden my bicycle to school that day, and left it outside. The windows had no screens, so I just jumped out the window, got on my bike and rode home."

The best part of the school year, however, came during the winter weeks when the Legislature convened in Santa Fe, in the young state of New Mexico. Her father was one of the lawmakers, and she joined him every day after her classes. He let her sit beside him as he tended legislative duties, and she loved being in the midst of the action. Noting his daughter's interest, *don* José arranged for businessmen and other leaders to meet with her once a week to explain the issues. Thus the Legislature provided an important part of her education—and it also presented her with a paradox. Why, she wondered, was the Legislature so easy to understand, when school was not? The Legislature followed a clear set of rules, and members of it were free to speak their minds, even to sharply disagree with each other. What's more, they could do so in either English or Spanish.

In those early sessions of the Legislature, education was a vital issue, as it had been for at least 200 years before New Mexico became an American state. An early historical reference to the subject was a 1712 order from the Spanish king, instructing the colonists to establish a school. Using his own funds, Gov. Mariano Martínez did so, hiring two teachers from Spain. In the earliest days of the American era, and even before, a headstrong priest in Taos named Padre Antonio José Martínez believed that girls as well as boys needed an elementary education, and he welcomed both sexes into the school he established. But opportunities for higher education remained scarce in New Mexico and throughout the Southwest, and wealthy Hispanic families sent their sons either east to Missouri for instruction or south into Mexico.

Small private and religious schools came and went in New Mexico during the Spanish era and also during the brief Mexican period. But it was the American era that brought one of New Mexico's greatest champions of education—who oddly enough was a Frenchman, and also a man of religion, in the Catholic Church. He was Bishop (later Archbishop) Jean Baptiste Lamy, who arrived in Santa Fe in 1851 to preside over church affairs in the territory. Placing great emphasis on education, Lamy opened a string of parochial schools around New Mexico, and established in Santa Fe both St. Michael's College—with the aid of the Christian Brothers order—and Loretto Academy—opened by six Sisters of Loretto who came to New Mexico from Kentucky at Lamy's invitation.

The Territorial Legislature also realized that education was important and voted in 1854 to provide a large parcel of land for a university to be built in Albuquerque—something that was not accomplished until 1889, when a new law also provided funding, not only for the Albuquerque campus but also for a school of mines in Socorro and an agricultural college

Cleofas Martínez Jaramillo, photo courtesy Museum of New Mexico, negative no. 9927

in Las Cruces. In 1860 lawmakers passed a mandate for compulsory public education, but in the reality of life on the frontier, much of the available schooling continued to be provided by churches, both Catholic and Protestant. In the 1890s a typical curriculum in a New Mexico school might include elementary and business English, Spanish, French, German phonology, writing, chemistry, instrumental music, and the study of minerals. The Fergusson Act of 1898, named for Harvey Fergusson, the U.S. representative who pushed it through Congress, provided generous funding and land for education, which was seen as essential if New Mexico ever wanted to achieve statehood.

One of the most revealing accounts of education in the 1890's included excerpts from a novel, *Romance of a Little Village Girl*, by Cleofas Martínez Jaramillo. At ten years of age, she was the youngest boarder of a school in Taos run by the Loretto nuns. Because she was so young, she was given the nickname "little piñon." Cleofas was forbidden to speak Spanish at school and the first English she heard was from the nuns when they told her "Put some wood in the stove."

In many rural communities the term "little red schoolhouse" really did apply, for most such buildings were painted that color. Often the schools had just one room for grades one through eight, with all pupils sharing the blackboard. In small communities students often sat on benches, at tables provided by parents. In larger districts, students had individual desks. But quality of teaching remained spotty, especially at rural schools, and in an alarming report to the governor in 1901, the Territorial superintendent of public instruction warned that many students were not getting a solid enough education to enable them to move on to higher learning. As always, he pleaded for more funding.

Yet the schools in Santa Fe attended by the Ortiz y Pino children in the 1920s were quite competent—even if Concha did not have an especially good time at hers. She did enjoy singing in her clear, sweet voice, not only at school but also on the Plaza bandstand, at Fiesta and on other occasions. And she did make friends at the academy, and enjoyed their company. A special one was mischief-loving classmate Angela Sosaya (who took the name Biddle after marriage). The girls spent long hours talking about clothes, boys, the nuns, and anything else they wanted to. *"Era una diablita,"* Concha now chuckles, looking back at her pal. "She was a little devil." Santa Fe friends were important to Concha during the long school term, when she stayed in the city. But her best friend and "sister" remained Bluebelle back in Galisteo, where the girls still spent summers together.

Bluebelle did not fare well at the public school in Galisteo. The word "strict," synonymous with schools everywhere, plagued the smart and spirited young girl. "Bluebelle always knew more than the teacher," Concha says. "They all hated her at school." One day

Bluebelle asked permission to use the outhouse. The teacher said no. Bluebelle persisted, but still the answer was no. Then Bluebelle wet her pants, and instead of being quiet and embarrassed about it, she showed all the other students her "mess." They all laughed hysterically. The next day *doña* Josefa kept Bluebelle at home, and hung her soiled pants on the front gate, for all to see. The punishment was not for wetting her pants, Josefa explained, but for disrupting the class. But looking back at the incident, Concha expresses stubborn admiration for her friend, and is sorry she was not there to stand up for Bluebelle. "I wish I would have told that teacher a thing or two," she says. "We were that way— Bluebelle would think of something, and I would say it."

The year 1928 eventually arrived, and with it graduation time for Concha. She, like the other girls, was radiant that day, with a long, new gown and cape, and a lovely fresh flower. But immediately after the ceremony, the nun who headed the school approached *don* José and said, "Mr. Ortiz y Pino, it is a disgrace that you wasted so much money on Concha's education here. I'm very sorry to tell you that she didn't get a thing out of it." It was just a final disappointment from Loretto Academy. "Of course, I disagreed," Concha grumbles, even now. "That school was a bad experience. But I did get to sing, and I learned a lot of folklore. I also met some wonderful people."

As a high school graduate with no particular plans, Concha returned to Galisteo. But that arrangement did not last long. "My father got tired of having me at home," she reports. "So he sent me back to school." This time she went far away—to George Washington University in Washington, D.C. There she enrolled in studies in philosophy and political science. But she still did not like school, and was distracted by other aspects of life in a big city. "School was OK for a while," she recalls. "But I tired of it." The things she did enjoy included museums, theaters, and Washington's social scene. "But when my father heard that I didn't want to attend classes, he made me come home."

Years later, Concha returned to college and eventually earned a degree. Before she did, however, she served as a member of the New Mexico Legislature, where she sponsored several bills to aid education. When that period of her life had passed, she enrolled at the University of New Mexico, in the new school for Inter-American Affairs—a program she had helped create as a lawmaker. She then became its first graduate, with a bachelor's degree in Inter-American Affairs and Political Science. "It took 10 years for me to finish college," she says. "I just had so many other things to do that I decided I'd go to school when I could."

In 1950 she accepted the position of dean of women at the College of St. Joseph in Albuquerque. (The now-defunct school later became the University of Albuquerque.) While there she taught freshman women a course called The Art of Graciousness. "It included Emily Post-types of things," she explains. Her students learned how to put on and take off gloves, to walk with a book on their head, and eat with the proper utensils. They also learned how to twirl spaghetti with a fork—a skill Concha apparently could teach, even though she never got the knack of it herself.

In 1975 the University of Albuquerque bestowed upon Concha an honorary doctorate. The accompanying citation said, in part: "It is appropriate that the University of Albuquerque has chosen to honor Mrs. de Kleven with a doctor of humanities. She has been a member of the Board of Trustees for 11 years, but her involvement with the school started long ago. When the University was located on South Second Street, Mrs. de Kleven scrubbed floors, waited on tables, and baked bread as part of her service to the school." The citation stated also: "This tribute is being made to a woman who has devoted her life to her community, church and state, and especially to people."

Capítulo 9
Raíces Políticas

Mucho antes de que el territorio de Nuevo México fuera aceptado como uno de los estados de la unión norteamericana, la familia Ortiz y Pino inició la tradición de su participación en asuntos políticos. Es una ironía que ese vínculo con la política tenga sus raíces en un acto de desafío en contra de los Estados Unidos de norteamérica. Ese vínculo remonta a Nicolás de Jesús Pino, hijo de Pedro Bautista Pino, que en 1811 se presentó en las Cortes de España un informe respecto a las condiciones en Nuevo México y a la vez solicitó ayuda para la provincia nuevomexicana.

Posteriormente, horrorizado por la violencia de una muchedumbre de indios en Taos que se rebelan y asesinan al gobernador del territorio de Nuevo México y torturan a docenas de norteamericanos, don Nicolás se arrepiente y promete que él y su familia, desde ese momento, prestarán servicio al gobierno de Nuevo México. En 1868, el primer cargo que desempeñó Nicolás Ortiz y Pino fue el de juez de paz. En seguida ganó los comicios para senador en la Legislatura del territorio, donde lo eligieron presidente del senado. También, dos hermanos de don Nicolás se distinguieron desempeñando cargos en el gobierno. Su hermano Facundo fue elegido varias veces al cargo de legislador donde fue presidente de la cámara de diputados y del senado. El otro hermano, Miguel fue elegido a la Legislatura en 1865. Otro descendiente de los Ortiz y Pino, don Nicolás, padre de José Ortiz y Pino, fue elegido a la Legislatura del Territorio de Nuevo México. José Ortiz y Pino, el padre de Concha, prestó servicios en la asamblea legislativa del estado de Nuevo México. Mientras desempeñaba el cargo de legislador, don José preparaba a Concha para que se prestara de candidata para servir en el cargo de legisladora.

Este capítulo contiene un excelente bosquejo histórico del derecho de sufragio femenino en los Estados Unidos de norteamérica y en Nuevo México. Cuenta doña Concha que pese a que ella no haya participado activamente en el movimiento femenino, ella cree que a toda mujer se le debe tratar como igual al hombre. Agrega ella: "He vivido una vida donde a veces yo era la única mujer que estaba involucrada en causas que afectan al público. Los hombres me trataron bien y a veces fueron mis protectores. Sin embargo, en otras ocasiones tuve que luchar para lograr las metas que me propuse."

Political Roots

Beginning long before New Mexico became one of the United States, and continuing ever since, was a bond linking the Ortiz y Pino family to the government of the state and the nation. Yet ironically that bond had its roots in an act of defiance against America. The link traces to *don* Nicolás de Jesús Pino, son of the renowned *don* Pedro Bautista Pino, who went to Spain in 1811 to plead for aid to his beloved province. *Don* Nicolás, who lived from 1819 to 1896, was born while New Mexico was still a colony of Spain, and he died just 16 years before it joined the American Union, as the 47th state, in 1912. Along the way, he lived through the entire Mexican era, from 1821 to 1846.

A man of great passion and devotion, *don* Nicolás was dismayed when the United States claimed New Mexico after the brief Mexican-American War. Quickly the young man joined a plot to overthrow the new, English-speaking government. But the plot was discovered—apparently the planners were reported to the American authorities by one alleged *doña* Tules, a flamboyant saloon owner in Santa Fe—and Nicolás was arrested.

A short while later, however, in January 1847, a drunken mob of Taos Indians, urged on by Mexican malcontents, staged an uprising in that northern town. They scalped and killed the U.S. Territorial governor, Charles Bent, and tortured and massacred a dozen other Americans. They then marched on Santa Fe, to seize the capital and inflame the whole territory to rebel. U. S. military forces confronted the rebels, and after a pitched battle vanquished them. Ten U.S. soldiers were killed and 52 were wounded, with several dying afterward. More than 150 Indians and Mexican loyalists were killed, many more were wounded, and several leaders were hanged after a brief trial.

Horrified by the violence, Nicolás changed his stance. He pledged allegiance to America, and further pledged that he and his family—then and in later generations—would serve in New Mexico's government. His first political office was as a justice of the peace in 1868, and he then moved on to the Territorial Senate, winning elections in 1869, 1873, and 1876. In the first of those terms, he served as president of the Senate.

Don Nicolás had two older brothers, both of whom distinguished themselves in government as well. Facundo was the first to serve, before Nicolás. Entering the Territorial Legislature in 1855, he won re-election several times, and was chosen both Speaker of the House and president of the Senate. But his career was cut short when he died young, in January 1863. His obituary from the *Río Abajo Weekly Press* states:

Hon. Facundo Pino

Died at Santa Fe, on the 28th *último*, after several weeks' illness, aged about forty years. At the time of his death, he was President of the Legislative Council; and it is worthy of mention, as a proof of the estimation in which his character and talents were held by that body, to say that, with the exception of one session, when a member, he was always chosen to preside over its deliberations. He was well educated, and an accomplished gentleman; and, had his life been spared, there is no telling the honors that might have been conferred upon him, not only by the people of this Territory, but by the United States, whose

Nicolás Pino, Concha's great-grandfather, and Juan Ortiz, her grandfather— courtesy Concha Ortiz y Pino de Kleven

institutions he loved with an ardor equaled only by that of one born and bred under them. *Requiescat in Pacem.*

The next Pino brother to serve was Miguel, who first was elected to the Territorial Legislature in 1865. Like his brothers, he became president of the Senate. When he died in June 1867 at the age of 45, a joint obituary was written about him and a man named *don* Simón Delgado. Taken from Concha's family scrapbook, the faded clipping declares:

> The spirit of Don Miguel Pino fitted life's hardest and most dangerous storms. He was quick, high, bold and defiant. In public life he was ambitious and aspiring and ever ready to contend against animosities, however violent and unjust they were. He knew the disadvantages under which his countrymen had been born and circumstances had placed them, and was ever keenly alive to wrongs, and oppressions, whenever inflicted upon the poorest of his poorest native countrymen by anyone born and educated under more favorable circumstances. This was natural to his proud and lofty nature, and a high merit in his character both he and Don Simón sympathized deeply with the people in all their sufferings and hopes, and longed to see education and improvements, elevate and bless the inhabitants. Both were devoted in their loyalty to the government and its faith, favor, forte and principals. Don Simón has left a widow with three children. Miguel has left a widow with no child. Our friends will long be fondly cherished by their friends and countrymen.

In Concha's direct line of ancestry, the next member of the Pino family to be elected to the Legislature was a grandson of *don* Nicolás, her father, José Ortiz y Pino—who served not a territory but a young state, as a representative in the Eighth Legislature, from 1927 to 1928. He was a member of the Republican Party, and his district included Santa Fe, Torrance, and Guadalupe counties. He carried a heavy load in the Legislature, serving on seven committees and chairing three of them. With all his other duties at his store, his ranch, and other businesses, and with no shortage of family responsibilities, José decided to leave the Legislature after just one term. But while there he was grooming his daughter Concha to follow him.

Nor was the official seat of state government in Santa Fe the only source of political preparation that Concha got as a girl and young woman. Even without fully realizing it, she was also influenced by the Women's Suffrage Movement—the battle for equal rights for women in America, in politics, in pay, and in other areas as well. Though barely aware of this struggle when she was a little Spanish-speaking child in Galisteo, Concha later learned a lot about it—and also did something about it, as a lawmaker.

Beginning with its origins, most of the young American nation treated women as decidedly second-class citizens when compared to men. In the English-speaking Eastern colonies, women could not sign contracts, own property, retain wages they earned, or seek divorce from their husbands, except in flagrant cases of adultery or equal outrages against society. Women were essentially considered pieces of property, owned by their husbands or fathers. Colonial governments recognized them as essential to building stable communities—something that fierce men with weapons could never do alone—but official appreciation for women did not go very far. In the conventional thinking of the day, even the Bible confirmed women to be inferior.

Yet more and more American women were being educated, often beyond their husbands' level, and more and more of them began questioning their status. Beginning in the early 1800s, with many women then working for pay—either from their homes or in factories—struggles for better wages, shorter hours, and other rights broke out in various places. Husbands, brothers, and other men often took the women's side. Then the Civil War, 1861–65, in which women played indispensable and often heroic roles as battlefield nurses and hospital workers, enhanced their standing dramatically.

Four years after the war ended, the American Woman Suffrage Association elected Henry Ward Beecher its first president in 1869. That same year, Susan B. Anthony and Elizabeth Cady Stanton founded the National Woman Suffrage Association. Later the organizations merged, and in 1884 nominated the first female candidate for president—even though women could not vote in presidential elections. Several states, however, had amended their constitutions to allow women to vote on issues such as school bonds and taxes. In 1889, Wyoming requested to join the Union as the first state with full voting rights for women. Then in 1919 the entire nation gave women the vote.

In New Mexico the official status of women had not been quite as bad as in some other states or territories, for under Mexican law they could own property in their own right, could inherit it, and could will it to whomever they wished, male or female. Yet the Spanish tradition, and then the American tradition, both kept women "in their place." But the frontier had harsh realities of life on the ground, and strong women as well as strong men could and did make their own place.

As the American national debate on women's rights was mounting in the 1880s, a baby girl who would lead the fight in New Mexico was born, in 1881. Her long name was María Adelina Isabel Emilia Otero, and she was called Nina. (She later married and divorced an American soldier, Rawson D. Warren.) Her family lines, Otero and Luna, included some influential members: a colonist during the de Vargas era after the 1692 reconquest, and her father, Manuel B. Otero, a prominent landowner.

The 1910 New Mexico Constitutional Convention, which hammered out the conditions for statehood in 1912, gave recognition to women's rights, allowing them to hold school offices such as superintendent, director, or member of a board of education. But it reserved

Nina Otero Warren—courtesy Museum of New Mexico, negative no. 89756

for men the power to decide whether women could actually vote in such elections. If enough men objected, the women could not vote. Between 1914 and 1920, Otero worked to win full voting rights for women, at the forefront of a suffragist group called Alice Paul's Congressional Union. More than half its members were married, a third were New Mexico-born, and two-fifths had moved to New Mexico from the Midwest, between 1871 and 1890. But the drive ended in disappointment, when the all-male Legislature rejected the New Mexico Suffrage Bill in 1917, by four votes. Yet in defiance of that verdict, Otero ran for and won the office of superintendent of public schools.

Two years later, Congress passed the 19th Amendment, calling for women to vote in all elections. Before it could become law, however, the measure had to be ratified by three-fourths of the states. When it came before the New Mexico Legislature in 1920, Otero defended it before the state Republican caucus for three hours—a shocking piece of behavior, as no woman had ever before appeared at a state political caucus. Shortly afterward, New Mexico voted yes, to help make women's suffrage the law of the land.

When the amendment was ratified, Concha Ortiz y Pino was 10 years old, just entering formal school in Santa Fe. "I don't remember any of the Suffrage Movement," she acknowledges. "Evidently it didn't extend to Galisteo, or we would have been involved—especially since Mamá Fita advised all the politicians. If I had known about it as a child, of course I would have approved."

The Women's Liberation Movement has come a long way since 1919. Concha never officially identified herself with it, even though her record has certainly advanced equality for women. "I'm not a woman's libber, but I feel that we all should be treated equally," she says as she looks back. "I've lived a life where sometimes I was the only woman involved. The men were very sweet to me, and sometimes protective. In other instances, however, I had to work very hard to accomplish my goals."

Capítulo 10

La crisis económica que azotó al país y la Caravana de Publicidad para elegir a Roosevelt presidente de la república

Cuando Concha estaba estudiando en la Universidad de George Washington, en la capital de la nación norteamericana, sucesos de grande escala tenían gran efecto en su vida. La segunda década del siglo veinte fue una de prosperidad en los Estados Unidos. Sin embargo, en 1929 empezó la crisis económica que afectó al país y a otras partes del mundo. Cuando la crisis económica estaba en su apogeo, Concha ya estaba de vuelta con su familia en Galisteo. Su familia, una de las pocas familias ricas en la comarca, tomaba medidas para ayudar a sus vecinos durante esa crisis.

Concha sentía la necesidad de prestar su ayuda y le dijo a su padre, "Tengo que hacer algo porque quiero prestar mi ayuda para que la gente logre mejorar sus condiciones económicas." En 1929, Concha y su hermana Mela establecieron la Sociedad de Artesanía Hispánica Colonial en Galisteo. Concha confeccionó un plan con el fin de que las mujeres que pertenecían a dicha sociedad vendieran su artesanía en una de las tiendas en Santa Fe. Este esfuerzo llamó la atención de otros grupos en distintas partes de Nuevo México. Por fin, el padre de Concha, don José, la convenció que cerrara la empresa. No obstante, don José decidió que Concha debía emprender una carrera política. Don José permitió que su hija acompañara, en capacidad de chofer, al político John E. Miles, que se dedicaba a la campaña de publicidad política cuyo fin era elegir a Franklin Roosevelt, presidente de los Estados Unidos. Concha, a la edad de 21 años, se unió a la Caravana de Publicidad pro Roosevelt con el fin de apoyar la campaña que dirigía Clyde Tingley, alcalde de Albuquerque, y otros políticos nuevomexicanos. Don José estableció reglas que le imponía a su hija Concha, al efecto de que ella asistiría únicamente a reuniones oficiales con fines políticos y nada más.

Roosevelt ganó la presidencia con gran mayoría de votos. Concha quedó emocionada porque había participado activamente en esa victoriosa campaña política que eligió a Roosevelt presidente de la nación. Concha se dio cuenta de que había encontrado la luz que alumbraría su trayecto en la vida.

The Depression and the FDR Caravan

While the impressionable young Concha was just playing at being a college student at George Washington University in the nation's capital in 1928, events on a grander scale were converging in a calamitous way that would affect her next years and all the rest of her life. The 1920s were a glittering decade in the U.S., and in much of the outside world. Referred to as the Roaring 20s, the New Era and the Decade of Prosperity, the 1920s rode high on mass industrial production, mass advertising, and massive credit, in a nation that always before had lived on thrift and savings. It was an economic bubble that had to burst sooner or later—and so it did, in October 1929, when the New York stock market crashed and the worldwide Great Depression began.

All across America, people could no longer keep up with installments on goods they had purchased with debt. Sales of new goods plummeted, and workers were laid off from idle factories. Banks began failing, and their depositors lost their savings. Farmers could not meet mortgage payments, and suddenly landless, their families streamed into cities, or into "golden destinations" such as California, which in reality provided no relief. The new arrivals, willing to work for a pittance, took jobs away from former white-collar employees now out on the streets selling bread made by their wives. A massive 10-year drought accompanied the Depression, and turned the fertile Midwest into what was called the Dust Bowl. Food shortages followed economic ruin.

New Mexico fared somewhat better than the rest of the country in the Depression, though barely. The drought did not hit the state as hard as it did the Midwest, and as a largely rural area, accustomed to meeting its own needs on small farms, New Mexico continued to eke out an economic existence. But outside cash, which fueled progress, growth, and stability, virtually stopped coming in. Galisteo, like all villages in New Mexico, faced harder times than anyone could remember, and survival was difficult. Concha was

Concha with Albuquerque Mayor Clyde Tingley to her left and the Roosevelt Caravan—courtesy Concha Ortiz y Pino de Kleven

U.S. Sen. Dennis Chávez with the Roosevelt Caravan at Vallecitos, N.M., in the 1930s— courtesy Center for Southwest Research, University of New Mexico, negative no. 000-457-0074.1

54

back home when the worst ravages of the Depression struck, and as one of the few prosperous families, the Ortiz y Pinos accelerated their efforts to help their neighbors. "Mamá Fita even made panties for the little girls," Concha remembers vividly. "She made them out of rags, just so they'd have something on themselves."

As an educated young woman now instead of a child, Concha felt a strong personal need to act. "I told my father, 'I have to do something to help people make money." She got him to provide a hilltop house that the family owned, and firewood to heat it. For three days Concha cleaned and painted the house, then opened it in 1929 as the Colonial Hispanic Crafts Society of Galisteo, with coffee and refreshments, courtesy of her father. Concha's sister Mela taught embroidery, someone else taught knitting, and her father hired an expert teacher in colonial arts and crafts. Concha, who could weave a bit, helped the women make small rugs. She also negotiated a selling outlet in Santa Fe.

"We used rosebuds to make perfume, and created luxury items," she smiles in memory. "We had teachers, a building, food and warmth, and an outlet for selling. With our school we could make items for ourselves and others, and earn some money. My aim was to revive long-neglected crafts and at the same time supply furniture, blankets, leather goods, and clothing for the trainees." The effort caught the attention of the New Mexico Department of Vocational Education, which sent six persons for training.

Other New Mexico towns, including Santa Fe and El Rito, launched similar projects. But after about a year, Concha's Galisteo operation shut down. "My father didn't feel that we were generating enough help for the participants," she recalls with regret. "I think it bothered him that I was always asking for money for ice cream and Cokes for everybody. He told me, 'Concha, eres tan entremetida.' ('You're such a busybody.') He wanted me to leave everyone alone to go on his or her own way. Finally he told me to close the school. I hated to do it, but I had lost my sponsor."

Her father's decision seemed stern, but he was aware of things that Concha did not know. One of them was that a man named Bruce Sewell was about to launch a much grander project to stimulate the state economy by preserving traditional arts. "He was to do for New Mexico what I was doing in Galisteo," she acknowledges. "His project grew and developed beautifully. On a personal level, I could walk away and do something else." And her father had decided that she should walk away into politics.

John E. Miles, a close friend of José and a rising politician in New Mexico, was traveling around the state in 1932, stumping for Democrat presidential candidate Franklin D. Roosevelt. "All of us felt hopeful that FDR could help us out of the Depression," Concha says. "Johnny Miles traveled in his own car, so my dad told him I could be his driver. We went to Las Cruces, Santa Fe, Las Vegas, Taos, so many places. We'd stop at the little *pueblitos* and talk to the people." Later that year the 21-year-old Concha also rode with the Roosevelt Caravan, a bus used by Albuquerque Mayor Clyde Tingley, Police

Concha with Frank Baca in 1929 at San Juan Pueblo—courtesy Center for Southwest Research, University of New Mexico, negative no. 000-457-0007

El Corrido de Gallo *and*
Baile *sponsored by Concha*
Ortiz y Pino de Kleven,
standing in the center with
back to camera and right of
the luminarias (bonfires), to
benefit the Galisteo Arts and
Crafts School, which she
founded during the Depression.
Photo by T. Harman
Parkhurst—courtesy Museum
of New Mexico, negative no.
133005

An invitation to the dance to
support the Galisteo Vocational
Crafts School—courtesy
Center for Southwest
Research, University of New
Mexico

Fiesta
Dinner and Baile

for Benefit of the New

Galisteo
Vocational Crafts
School

Sponsored by Miss Concha Ortiz y Pino

Galisteo, N.M. Oct. 22, 1933

FREE FIESTA ALL DAY

Featuring a

CORRIDA DE GALLO

(CHICKEN PULL)

Galisteo Boys vs. Santo Domingo Indians

Free Dancing All Afternoon

Spanish Dinner and Baile in Evening

Admission $1.00

Come, have a good time and help this worthy school.

Chief Ben Martínez, and other New Mexico politicians.

A strict José Ortiz y Pino, cognizant of his daughter's youth and vulnerability, laid down stern rules concerning her. She could travel with the Miles car and the FDR Caravan, but after arriving in towns she could not socialize with her fellow campaigners. She could attend official meetings, but anything beyond political purposes was out of the question. He put Chief Martínez in charge of her well-being. Concha went along with the restrictions. Looking back, she says she liked the traveling and driving, but when called on to speak in public, at first she was afraid. "But one time in Taos, all that changed. I was scared, but the people were so nice that I relaxed. I started telling them about Mr. Roosevelt and how he could help all of us. They listened and even applauded when I finished speaking. By the time we were done, I felt confident that I could do this again. In the end, I spoke many times." Concha wouldn't have said so at the time, but she was mastering the art of persuasion.

The Miera y Pacheco map—courtesy Museum of New Mexico, negative no. 154985

Roosevelt defeated incumbent Republican President Herbert Hoover in a national landslide in 1932, and quickly began implementing his New Deal programs to battle the Depression. Agencies that had special impact upon New Mexico included the Federal Emergency Relief Act (FERA), which provided employment; the Civilian Conservation Corps (CCC), which undertook a massive program to construct trails, bridges, parks, recreational facilities, and other public works; the Agricultural Adjustment Act (AAA), which aided farmers; the Works Progress Administration (WPA), which built public buildings such as schools, courthouses, libraries, and government offices; and the Federal Art Project (FAP), which commissioned writers, painters, photographers, and other artists to record, preserve, celebrate, and honor the country's regional artistic heritages.

In New Mexico, as well as in the rest of the nation, the arts program brought a virtual renaissance for learning. Music, painting, sculpture, and theater all benefited, and the artists were paid a government salary for their efforts. Photographer Ansel Adams recorded life in Mora, Peñasco, Pie Town, Hernández, and other small villages. Writers Reyes Martínez, Loren Brown, and Blanche Grant, among others, put down on paper life as it was lived in the 1930s, and before. An ancient 1779 Miera y Pacheco map of New Mexico had been discovered by a shepherd near Velarde; the Federal Art Project preserved it for posterity. The Historical Social Archives produced a state guidebook under the direction of Ina Sizer Cassidy. Aurora Lucero-White gathered collections of folklore. The Federal Music Project hired Helen Chandler Ryan to record and revive New Mexico Hispanic music. Artists Patrociño Barela and Juan Sánchez carved *bultos* to preserve sacred art with wood. The lists of New Mexico artists goes on and on.

As these bold and imaginative programs began strengthening New Mexico as well as the rest of the country, Concha was thrilled. She also was thrilled that she had played a part in backing President Roosevelt, and in helping convince her state to support him. She had breathed deeply of the heady air of politics, and was electrified by it. An aimless young woman no longer, she had found a course in life.

CAPÍTULO 11
Los años de legisladora

Concha sabía que la tradición de la familia Ortiz y Pino conllevaba la promesa de que por lo menos uno de los familiares iba a prestar servicio al gobierno del estado. Concha había cumplido 21 años. En esa época las expectativas normales de una joven de su edad era aspirar a una vida de mujer casada, la maternidad, una vida en familia, participación en asociaciones como la de padres y maestros, prestar ayuda a las asociaciones comunitarias, y formar parte de organizaciones de índole social. Pero, su participación en la campaña política para elegir a Franklin Roosevelt presidente había inspirado en Concha deseos de participar en la política. Su padre no se opuso. Al contrario, le inspiraba ánimo a su hija Concha.

En 1936, Concha decidió lanzarse de candidata para el cargo de legisladora en la asamblea legislativa de Nuevo México. Ganó los comicios y era la tercera legisladora hispánica que fue elegida a la asamblea legislativa de Nuevo México. Sus colegas en la legislatura la nombraron que prestara servicio en cinco comités importantes. Reelegida a la asamblea legislativa varias veces, llegó a ser líder del partido mayoritario en la cámara de diputados, la primera mujer que logró desempeñar ese cargo en el país. Al recordar su carrera de legisladora Concha dice: "La mayor parte de la legislación que presenté fue con el fin de que hubiera cambios respecto a la mujer y en el sistema educativo." Respecto al idioma español, Concha presentó un proyecto de ley al efecto de que a los estudiantes en escuela primaria del séptimo y octavo nivel, les ofrecieran clases de español. Al nivel nacional, logró conseguir el apoyo de dos educadores y distinguidos líderes políticos. El propósito de la legislación era que los estudiantes deberían dominar más de un idioma. Respecto a la educación a nivel universitario, Concha presentó un proyecto de ley a fin de establecer la Facultad de Estudios Inter-Americanos en la Universidad de Nuevo México. Después de cumplir tres términos de legisladora, decidió no seguir en esa carrera y se matriculó en la Universidad de Nuevo México. Se especializó en las materias que ofrecía la Facultad de Estudios Latinoamericanos, y en esa especialización académica recibió su licenciatura.

The Legislative Frontier

11

Concha knew that the Ortiz y Pino family heritage carried with it the promise of generation after generation serving New Mexico state government. When her father José was elected to the Legislature in 1927, she thought that he would bear the banner in a major way. "People wanted my dad to run for governor," she says. "But this is what he said: '*Soy de mi gente. De mi gente voy a ser.*' ('I am of my people. Of my people I will be.') He wanted to remain an average citizen, Spanish-speaking, in Galisteo. He refused to run for governor, and left the Legislature after only one two-year term. But instead he encouraged *me* to run for the Legislature."

As a young woman in her 20s, Concha lived at a time when normal expectations for her were pretty much limited to marriage, parenthood, family involvement, being active in the PTA, helping at community fund-raisers, and belonging to the right social circles. But her statewide participation in the 1932 presidential campaign of Franklin Roosevelt had excited her to the core, and whetted her appetite for politics. Pushing her along in this direction was her father. Although he was elected to the Legislature as a Republican, the political landscape in northern New Mexico underwent a transformation with FDR, the Depression, and the New Deal. That part of the state became more Democratic than Republican, and has remained that way.

In 1936, when Roosevelt was seeking his first re-election as president, 26-year-old Concha decided to seek political office for herself, as a member of the state of New Mexico's House of Representatives, from Santa Fe County's District 4. Roosevelt won his race in November, and Concha won too, becoming the state's third female legislator. The first two, who served in the 1930–31 session, were Fidelina "Faye" Lucero of Mora County and Porfiria Paiz from Quemado. They were the nation's first Hispanic women elected to a state legislative body, and Concha followed in their pioneering footsteps.

When the 13th Legislature convened in 1937, Concha was assigned to five committees: corporations and banks, educational institutions, judiciary, livestock, and roads and highways. She won re-election to another two-year term in 1938, and then was named to five more committees: appropriations and finance, oil and gas, privileges and elections, public lands, and taxation and revenue. She was re-elected yet again in 1940, and served on still more committees: interstate cooperation, mines, public lands, rules and order of business, and the committee on committees—which decides who will serve on which panels. Moreover, she represented New Mexico for four years on the Interstate Council of State Governments, and was New Mexico's official delegate to the New York World's Fair in 1940. There were few areas of government in which the young legislator from Galisteo and Santa Fe was not deeply involved.

In addition to gaining experience and seniority with her re-elections and committee work, Concha was developing impressive qualities of leadership, a fact that did not go unnoticed by the leaders of the Democratic Party. When the party held its legislative caucus in 1941, Concha was named its majority whip in the House of Representatives. The holder of this important floor-leadership post has the duty to constantly interact with all the party's other elected representatives, keeping them aligned with the party's official position on issues and votes. While still in her 20s, unmarried, Hispanic, and female, Concha made history by becoming the first woman ever to serve as majority whip in any state legislature in the nation. Barely two decades after women won the right to

15th LEGISLATURE STATE OF NEW MEXICO

1941   1942.

Photo by De Castro

Gov. John E. Miles

Sylver Lorenzo

Don G. McCormick

Whip
Miss Concha Ortiz y Pino

Speaker
Frank McCarthy

Floor Leader
Gilbert Lopez

Carles E. Tomich

15th New Mexico State Legislature, with Concha Ortiz y Pino, first female majority whip in the United States in 1941—courtesy Concha Ortiz y Pino de Kleven

vote in 1919, she had cracked a significant political "glass ceiling."

Of the various bills that she herself sponsored, Concha took the greatest satisfaction from ones that promoted women and education. "All the legislation I introduced was to change things," she reflects. "For example, women had been able to vote since the 1920s, but they still could not serve on juries. I thought this was unfair, so I fought to equalize the situation. My law passed." She fought also to equalize educational funding for schools in both rural and urban areas. That measure too became law.

"I was able to pass proposals because I worked well with my fellow legislators," she says, revealing a secret of her success. "In order to win the vote, I had to explain my positions well. I met weekly with key citizens to keep myself apprised of the latest developments, and to learn. I also used the art of compromise. It worked. I was so young and the only female representative at that time, so the men were very protective. Everyone helped me."

On at least one occasion, however, one man was not at all helpful. Ironically, he was the old family friend Johnny Miles, who was elected New Mexico governor in 1938. Knowing that Concha disagreed with him on a bill that was coming up for a vote, Miles invited her to visit him in his executive office. She was glad to do so, but after she got there, the governor began chatting aimlessly and at great length on topics that did not seem pertinent to her. She began to worry that she should be on the House floor doing her duties, but she did not want to be rude by interrupting the governor. Then, before she could politely excuse

STANFORD UNIVERSITY, CALIFORNIA

February 12, 1941

Miss Concha Ortiz y Pino,
Santa Fé, New Mexico.

Dear Miss Ortiz y Pino:

I am in receipt of your recent letter, in which you ask me for an opinion concerning the teaching of Spanish in the Public Schools of New Mexico, in the 5th-8th grades. I am of course very glad to comply with your kind request in view of the fact that it is a subject that has interested me for many years, in fact all my life as a teacher and investigator of linguistic problems in New Mexico.

The study of Spanish in the schools of the United States is of the greatest possible importance. As Herbert Hoover said many years ago, when he was Secretary of Commerce, "Spanish has an importance in this Continent second only to that of English, and , if not made compulsory, should at least be made available to all our students of high school and college." At the present moment Spanish has become almost of equal importance in this Continent to that of English. English is being introduced in most schools of South America, and in the United States it is now by far the most important language in our schools next to English. Those who do not wish to recognize this have obviously no vision. We must make all possible efforts to make the Spanish language the second language of all America. This is no longer a hope or a plan; it is becoming a reality, and it is absolutely necessary for National Defense and for the future prosperity, peace and good will of the Americas.

Now, what is the relation of all this to the problem of teaching Spanish in the 5th-8th grades in New Mexico? Very much indeed. In New Mexico, unfortunately, some of our leaders did not have the vision to look ahead. Many years ago, Spanish should have been taught in the grades. But it is still possible to save much of the Spanish linguistic heritage that New Mexico possesses. Many people from New Mexico still speak Spanish, the great and beautiful language of the Conquistadores and Castilla, the language that is spoken today by millions upon millions of our best friends and neighbors in the Carribean, in Central and South America, and our distant friends in Spain and in the Philippines. Therefore, it is high time that we in New Mexico make an effort to coordinate with the national defense program and teach Spanish in the grades, where it can be done with such great advantages on Old Spanish soil and with the powerful backing and enthusiastic efforts of a native Spanish-speaking population that love that

language as much as they do English. In Canada French is taught in the grades as well as English in all communities where it is desired. Spanish-speaking children in New Mexico in many cases learn Spanish with great difficulties. The State should take advantage of this interest and this great heritage as the starting-point for a drive to have Spanish officially declared as the second language of New Mexicans. Placing Spanish instruction in the 5th-8th grades will do exactly that. And with that foundation the interest for Spanish will grow and it will be more popular in high school and college.

There are some books already available for these grades. They should consist for the most part of reading and writing Spanish, as well as speaking, and for speaking, what better laboratory than the daily contacts and conversation with Spanish-speaking children? We have the ideal situation for this in New Mexico. And do not worry about the type of Spanish that is spoken in New Mexico. I have travelled all over Spain and parts of Spanish America, and I can assure you that the Spanish spoken in New Mexico is all right. It is a little archaic in its vocabulary and grammar, but it is good Spanish. That is why it makes a good foundation on which to build. It is a solid and firm foundation. It is for you, the leaders of the land, to see to it that this great language be not lost in the land of the Conquistadores, but rather improved, enriched and made available to young people in the grades, when they are at the plastic age when languages come easy to them. Silver Burdett and Company have a few easy books that can be used in 5th-6th grades in Spanish classes. Oxford University Press is now publishing a fine series, under my own general editorship, designed for the 8th and 9th grades. I should be glad to ask them to send you some of those already published. Of course new ones could be prepared by the Oxford University Press if you need them.

Under separate cover I am sending you a little pamphlet that will give you additional information. I am strong for the project now before your legislature. Please tell your legislators that an old freind of New Mexico, one who has devoted all his life to the linguistic and folkloristic and general cultural problems of this blessed land of the conquistadores, votes yes on the project, and it is his hope that the vote will be unanimous.

Very sincerely and devotedly yours

Aurelio M. Espinosa

Executive Head of the Department of Romanic Languages and Corresponding Member of the Royal Spanish Academy

A letter from Dr. Aurelio Espinosa in support of bill sponsored by Concha Ortiz y Pino to allow the Spanish language to be taught in New Mexico public schools— courtesy Center for Southwest Research, University of New Mexico

herself, someone came in with the news that the vote on the bill had already taken place. "I missed the vote," she fumes even now. "I knew that the governor had purposely kept me away."

Such stratagems did not often fool Concha, however, and she could be adamantly stubborn for causes she believed in. One such cause was the Spanish language. She remembered with resentment that she had been punished for speaking it at the Loretto Academy, and she did not think New Mexican students should be penalized that way. But as a legislator, she learned that an English-only policy was still being strictly enforced in many schools. "I think that people believed they were helping by forcing the children to speak only in English— making them blend in with their fellow Americans," she says. "What they didn't realize was that they were actually robbing the little ones of their culture." So typically, she decided to address the situation.

Her proposed solution was to pass a state law requiring formal instruction in the Spanish language for all seventh- and eighth-grade students—Anglos as well as Hispanos—in schools that would conduct their other classes in English. "I thought this bill was a no-brainer, not controversial," she recalls. "But, boy, was I wrong! The Spanish public did not love the idea. The LULACs (League of United Latin-American Citizens) worked against me, and kicked me out of their organization twice. It made my father feel very bad to know that because I fought for the bilingual bill I received these problems. He knew that the LULACs were mean to me."

A letter that appeared in the Albuquerque Journal in support of the bill to have the Spanish language taught in New Mexico public schools— courtesy Center for Southwest Research, University of New Mexico

As opposition mounted, Concha worked all the harder on behalf of her bill. To help her, she enlisted the support of powerful and influential allies. One was a well-respected educator, Dr. Aurelio Espinosa, formerly of the University of New Mexico and then a professor at Stanford University. He wrote a letter endorsing the idea. Another major backer was one of New Mexico's U.S. senators, Dennis Chávez, who addressed the Legislature urging passage of the bill. She had gotten to know Chávez who was a friend of her family, during her brief time in Washington, when he was a member of the House of Representatives. Sen. Chávez (who now is one of two New Mexicans memorialized in a sculpture in the Hall of Statuary in the nation's Capitol in Washington) and his wife frequently took the young Concha to church with them. Another U.S. senator from New Mexico, Bronson Cutting, who preceded Chávez had also shared long conversations with Concha about political-science education. "We discussed the fact that we were creating Americans," she says. " We had to encourage boys and girls to vote. We had to help them learn much."

In Concha's mind, her bilingual bill would help all New Mexico students in the process of becoming American citizens. Thus the determined opposition surprised and perplexed her. "Some people actually believed that I was against students learning the English language, that I wanted to keep them dumb. How absurd! That was untrue. I never felt it was bad for students to learn English, but I also believed that people became more valuable and more educated when they knew more than one language." She stuck to her guns, refused to back down, and saw her bill voted into law.

But the success came at a price. "When my bill finally succeeded, I wondered whether or not I was victorious," she reflects. "Someone wrapped toilet paper around my door. The police had to escort me from the building on the day of the vote, because of the threats I had received." Now six decades later, she still ponders the same question. "Today, some of the students are once again leaving their Spanish language," she muses. "I hope they don't regret it later."

VOTE FOR

Concha Ortiz y Pino

Candidate for
State Representative

_____

Pledge

1. *Educational* Improvements

2. No Additional *Taxes*

3. Proper Distribution of *Relief*

4. Interest in *Livestock* Industry

Much of Concha's legislative work benefited the University of New Mexico. "I went east and lived in a dorm in Washington, but when I came home for Christmas I decided I liked UNM better. There were 2,000 people attending the school at the time. The professors were nice. There were lots of brick buildings. I liked everything about it. When Dr. James Zimmerman, the university president, came to me with requests for help, I had no problem saying yes. I also helped another president, Dr. Tom Popejoy."

One of Zimmerman's most deeply held beliefs was that people in the United States should make a concentrated effort to understand their Latin-American neighbors, and that higher education should help achieve that goal. He wanted the University of New Mexico to establish a special school for that purpose. Concha agreed, and worked in the Legislature to make such a school a reality. Zimmerman's dream came true and the school of Inter-American Affairs is now a part of the campus. Concha also worked with Zimmerman to obtain a collection of rare books on Mexican history, which UNM acquired for its library, in competition with several other historical institutions.

Not all of Concha's efforts for the university worked out to her liking. "I once introduced an appropriations bill to provide $90,000 for the UNM library," she recalls a bit ruefully. "I worked hard to gain this money. But somehow the university mysteriously used it for a golf course instead of for the library." She has nothing against golf, she says, but feels that far more people would have benefited from the original library plan. "The numbers don't compare. In the Legislature we all knew that our work could undergo changes, amendments, etc. However, I don't think any of us ever anticipated an outright change in spending once the lawmakers voted on where the money was to go."

In 1942, after three two-year terms in the House of Representatives, Concha, now 32 years old, decided not to seek re-election. Her work in the New Mexico Legislature was done, and now she wanted to achieve a goal she had earlier set aside, to await its proper time in her life. She wanted to earn a college degree—and the place where she decided to get it was the University of New Mexico, in the new Inter-American Affairs Institute, which she had been instrumental in founding.

Concha Ortiz y Pino's campaign literature—courtesy Concha Ortiz y Pino de Kleven

Capítulo 12
El hombre, Victor Kleven

Joven atractiva de eminente y acaudalada familia, Concha seguramente había captado la atención de muchos pretendientes. A la vez joven reservada, discreta, se crió durante la era pos-victoriana, Concha es reacia hablar respecto a relaciones amorosas que hayan ocurrido antes de que conociera y se enamorara de Victor Kleven, profesor y administrador en la Universidad de Nuevo México. Como era hombre inteligente y bien parecido, Concha quedó encantada de Victor cuando lo vio por primera vez.

Recuerda doña Concha que asistió a una conferencia dictada por el Profesor Kleven, hombre inteligente, maravilloso, de mucho talento. Concha quedó encantada al conocerlo. Cuenta Concha que dentro de poco tiempo se enamoraron. "Conversábamos inteligentemente sin discordar." En diciembre 1943, el Padre Theo Mayer pronuncia las nupcias entre el Dr. Victor Kleven y Concha en la Catedral de San Francisco en Santa Fe. Fiel a sus tradiciones, Concha le agrega a su apellido familiar el apellido de Kleven. El matrimonio no procreó hijos y trataron de adoptar el hijo de una de las empleadas de la familia. Antes de que terminara el proceso de adopción, la madre decidió poner al niño en un orfanato. El profesor Kleven y el niño siguieron comunicándose por carta.

En esos días, Concha y Victor decidieron construir su propia casa en el rancho de Galisteo. La noche que iban a celebrar el estreno de la casa, Concha y Victor fueron a llevarle un regalo de cumpleaños al niño que hubieran adoptado, que ahora estaba en el orfanato. Encantado al recibir el regalo, el niño cariñosamente les dio un abrazo.

Mientras que Concha y Victor iban de regreso a su casa, Victor se desplomó en el asiento del automóvil. Con mucha prisa, Concha lo llevó al hospital en Santa Fe. Cuando llegaron al hospital, ya Victor había fallecido. El año era 1956. Victor murió a la edad de 59 años.

The Man, Victor Kleven

As a strikingly attractive young woman from a prosperous and prominent (some would say aristocratic) New Mexico family, as a history-making female legislator decades ahead of her era, as an intelligent and courageous fighter for causes she believed in and as someone who packed more living into her first 30 years than most people do in a lifetime, Concha surely turned many a young man's head in her youth, and set many stalwart male hearts to fluttering. Yet with a reticence tracing to the proper post-Victorian age in which she grew up, she is reluctant to talk about whatever romances she may have had before the one great love of her life—a man named Victor Kleven—came along.

Even her family scrapbook—teeming with photos, certificates, souvenirs and mementos not only of her own nine decades but also decades that preceded her—holds tantalizingly scant evidence of romantic liaisons. One keepsake is a typewritten and lovelorn poem composed for her by a swain who identified himself merely with his initials: "S.E.D.D." Apparently he considered Concha *"une belle dame sans merci,"* as the French might say—a beautiful woman without mercy—for he wrote:

Concha Ortiz y Pino—photo by Robert H. Martin

> For months and years I've waited now,
> Hoping that we'd meet somehow,
> Discouraged 'cause you do not write—
> Inspired by love to keep up the fight.
>
> A thousand plans I've had for you,
> But then I'd not know what to do,
> Because for months I had not heard,
> One single, little, lonesome word.
>
> I've written letters, sent you flowers,
> And thought of you at times for hours—
> I walked again, my hand in yours,
> At Fiesta time, among the flowers.
> —Adored your picture (so serene)
> In the New Mexican magazine—
> Oh, I could not begin to tell
> How much I've lived within the spell,
>   Of adoration.

DARLING:

For months and years I've waited now,
Hoping that we'd meet somehow,
Discouraged 'cause you do not write--
Inspired by love to keep up the fight.

A thousand plans I've had for you,
But then I'd not know what to do,
Because for months I had not heard,
One single, little,lonesome word.

I've written letters, sent you flowers,
And thought of you at times for hours--
I walked again, my hand in yours,
At fiesta time, among the flowers.
--dored your picture (so serene)
In the New Mexican magazine---
Oh I could not begin to tell
How much I've lived within the spell,
Of adoration.

--2--

Sometimes we think she does not care,
And by her absence way out there
Has thought it best just to forget
Or let events go on and drift.
Of course we know her philosophy
"That what's to be is going to be,"
But fear that it may not inspire,
A genuinely deep desire
To keep alive that spark divine
Which she again may never find.

A love that full and wholesome is,
     cannot be denied,
Unless it's crushed and trampled down,
     or cruelly laid aside.
A woman knows this in her soul,
As nature cries: "That is your goal"--
For women who do not live and love,
Have missed God's message from above.

Of course there is your own career,
Which I do wish for you, my dear.
I know you'll soon be proud and great
And hold bigger offices in your state,
And even come to Congress--Yes,
And be a Senator then, I guess.
I wish for you these things and more,
And know you're trying hard to soar
And utilize your charm and grace
To help your people and your state.

But all the while, I hope you'll see,
You cannot faithful to your people be,

Unless unto yourself you're true,
And do what God would have you do:
To love, - to rear a tousled head-
to wash a dish---to make a bed--
And hundreds more of little chores
That are filled with what love hath
                         in store.

Then,too, I may have overlooked,
Another page upon our book,
Which says you've found someone else,
With whom your soul has deeply felt,
     the touch of love.
And rather than spend the passing years,
In futile hopes, in sighs and tears--
You may be want to go ahead
And neglect our love until its dead.
But this I ask, Why is that so?
Whatever you do, where'er you go,
Why can't you inspiration give and gain,
And get relief from life's sharp pains,
Even if you communicate with him, and
nothing more,
Or write to him each month or so.

Oh,Concha,Darling, don't you see,
"What's meant to be is meant to be,"?
Why don't you stop and write just once,
And tell me how you feel
And ask me for a kiss,to seal,
Our love.

--4--

And send our token
So that I may keep it close
Until you and I can meet again.

V.E.D.D.

Some poetry written for Concha—courtesy Center for Southwest Research, University of New Mexico

The piteous and somewhat lengthy lament continues in this vein for seven more verses, in which the forlorn suitor's heart is left bleeding on the page. A sampling:

> A love that full and wholesome is,
>   cannot be denied.
> Unless it's crushed and trampled down
>   or cruelly laid aside.
> A woman knows this in her soul,
> As nature cries: "That is your goal"—
>   For women who do not live and love.
> Have missed God's message from above.

Obviously familiar with her legislative accomplishments, he notes:

> Of course there is your own career,
> Which I do wish for you, my dear.
> I know you'll soon be proud and great,
> And hold bigger offices in your state,
> And even come to Congress—Yes,
> And be a Senator then, I guess.

Yet he makes plain that he wishes to share domestic bliss with her:

> …To love,—to wash a tousled head—
> to wash a dish—to make a bed—
> And hundreds more of little chores
> That are filled with what love hath in store.

Suddenly a dismaying suspicion overcomes him:

> …Then too, I may have overlooked,
> Another page upon our book,
> Which says you've found someone else,
> With whom your soul has deeply felt,
>   The touch of love.

He pleads with her, however, to forsake all others:

> Oh, Concha, Darling, don't you see,
> "What's meant to be is meant to be"?
> Why don't you stop and write just once,
> And tell me how you feel
> And ask me for a kiss, to seal,
> Our love.

But apparently his fervent appeal went for naught.

Another aging piece of paper preserved at the Center for Southwest Research, UNM, is a letter sent to Concha in 1943, from a man named Chad. It was mailed from Honolulu, Hawaii, where perhaps he was stationed in the Pacific Theater of World War II. Half a statement of friendship and half a declaration of love, the letter reminisces fondly about experiences that the writer and Concha shared in Santa Fe—visits to St. Francis Cathedral, strolls along little streams—and inquires about her parents. It goes on to say:

> Dear Concha, you were sweet to write. Always do so when you can, for I love to read your words. I love even more. Do you mind if I tell you who? Not even if I tell you I love you?…And when you write you will send a snapshot please—a picture all about you.… I love to imagine myself so near—there with you so sweet and pretty—hazel eyes—cheeks of autumn tan.…The bells of old Santa Fe will ring a new Christmas soon. I'll send you something, for I cannot be with you then. Goodnight, dear Concha. With lots of love for you—adios—aloha—sweet dreams.

Yet another saved message in Concha's book of memories is a rather startling one, for it came from one of the most famous movie stars ever. Handwritten on stationery from the Biltmore Hotel in Los Angeles, and undated, it is not a love letter, but says:

> Dear Concha:—
> From all the nice things I have heard about you I am sure I would like to meet you. I believe you are just the kind of young lady who would pass the screen test with flying colors, and I am looking for a very good-looking leading lady in my next picture. When you come to Hollywood be sure to call on me: and if I am in Santa Fe in the near future, I will be sure to look for you.
> Yours, Clark Gable

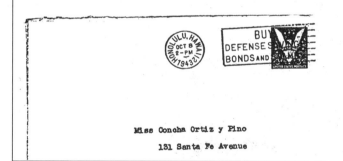

A love letter to Concha from gentleman in Honolulu, Hawaii—courtesy Center for Southwest Research, University of New Mexico

From the vantage point of years and decades later, it is impossible to say whether Concha might have made it big in Hollywood, or if she might have been a good and loving wife for either "S.E.D.D." or "Chad." But all such questions became moot one day in 1942 on the campus of the University of Mexico in Albuquerque, where Concha went to resume her college studies. Everything changed for her the day she met Victor Kleven.

Kleven was a professor and administrator at UNM; and one of Concha's friends invited her to attend a lecture by him. "He's great. You should hear him speak," Concha remembers her friend saying. Sitting in the audience, Concha agreed wholeheartedly. "Oh, he was just wonderful, so brilliant," she remembers, a huge smile lighting up her face. "I was enthralled. After the lecture, I remained to speak to him. He was very nice and answered all my questions. Then he invited me to dinner so we could talk some more. I didn't usually say yes to go out with men I had just met, but with Victor it felt so right. I accepted." Much of their talk that evening was about Latin America, a subject—like many others—about which Kleven knew a

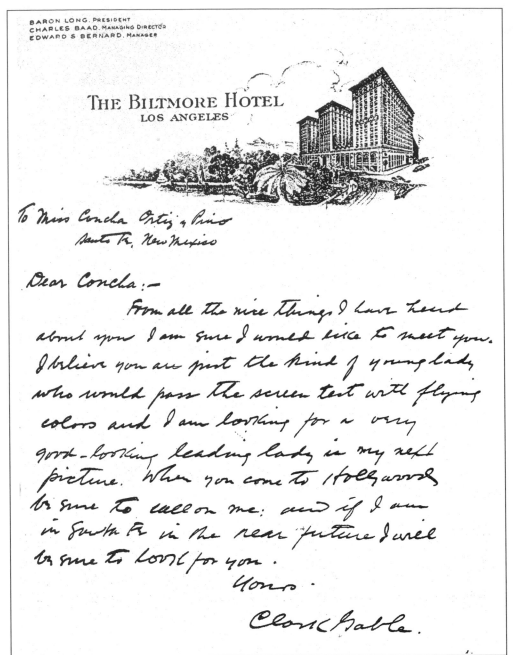

THE BILTMORE HOTEL
LOS ANGELES

To Miss Concha Ortiz y Pino
Santa Fe, New Mexico

Dear Concha:—

From all the nice things I have heard about you I am sure I would like to meet you. I believe you are just the kind of young lady who would pass the screen test with flying colors and I am looking for a very good-looking leading lady in my next picture. When you come to Hollywood be sure to call on me; and if I am in Santa Fe in the near future I will be sure to look for you.

Yours,

Clark Gable.

A letter to Concha from legendary actor Clark Gable, wanting to meet her—courtesy Center for Southwest Research, University of New of New Mexico

great deal. "He was intelligent, handsome and brilliant. I enjoyed myself immensely."

Victor was about 13 years older than Concha. He was born in Minnesota shortly before the 19th century moved on into the 20th, and he attended elementary and high school in the Midwest. His father was a Minnesota state judge. A highly intelligent young man, he chose Canada as the place to attend college. He had a brilliant undergraduate career, culminated by one of the college world's highest distinctions, being chosen a Rhodes Scholar to study at Oxford University in England. There he studied law, and graduated first in his class. As an attorney he joined the Canadian Army, with the rank of lieutenant. He served through the end of World War I, in 1919, then joined a law firm in Saskatoon, Saskatchewan. He quickly became a partner, and his name was added to the company's official title. He also joined the law faculty of the University of Alberta.

As a soldier in the Great War, Victor believed he was helping "make the world safe for democracy." He kept working on that goal after the war, taking a position with the idealistic new League of Nations, which emerged from the Versailles Peace Conference in 1919. Three years later, in 1922, the League established the Permanent Court of International Justice, also called the World Court, at The Hague in the Netherlands. As a court official, Victor kept busy in both London and Geneva, Switzerland, and he kept learning more and more about international politics.

Yet despite its high purpose, the League never truly jelled as a major worldwide organization. It lacked military enforcement powers for its decrees; and its financial sanctions sometimes worked and sometimes did not. The League suffered its greatest setback when the United States Senate failed to ratify membership in it, even though President Woodrow Wilson had been a driving force in its creation. After working hard on its behalf, Victor eventually left the League to become an adviser to the Polish Army. He also practiced law in England, Canada, and the United States. In 1940 he accepted an appointment as head of the University of New Mexico's Department of Government, and also in Albuquerque, was a founder of the College of St. Joseph.

The Man, Victor Kleven

After first encountering Victor, Concha enrolled in several of his classes; and he often pulled her aside for further conversation afterward. Soon they were meeting on a daily basis, and dated at every opportunity. Their courtship had begun. "We fell in love," Concha says, simply and eloquently. "He was a person easy to be with. Neither of us was domestic, but we didn't care, because we were in our own world. We shared a philosophy of government and history. We discussed things intelligently, but never fought. We never used a cross word on one another. He was a very patient man."

In December 1943 Concha and Victor married. The Dec. 12 issue of the *Santa Fe New Mexican* described the event, which took place at 9 a.m. in St. Francis Cathedral, with the Rev. Theo Mayer officiating. The organ was played by Mrs. Elsie Hammond, while Concha's sister Mela, a music major in college, sang "Prayer Perfect," "On This Day, Oh Beautiful Mother," and Gounod's "Ave María." Victor and his best man, Concha's brother Frank Ortiz y Davis, waited patiently as the bride and her maid of honor entered. Concha wore a British flannel gray-and-white-pinstripe outfit, topped by a Lily Dasche hat of black shiny straw, with a high brim and a swirling ornament of black coque feathers. Maid of honor Marie McGrath wore a black crepe gown with white lace and a shoulder corsage.

The newspaper described at length the clothes of the other women in the wedding party. Concha's mother Pablita wore a black gown heavily embroidered with steel nail heads forming a floral pattern. A shiny black straw hat adorned her head, and silver fox furs shielded her from the winter chill. Sister Mela wore a tailored beige wool suit, trimmed in blue. Another sister, Josefita, wore a navy blue outfit with matching accessories. Niece Pauline Gómez came in powder blue and white. Mrs. Frank Ortiz y Davis wore a black-and-white polka-dot ensemble. The men's clothes were not noted.

Rhodes Scholar Victor E. Kleven—courtesy Concha Ortiz y Pino de Kleven

After the ceremony the wedding party and close friends moved on to a breakfast at La Fonda. There Mela entertained the group with "I Love You Truly" and "At Dawning," accompanied by Mrs. Hammond on piano. Three long baskets of flowers—Easter lilies and pale yellow andragons with white stock—added décor, as did lighted ivory candles. The wedding cake featured tiered squares, dainty white trellises and rosebuds, all topped by a miniature bride and groom under a wedding arch. Concha and Victor cut the cake and slices were served with a solid gold fork, a wedding present.

A champagne toast was lifted, then the wedding couple, with Concha wearing a tailored traveling outfit and two lavender orchids as a shoulder corsage, left for a quick honeymoon to Denver. While there, Victor also attended a meeting of the War Labor Board, on which he served. The couple's second honeymoon—the "real one" in their assessment—had to wait until later, after Concha won her bachelor's degree in Inter-American Studies. This time they went to Mexico City, for two wonderful weeks.

The lengthy wedding article in Santa Fe's daily newspaper was indicative of the social customs of the day, and also demonstrated the high stature of the Ortiz y Pino family in the

Victor E. Kleven as a high school student in Minnesota— courtesy Center for Southwest Research, University of New Mexico, negative no. 000-457-00651

community. For readers, it represented a "fairy-tale" romance, which seemed only appropriate—not only for Concha but also for her distinguished husband. One writer in attendance, representing a publication of the University of New Mexico, stated: "Without any doubt, I venture to say that in spite of his exciting and interesting career, Dr. Kleven's biggest moment came when he married Miss Concha Ortiz y Pino of New Mexico."

Although her maiden name was rather lengthy, Concha decided to extend it even further after marriage. In keeping with an old Hispanic custom that was fading from regular usage, she proudly added "de Kleven" to her previous name. As always, she honored her traditions.

The new couple's married life in Albuquerque, naturally enough, was centered on the university. Concha quickly became president of the faculty wives club, dedicated to advancing their husbands' careers and to the cause of education in general. She also joined Victor in a committed involvement in the success of his students. Several of his courses focused on the tumultuous world events of the day, with special attention to rulers who violated their constitutional obligations. He taught students how to critically evaluate propaganda, but did so in an engaging—not a strident—manner. A profile in a UNM publication characterized Victor as "expert, jovial and cheerful."

"Victor's students did very well in class," Concha reminisces. "Some of his colleagues didn't know his secret. They didn't realize that he was always available to his students, morning, noon, night, weekends and holidays. Sometimes he would tell me, 'Concha, my students are preparing for a very important examination. We must help them.' We had a huge back yard near the university, and we made our home accessible to the students. He told me to rent folding chairs and tables for use in the yard. I was also to prepare pitchers of water and iced tea. He said that the students would come to the house, eat sack lunches they brought, and then quietly study in the yard, with his help."

Concha liked Victor's plan, but thought she could improve upon it. She slipped the word to his students that when they came to the house they need not worry about bringing a lunch. She would provide one, and it would be good. "Don't tell Dr. Kleven," she made them promise. "Let's surprise him. But you better get A's, or he'll kill me." The students did fine, Victor was pleased with his wife's abilities as a hostess, and it was a win-win situation all around. "All his students adored him, especially the girls," says Concha. Many of them went on to distinguished careers in government, law and business.

"Days with Victor were heavenly and spiritual," she says tenderly. "He had a love for students and all human beings. His students were like my kids, my pals. I'm glad I got what I did. I learned so much from the young people, and also from Victor. He was wonderfully charismatic. He did wonderful things, but he never showed off."

In her unique role as wife, Concha confesses to a coquettish side. "I knew I wasn't slow.

I did well in school. But I loved discussing government and politics with Victor. I absolutely loved his mind, so sometimes I would say, 'Victor, I don't understand this. Could you please explain it to me?' Then he'd go on, telling me whatever it meant, even if I knew the explanation all along. I so enjoyed those moments. At other times we'd have long discussions because we both wanted to do so. He had confidence in me, that we could discuss such things deeply."

After World War II ended in 1945, Victor used his first-hand knowledge of the now-defunct League of Nations to present himself as an expert on the new organization trying to coalesce to replace it, the United Nations. He traveled around New Mexico and to many other places speaking to explain the issues. Yet a time in his life had come when he wanted to step back from intense professional involvement. In 1947 he withdrew his name from consideration for the dean's post at the UNM law school. Instead he worked in a Santa Fe law office as a consultant.

More and more, Victor seemed drawn to the elemental New Mexico life that he had married into, which Concha represented and into which she had introduced him. A major property owned by the Ortiz y Pino family was the sprawling Agua Verde Ranch, stretching across areas of Santa Fe, San Miguel and Torrance counties. In 1951, with her father José wheelchair-bound from the ravages of Parkinson's disease, Concha was appointed

Victor E. Kleven—courtesy Concha Ortiz y Pino de Kleven

director of the ranch, after a sharp family dispute with her brother Frank. Victor and Concha discussed the situation, and agreed that the only way she could really run the place was to go live there. So she moved from their Albuquerque home out to the ranch. Victor's duties kept him in town, but as often as he could, on weekends and other breaks, he joined his wife at Agua Verde. He very much enjoyed being there, and the ranch hands liked his company. "The men would take him to the bar for a Coke or a drink, and paid for it," Concha remembers. "I made him leave his money at home. They took him everywhere. He also rode horses very well. In fact, he loved to ride."

While Concha and Victor were contemplating the future course of their joined lives, they were also contemplating questions of family. Their marriage had produced no children, and they started to consider adoption. "We thought we'd be wonderful parents, and we wanted to share our home with a little one," she says. "About the time we were discussing this, one of the employees of the family became pregnant. She wasn't married and didn't know what to do. Victor and I decided to adopt the baby." When the infant boy was born, Concha says, "he was the most perfect child you could find anywhere. He was so lovable. We loved him and he loved us. Antonito was strikingly good-looking. Victor could hardly wait to come home for lunch so we could feed the baby together."

The infant lived with Concha and Victor long enough for them to become very attached to him. But then one day the mother came to their home to reclaim him. An adoption process had been started, but it was not final. Victor and Concha had not established firm parental rights, so they reluctantly returned the child. They pleaded with the mother not

Concha and Victor in front of their Albuquerque home, circa 1950. Photo by Robert H. Martin—courtesy Center for Southwest Research, University of New Mexico, negative no. 000-457-0012

The Man, Victor Kleven

Victor E. Kleven in 1932—courtesy Concha Ortiz y Pino de Kleven

Groundbreaking for St. Joseph's College, left to right: Mother B.A. Reginalda, Dr. Victor E. Kleven, unidentified priest, and Archbishop Byrne, June 12, 1950—courtesy Center for Southwest Research, University of New Mexico, negative no. MSS 507BC

The Man, Victor Kleven

A night on the town: Robert H. Martin, Victor E. Kleven, Concha, Mela, and Pablita— courtesy Robert H. Martin

to take Antonito from them, but she left with the baby. Not long afterward, Concha and Victor learned that the mother and her boyfriend had placed the little boy in a nearby orphanage. The Klevens then made payments to the orphanage to help defray the child's costs, asking nothing in return but occasional visits. Yet when the mother learned of this arrangement, she removed her son, and Concha and Victor never saw him again. Concha still gets tearful when remembering her brief time as a mother.

As Victor gravitated more and more to the Agua Verde Ranch, he formed a special bond with a boy who lived nearby. The professor and the child wrote letters to each other while Victor was out of town. Concha and her husband built for themselves their own home on the ranch, where the couple had decided to live full-time as soon as Victor could wrap up his city work. They were planning a special celebration to christen it on a weekend evening when Victor arrived from Albuquerque. But the boy's birthday was happening at the same time, and Victor wanted to go surprise the child first. "When I went to change my clothes, my husband insisted that I wear a blouse from Paris with a pair of slacks," Concha recalls. "The top had big, puffy sleeves, and I called it my clown blouse. I hardly ever wore it, but Victor loved it on me. He'd say, 'I like those wild things.' So I wore the outfit just because he asked me to.

"The little boy loved his gift and hugged Victor. Then we got into the car to return home. Victor slumped over. I was terrified, but I tried to make him comfortable. I took off to the hospital in Santa Fe. I was speeding when I passed a state policeman. I honked and yelled, 'Victor!' The officer knew us, and provided me with an escort. When we arrived, Victor was already dead. There was nothing I could do. Here I was, alone at the hospital, looking like a clown, an unwilling widow. Here it was, 1956, and Victor was dead, at age 59."

Capítulo 13
El rancho Agua Verde

La familia de los Ortiz y Pino se ganaba la vida criando rebaños de ovejas y ganado vacuno en el rancho. Juan, el abuelo de Concha, además del rancho tenía una tienda. Don José, padre de Concha, logró negociar y adquirir terrenos que le pertenecían a muchos terratenientes de la comarca. Acumuló terrenos para formar un rancho que se extendía por partes de los Condados de Torrance, San Miguel, y Santa Fe. Don José decía que su rancho era "un estado dentro de un estado." Además aprovechó los subsidios que el gobierno otorgó a los dueños de ranchos donde criaban ganado vacuno y rebaños de ovejas.

Su rancho era un imperio bien administrado por caporales, veladores, pastores, camperos, y cocineros, con quienes mantenía excelentes relaciones a medida que éstos atendían a sus tareas especializadas. Conjuntamente, todas esas personas bajo el mando de don José lograban administrar un rancho que prosperaba. Su hijo Frank Ortiz y Davis era el contable de las varias empresas de don José. Don José decía que Frank era su "socio." Así mismo, decía, "Concha es mi "socia."

Durante la época cuando don José estuvo dirigiendo Agua Verde, las grandes tenencias llegaron a abarcar más de 100,000 acres de terreno. Entrado en edad, don José sufrió con la enfermedad parkinsonismo y ya no podía administrar las cosas como antes, y era incierto el porvenir del rancho. Don José decidió que Concha debe administrar el rancho y los terrenos que él había acumulado. Su hermano Frank se sintió ofendido con la decisión que Concha iba a administrar el rancho. Concha tomó su nuevo cargo muy en serio.

Sin perder tiempo, Concha se dio a conocer a cada uno de los empleados del rancho. Muchas familias vivían en el rancho conforme a los arreglos que habían concertado con don José. Algunos tenían el derecho de vivir el resto de su vida en el rancho, otros eran partidos o eran pastores que habían inmigrado a Nuevo México de la región Vasca de España.

Pese a las dificultades que tuvo de administradora del rancho, doña Concha logró mejorar las cosas. Modernizó e instaló muchas comodidades en el rancho. En cinco años logró que el rancho tuviera bases sólidas.

En resumidas cuentas doña Concha dice: "Todo se hizo sin descuidar los aspectos espirituales y tradicionales de la gente que allí en el rancho vivían ni sin atender a los aspectos espirituales y tradicionales de los vecinos." Entre otras cosas, durante el tiempo que doña Concha estuvo administrando el rancho, mandó que se reconstruyera una de las moradas más antiguas en Nuevo México, que estaba ubicada en terreno del rancho.

Agua Verde Ranch

The family had always been in the ranching business, it seemed. As far back as anyone knew, sheep and cattle had been essential. Much of the wealth of the illustrious *don* Pedro Bautista Pino, who went to Spain in 1811 to plead the cause of the New Mexico colony, came from his many flocks of sheep. When Capt. Sylvester Davis moved west upon marrying Josefa Pino after the Civil War, he took advantage of the U.S. Homestead Act to claim 160 acres for his own ranch, and then his sons became ranchers in their own right. Other branches of the family also ranched. It seemed only natural.

Concha's grandfather, Juan Ortiz, was a rancher in addition to running Galisteo's general store. In rural San Miguel County, Juan's huge ranch covered 88,000 acres, with four or five scattered settlements complete with haciendas, where his men lived and tended the cattle and sheep. He also ranched land closer in to town. In the late 1800s, jobless Europeans streamed into the vast open lands of the American West, in search of opportunity. Some who came to New Mexico were Basque sheepherders from Spain, with whom Juan made arrangements to care for 100 of his sheep, with profits to be divided after lambing and wool shearing. Galisteo became a major livestock center.

When Juan died in 1929, his land holdings were divided among his heirs. José received parcels in the village of Galisteo, and grazing lands along the river. He wanted more, so he expanded his property through use of the U. S. Homestead Act, which was still in effect (it was not terminated until 1935). But instead of merely claiming another 160 acres for himself, José devised a clever stratagem to acquire far more land. Because the law gave 160 acres to any homesteader who lived on the land five years and built a home there—even a tiny one-room home—José struck deals with many financially poor people to inhabit the land long enough to gain ownership, then sell it to him. He paid their $10 homestead filing fee, provided them with a house and livestock, and shared profits with them, until the time came for him to take possession. Even then, he agreed to let his *partidarios*, as the settlers were called, continue to live on the land throughout their lives. His plan was all legal and aboveboard, and under it a vast amount of land accumulated to the ownership of José Ortiz y Pino. He called it "a state within a state."

A major goal of his acquisitions was to put together contiguous acreage that would grow into a huge ranch stretching across parts of Torrance, San Miguel and Santa Fe counties. Its sprawling location was hard to describe, except to say that it was 76 miles from Santa Fe, Albuquerque, and Las Vegas. He called the ranch Agua Verde—Green Water. The name was somewhat misleading (or maybe just a little hopeful), because his most reliable source of moisture was along the river in Galisteo, not out in his "green water" area. Because cattle needed more water per head than sheep, he used his Galisteo land mainly for cattle, and concentrated his sheep flocks at Agua Verde, where they could fare reasonably well despite their sharp hooves digging up the grass. The big ranch out there, however, still had enough resources for some cattle to be raised as well.

As José was establishing himself as a rancher, his efforts were assisted by a Depression-era governmental policy that considered raising livestock a liability, although a necessary one. Under this program, ranchers received $5 per head of cattle that they raised, which were then slaughtered and given to poor people for food. The canny José was always quick to turn a government program to his advantage—whether it was the Homestead Act, the Depression livestock policy, or, later on, the gasoline-and-tire-rationing rules during World

War II, which sharply curtailed supplies for most citizens but imposed no restrictions on food-producing operations, such as José's ranch.

A full-fledged Western rancher cut from the legendary stereotype, José inherited the legacy of the Range Wars, but came along just long enough after them that he did not personally contend with violence. Before his time, the Wild West was the scene of often violent hostilities pitting ranchers and sheepherders and farmers against each other on the range, scratching and clawing fiercely to stake claims on the land and its scarce sources of water. Barbed-wire fences were strung and then cut down. Herds were rustled or stampeded or driven over cliffs by gun-wielding cowboys. Camps were dynamited and burned. Livestock was shot, clubbed, poisoned and drowned. Men were shot and lynched. But José fortunately missed that era, and he presided over a large and peaceful empire.

A key element of José's success was his personal management style. Each morning he ate breakfast in the chowhouse with his men, then met with the foremen—called *caporales*—he had appointed to preside over different parts of the operation: sheep, cattle, headquarters, homesteaders. In other specific positions of responsibility, a *mayordomo* (caretaker) served as supervisor; *veladores* (night watchmen) guarded the camp; *pastores* (shepherds) each watched over between 800 and 1,000 ewes, lambs, yearlings and rams. The *campero* (camper) moved the camp as needed for better grazing. A key person for overall morale was the *cocinero* (cook), for if the *costillas de borrega* (rack of lamb ribs), *frijoles* (beans), *papas fritas* (fried potatoes),

Son of an Agua Verde ranch hand with a Karakul lamb— courtesy Museum of New Mexico, negative no. 59019

Branding day on Agua Verde ranch—courtesy Jerry Ortiz y Pino

Cattle Sanitary Board of New Mexico:

CERTIFICATE OF BRAND.

I hereby certify that the following, as shown on the cuts below and hereto annexed, is a transcript of the brand and mark

LOCATION OF BRAND ON CATTLE
Left ribs

LOCATION OF BRAND ON HORSES, MULES AND ASSES
Left shoulder

of _____Jose Ortiz y Pino_____ of _____Galisteo_____ County

of _____Santa Fe_____ and Territory of New Mexico. Recorded in Territorial Brand

Book No.____9____, Page____40____, this ____13th____ day of ____September, 1910.____

W. J. Linwood
Secretary Cattle Sanitary Board,
Albuquerque, New Mexico.

A 1913 livestock certificate given to José Ortiz for the Ortiz y Pino ranch—courtesy Center for Southwest Research, University of New Mexico.

SHEEP SANITARY BOARD OF NEW MEXICO:

CERTIFICATE OF MARK

I hereby certify that the following as shown on the cuts below and hereto annexed

Ear Marks

A 1948 livestock certificate given to Concha Ortiz y Pino de Kleven for the Agua Verde ranch—courtesy Center for Southwest Research, University of New Mexico.

BRANDS { Paint _____ * * * NONE * * * _____
{ Fire _____ * * * NONE * * * _____

is a transcript of the brand and ear mark, recorded in the STATE BRAND BOOK No. 7 * * PAGE 4 * *

on the ____1st____ day of ____JUNE, 1948____ as the brand and ear mark of

__CONCHA ORTIZ Y PINO DE KLEVEN__ of 1506 Las Lomas Road, ALBUQUERQUE, N. MEX.

County of ____BERNALILLO____ and State of New Mexico.

Albuquerque, New Mexico ____June 1, 1948____

Tom Snell
Secretary.

José Ortiz y Pino III fixing a fence on the ranch in Galisteo, circa 1950—courtesy Museum of New Mexico, negative no. 111675

and *melaz* (sweet molasses) coming from the kitchen were not tasty, grumbling swept through the camp.

Lambing season was a period of intense activity. Huge herds of sheep were rounded up and set aside for birthing. Ewes ready to give birth were separated from the larger herd, and were fenced off in their own area. If the weather turned bad, the ewes had to be placed in sheds. Many of the births had to be assisted with hands-on help from the men. Every effort was made to preserve the life of both mother and child, but even so, many lambs came out stillborn, and many ewes died giving birth. The dead lambs were skinned, and their pelts were placed on the backs of orphan lambs in an attempt to make the mother ewe think the lamb was her own so she would feed it with her milk. New mothers and lambs were held in special pens and watched 24 hours a day, until the crucial post-birth period had safely passed. Any dead lamb was a defeat.

After lambing season, the station was disbanded and the herds again dispersed under the care of their *pastores*, not to come together again until the next phase of intensive work: shearing. Sheep whose wool was to be harvested were driven into corrals and pens, and traveling men who specialized in shearing came from as far away as south Texas to join the Agua Verde ranch hands for this huge task. Using clippers that looked like stubby scissors, the shearers worked under a tent for shade, and trimmed the animals one at a time. Pay was based on each man's tally of sheep, and the fastest shearers moved along at the rate of about

Agua Verde Ranch

José and Pablita with their Karakul lambs—courtesy Concha Ortiz y Pino de Kleven

Concha arrives in Agua Verde with a box of Kotex in 1951—courtesy Concha Ortiz ye Pino de Kleven

60 per day, working from sunup to sunset. (Like the steel-driving man John Henry in the folk song, who finally gave way to a machine, these shearers eventually were replaced by machines that could mow 100 sheep a day.) The wool was packed into big ten-foot burlap bags weighing about 500 pounds, which were sent to José's wool warehouse along the tracks in Galisteo, awaiting shipment to distant markets.

Another grueling task was castrating and branding the livestock. The former process was done to control the size of the herds, and the latter process marked the animals for identification after long periods of grazing freely around the open range. These tasks were performed before the hot weather of summer, and usually after a rain, because recently branded and castrated animals were susceptible to flies and worms. In true Old West fashion, *vaqueros* (cowboys) roped the calves and tied their legs, and red-hot branding irons left an indelible mark on both cattle and sheep (although rustlers often altered the brands, if they could). José's ranch used the Bar JO brand—his initials. Castration took place at the same time, and the men cooked and ate the testicles (Rocky Mountain oysters). And when their long, hard work of lambing, shearing, castrating, and branding was done, the men enjoyed heading for the bars of Santa Fe and Las Vegas, including *La Mariposa* (the butterfly) and *El Cid* (the king), George King's Bar, and the nearby brothels, including *La Mula* (the mule), *La Yegua* (the mare), *La Chispa* (the spark), and *La Take It Easy* (which needs no translation).

As a modern 20th-century rancher, José liked trying out innovations. A notable one that he brought to the Agua Verde Ranch was an exotic breed of black-wool sheep, called Karakul. A 1940 article in *New Mexico Magazine* described this experiment at the ranch. The Karakul breed, which traces to the Kohara region of central Asia, fared well in the New Mexico high desert. It was relatively disease-free, it fattened up quickly on less feed than traditional sheep, and its black wool was double the traditional length. At the time of the article, José owned 600 ewes, with more lambs on the way. He was highly enthusiastic about the venture, but it did not prove to be a success. Buyers for the dark-colored wool were hard to find, and in the end, José gave away all his Karakul stock—but not before his wife Pablita made luxuriant black coats for all the members of the family.

The Agua Verde Ranch and its owner were memorialized in a 1997 book written by a grandson, José Ortiz y Pino III. Titled *Don José: The Last Patrón*, the book reflects upon the endless march of the seasons, and the purposes for each. Spring brings promise and life, the author said. Summer brings growth and progress. Harvest time comes with autumn. And the winter months are for resting and planning. Obviously *don* José Ortiz y Pino is the book's focus and central character. But also featured prominently is his right-hand man at the ranch, his son Frank Ortiz y Davis. Frank kept the books for his father's various holdings, reviewing ledgers and accounts daily. He was his father's driver on trips from Galisteo to the ranch, and the men prayed two rosaries along the way. Frank also got down and dirty with hands-on physical work; among other things, he was one of the principal castraters during that grueling season. José called Frank his "partner" at the ranch. But he also used that term for his daughter Concha.

Between the death of his father Juan in 1929 and his own death in 1951, José presided over a time of enormous growth for his land holdings in general and his Agua Verde Ranch in particular, which ultimately encompassed more than 100,000 acres. Yet in his later years José was afflicted with Parkinson's disease, a relentless degenerative condition that brings its victims trembling of the arms and legs, imbalance, and difficulty in walking, talking and thinking. José could not manage things as he had before, and his various operations steadily began slipping. The ranch fell into debt. The financial future of his wife was shaky. The future of everything was uncertain. "My father was ill and couldn't do the work he used to do," Concha says. "His attorney was the one who suggested, 'Get Concha to run the ranch.'" And that is what *don* José decided to do.

His decision shocked and hurt his son Frank, who had assumed that he would be given that duty. Yet much of the ranch's decline had occurred with Frank second in command, and José apparently felt that new direction was needed. A bitter family rift erupted over the matter. Unable to resolve it among themselves, the Ortiz y Pino clan sent it to New Mexico

Frank, Concha, and Manuel on horseback in Agua Verde in 1935—courtesy Center for Southwest Research, University of New Mexico, negative no. 000-457-0010

District Court in Santa Fe for ajudication. More than unusual, the move was almost startling, for the customs of the time—especially among proud Hispanic families—called for such conflicts to be kept behind closed doors. Once in court, these matters became public record, and privacy was no longer an option. Yet the stakes in this dispute were extremely high, as spelled out by a realtor from Taos: At 100,000 acres, Agua Verde Ranch was about the same size as the cities of Los Angeles or Houston.

Shortly before José's death in 1951, the judge ruled that Concha should take over the ranch. Rather than selling it for quick cash, she chose a different course. "Our family ranch was overburdened by debt, and we were going to lose thousands of acres," she said later in a magazine interview. "Someone had to step in, and feeling an obligation to my mother, I decided to save the property." Neighbors pledged to assist her. "The big ranchers of the time, Albert Mitchell and Floyd Lee, told the judge they would help me."

The ruling was controversial for the times. Women back then seldom ran any large business, let alone a huge ranch. Even more surprising was that the woman chosen for the job was experienced mainly in legislative service, community activities and teaching. Frank took the decision very hard. He felt robbed of his birthright as the eldest and only surviving son. The tradition in old Spanish families was to pass down the major portion of an estate to the first-born son, unless there were specific reasons not to. Frank felt he had been a dutiful son, working and learning at his father's side. Female family members, however, were slowly taking the view that inheritances should be divided equitably among both men and women. Concha sums up the situation by saying: "Frank was very business-oriented. I was people-oriented."

Frank came away with various holdings, including the bar and store in Galisteo, and other ranch property. He also had considerable holdings with his own property and livestock. But he did not get what he expected: Agua Verde Ranch. "Frank suffered great hurt," Concha realizes. "It was difficult for him to see an end to the accumulation of so many years of work. But truly he was the son of *don* José, and he decided to begin anew." Frank restored his grandmother's hacienda, managed the store, the *cantina* and his livestock business. At his ranch he enlarged the house and added barns and a corral. Until he died in 1974, he led a comfortable life. But after the rift, the family was not the same.

Nor did things remain the same for Concha after the 1951 decree placing Agua Verde under her direction. She took the task very seriously, and she felt that the best way to reverse the ranch's decline was for her to move there full-time and preside over day-to-day operations. She and Victor discussed the situation fully, and agreed she must relocate to the ranch, although his work would not let him join her. She approached the challenge with optimism—and a bit of planning ahead. A black-and-white photo from her scrapbook shows her first arrival at the ranch as boss, wearing pants, a coat and a scarf on her head, and a big smile on her face. Under her arm she carries a cardboard box.

"Guess what was in there?" she asks. "Kotex. At least 200. I figured that if I was the only woman on the ranch, there was no one from whom I could borrow. I decided to take plenty,

Agua Verde Ranch

because I'd be far away from any store." The decision turned out to be fortuitous many times, she adds, because when ranch hands needed first aid for injuries or bites from animals or insects, she tore the Kotex into strips and used them as bandages. "We never had enough cotton at the ranch," she says. Nor did they have enough of hardly anything else; but when her sister Mela suggested that their mother send money to help out, Concha laughed and replied: "If I had any money, I'd just spend it right away. So the answer is no. No money at the ranch!"

The two-room house she moved into at the ranch had no furniture, plumbing, gas, or electricity. "It did have a hall and a fireplace," she concedes. "I took jeans, good shoes, a narrow bed from home, and a metal cabinet. Also in her truck were rubbing alcohol, sheets, dishes, medications, toothpaste, and gum. "My mother sent lots of candles and flashlights by the dozen." Foodstuffs she brought with her included candy, cookies, and canned goods, with a plentiful supply of sardines. Her first nights at the ranch were just about the worst she ever spent there, she recalls, because occupying the house with her were a bat colony and thousands of *chinches* (bedbugs). Between the whirring wings and the painful bites, sleep was out of the question until she fumigated both pests.

Concha and Frank take a break from work at Agua Verde—courtesy Concha Ortiz y Pino de Kleven

Concha set out at once to get to know the ranch's employees. Many families lived there under previous arrangements with José. Some were homesteaders who had helped him acquire the land, and now were entitled to live out their lives there. Others were *partidarios*, who cared for a certain number of animals and shared profits with the ranch owner when selling time came. A group that Concha got along very well with was *los españoles*, hard-working immigrants from the Basque region of Spain. Concha was careful to uphold every agreement that her father had made.

The new lady boss wanted to establish friendly relations with all her employees. "But many of the men were antagonistic at first," she remembers. "They resented taking orders from a woman." Her biggest problem was the foreman, a Texan recommended by her friendly neighbor Albert Mitchell, because the fellow had worked out well at that ranch. Yet Concha detected hostility in the man. "He was mean. Rumor had it that he had come from an insane asylum. One time he gave me wrong directions when I needed to drive somewhere. Some of the men were out on horseback looking for lost lambs. When they saw me driving toward the mountains instead of the highway, they waved me down and told me the way I was going was dangerous, and then led me to the road. I never knew whether he had done that on purpose. But he was brilliant with sheep and cattle. Mean as he was, he was also a good worker and kept things in line. So I didn't fire him."

She remembers Bernardo the cook very fondly. "He'd get up at 5 a.m. to make coffee, then get going on breakfast." Like her father before her, Concha made a point of sharing a hearty breakfast of sausage and eggs with the ranch hands every morning. But sometimes at night, when he was not tending to the men's hungry stomachs, Bernardo was overindulging his thirst at bars in Las Vegas and Santa Fe, a weakness that afflicted other ranch hands as well. With some regularity Concha would notice some of the men missing at morning chow—and if Bernardo was among them, breakfast would be missing too. With no phone at the ranch, she would drive to the highway intersection at Clines Corners, and call around to various lockups until she had located the miscreants. Then she would go bail them out and drive them back to the ranch in stern and stony silence. Looking back, however, Concha says: "Oh, I loved the men, despite their little mess-ups."

Half a mile from the ranch house stood a tall windmill, which pumped water from the ground to fill two big tanks. The water was used for basic needs: cooking and washing, and watering the livestock. But dry outhouses sufficed for bathroom purposes. Concha once reminisced for a magazine writer: "In that expansive land, nothing is lonelier than the sound of a windmill when you're alone—that screech, screech, screech. And, you know, it's never-ending. If I had allowed selfishness to take over, I would have despaired. Out there my diet was different. I spent months without reading—I hated those kerosene lanterns. I had no one to converse with except about what was necessary at the ranch. I couldn't do anything that I was accustomed to doing before." Her husband joined her at the ranch as often as possible on weekends, but his other duties limited such visits.

Living this harsh existence of work and deprivation, Concha saw her values refocus on the simplest, and deepest, things in life. She loved the dignity and humility with which the people around her tended their daily work. Beauty became associated with a well-built fence, or fat and healthy calves and lambs. Her religious faith supported her. She was sure that María Santísima (Holy Mary) and El Santo Niño (The Holy Infant) were looking after her causes. From time to time she attended religious processions in nearby communities, and came back reassured that the saints would intercede for her.

Under her direction, the fortunes of Agua Verde slowly improved. Losses were cut, debt was paid down, and money became available for improvements. Concha's cramped, two-room ranch house sorely needed replacing, but so did the men's living quarters, so she tended to their structure first. As electric power lines kept spreading across the land, Concha arranged for the ranch to be wired into the system. Drillers came and dug a deep well. Indoor toilets, wash basins, and tubs followed. The ranch got a telephone. Then one day Concha came back from town with a television set.

The television was a tiny black-and-white model, with scant resemblance to the big color consoles of today. But to the ranch hands, many of whom had never seen such a thing, it was "the magic little box." She placed it in her bedroom, and allowed the men to watch it at specified times. When her bedtime came, she firmly turned it off. "If I hadn't, I never would have slept!" she exclaims. She also used it, as she says, to "bribe the men," by offering extra TV time for extra chores like milking the cow. "With TV we all went crazy," she laughs, "We watched cowboy shows and mysteries and everything else. There weren't enough chairs, so the men sat on the floor. It got real crowded in there."

As time passed, Concha the lady boss won the full confidence and respect of her employees—and not least because they knew she would stand up for the ranch's interests just as strongly as any man ever would. One time a state worker showed up at the ranch to tell her that the highway through the area was going to be rerouted, that the access roads to Agua Verde were going to be cut off, and that she would have to build new roads at her own expense. She quickly sent him packing, by saying: "As you can see, we're all busy here castrating. We have very sharp knives. You'd better leave."

Not long afterward, she was leaving the café at Clines Corners when she encountered another Highway Department man who did not recognize her. He asked for directions to the ranch of some "son-of-a-bitch woman" who was making trouble by demanding new state-built roads to her place. The Highway Department was going to get rid of her, he confided, by building her a beautiful gate out at the edge of the road. "Sir, I am the son of a bitch you're looking for," she replied. "I've never taken a bribe in my life, and I do not intend to now." In the end, the state built new roads to the ranch.

After the five hardest years she had ever lived, Concha had the ranch back on a solid footing. And soon, her life out there was finally also going to get really good. Her husband had steadily been scaling back on the duties that kept him in town all the time, and more

Concha tending to spring lambs with a worker— courtesy Museum of New Mexico, negative no. 59021

and more he was gravitating toward life on the ranch. What's more, he found he enjoyed the ranch greatly and had a real feel for the men and the work. He and Concha chose a beautiful site and built themselves a new home on it. But the very first night they planned to spend there, Victor died suddenly from a cerebral hemorrhage.

With that tragedy, Concha lost her desire to remain at Agua Verde. She put it up for sale, and with all the improvements she had made, it was snapped up quickly, by millionaire oil man Robert O. Anderson. On a résumé she later put together, Concha described the years 1951 to 1956 with these few words:

> **Sent by court order to manage, operate, and rebuild 100,000-acre family ranch named Agua Verde, 76 miles from Albuquerque, Santa Fe and Las Vegas. Restored and rebuilt physical part of ranch. Restored herds of cattle, sheep, and horses and updated them into the most modern herds in the state. All this was done without neglecting the spiritual and traditional facets of both the people living within the ranch and also its neighbors. Also, one of New Mexico's oldest *moradas* (place of prayer for the penitentes) was rebuilt.**

After leaving Agua Verde, Concha never went back. "However," she says, "I would wish that kind of life for everyone."

Agua Verde Ranch

Capítulo 14
La Familia

En Nuevo México, para muchas personas de ascendencia hispánica, el linaje de sus familias es muy importante. Para Concha nada le queda más cerca. A partir de su propia generación, Concha puede delinear su estirpe atravesando nueve generaciones en Nuevo México. Anterior a esas generaciones que vivieron en Nuevo México, los familiares de Concha remontan a la época de los antepasados que vinieron a este continente de España. Desde que nació Concha, durante por lo menos cinco generaciones, la familia Ortiz y Pino sigue causando impacto. Concha tiene más de 90 años de edad, y durante su vida ha dejado sus huellas en el Estado de Nuevo México y al nivel nacional.

Entre la progenie de José Ortiz y Pino y Pablita Ortiz y Davis, Concha es la tercera hija entre tres hermanas y un hermano. Josefita era la mayor, a quien le siguen su hermana Margaret y su hermano Frank. La mayor eligió casarse y fue buena madre, dedicada a su familia y a sus quehaceres domésticos. La menor era Manuelita que tenía el sobrenombre de Mela. Ésta se casó con el fotógrafo Robert Martin, mencionado en otro capítulo de este tomo. Todos los hermanos y hermanas de Concha han pasado a mejor vida.

El capítulo Rancho Agua Verde de este tomo menciona a Frank, su hermano mayor, que le sigue a Josefita. Por derecho propio, todos los hermanos y hermanas de Concha fueron personas notables. Se distinguieron desempeñando cargos en el gobierno, en humanidades, la religión, en el mundo de las finanzas al nivel internacional, fueron comerciantes, estancieros-ganaderos, meteorólogos, siempre ofreciendo servir a la comunidad mientras se ocupan en sus oficios y profesiones. La vida de los Ortiz y Pino fue una vida llena de dolor, alegría, tragedias, triunfos, abundancia, necesidad, amor, venganza, desesperanza, esperanza, y fe. Pese a todo lo dicho, los familiares de Concha siempre han estado dispuestos a servir en cargos del gobierno y siempre han seguido prestando su ayuda al prójimo.

The Family

14

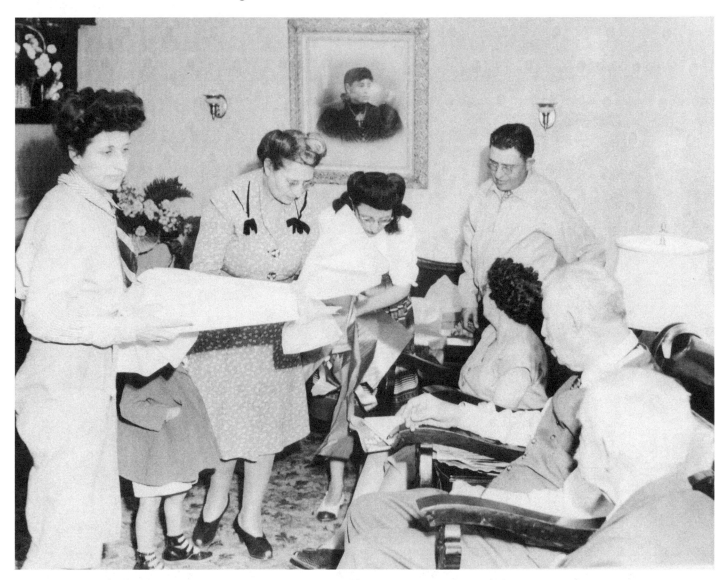

Concha, Margarita, Josefita, Mela, Frank, Pablita, José, and Mr. Turro—photo by Robert H. Martin

If anything is more important than family to the old Spanish clans of New Mexico, no one has ever learned what it is. For Concha Ortiz y Pino de Kleven, nothing else comes close. From her own generation she can trace her lineage back through nine previous generations on New Mexico soil alone, and back into the distant soil and distant past of Spain before then. And at least three more generations of the Ortiz y Pino family have followed in the more than 90 years she lived in and left her mark upon New Mexico.

The bloodlines are deeply imprinted upon members of this proud family, and present no mystery to them. To interested outside observers, however (and many outside observers are interested), tracing the family tree quickly gets confusing, if not downright impenetrable.

Wedding picture of Concha's sister, Josefita, and Ramón Gómez—courtesy Susan Varela

The Family

Generation after generation named newborn babies after beloved and honored ancestors with strong and simple names: Nicolás, Juan, José, Pedro, Antonio for the boys, and for the girls, Juana, Rosa, Ana, Concepción, Josefa, María. As these infants grew into their own lives, they in turn saw their names passed down to descendants. Links became only more complex as cousins sometimes married cousins. In addition, the Ortiz y Pino family began intermarrying with Anglos, bringing Anglo-named children

José Ortiz y Pino and Pablita Ortiz y Davis were cousins who fell in love and married; so their combined family lines, before and after, are tangled indeed. The scope of this book is not nearly broad enough to trace all the relatives. But to overlook Concha's brothers and sisters would be to fail to tell her story.

Concha was the third of seven children born to her parents (Pablita had twenty-two pregnancies), and one of four who lived to adulthood. Twelve years older was her sister Josefita. Two years older was her brother Frank. Then came Concha, followed by Margaret. Concha was eight years older than the "baby of the family," little sister Mela. Younger brothers Josécito and Juanito died in early childhood. Of all the children born to *don* José and Pablita, Concha is the only one still living.

The first of Concha's siblings to grow up and get married was Josefita. Her husband was Ramón Gómez. The life that Josefita chose and wanted was devoted wife and mother, and that is the life she led. As a member of one of Santa Fe's prominent families, she often saw her name in the society pages of *The New Mexican*. But she did not make headlines in her own right. She and Ramón had two children. Their daughter Pauline was blind, but owned and managed a nursery school, and won awards for her work. Their son Frank Gómez returned from World War II to found a real estate firm.

Concha and Mela, second and third from left, in Chapúltepec Park, Mexico City, circa 1930—courtesy Center for Southwest Research, University of New Mexico, negative no. 000-457-0008

A 1926 wedding for Adela, an African-American woman raised with the Ortiz y Pino family in Galistero—courtesy Jerry Ortiz y Pino

Concha's brother Frank Ortiz y Davis (who followed the old Spanish custom of combining his father's and mother's surnames into his own) married María García in a large Catholic ceremony. They had five children. The wife's family was also a prominent one in New Mexico, with her grandfather Samuel Ellison coming from Kentucky to help establish a court system early in the American era. Frank's career was discussed earlier in this book, in the chapter about Agua Verde.

Concha's youngest sister Mela was by far the closest in the lives they shared. Like Concha before her, Mela (her nickname from her given name Manuelita) graduated from Loretto Academy, an all-girl school in Santa Fe. During her school years Mela developed serious sinus problems, similar to the ones that killed her sister Margaret, who died as a young girl. Her alarmed parents sent her for treatment to Denver, where she recovered, and continued her education there at Loretto Heights College. Recognized as a beautiful singer, Mela also joined the Denver Music Society. After completing her studies in Denver, Mela came to the University of New Mexico for advanced music and voice training. She also trained at Columbia University in New York City. World War II was raging when she got out, and Mela took positions as assistant club director at USO (United Service Organizations) clubs in Tyler, Texas, and Roswell, N.M. Then her mother Pablita became ill, and Mela returned home. Just as the war ended, she became USO program director in Santa Fe.

Five days after the Santa Fe USO center opened, a young Army photographer named Robert Martin dropped by. He had come to New Mexico to work as a photographer in Los Alamos, where the just-detonated atomic bomb was created. Mela assisted with the project. After a lengthy courtship, they married in 1950. Looking back at their union, Martin chuckles: "Mela was a Democrat, a woman, Catholic, and Hispanic. I'm a Republican, a man, Lutheran, and Anglo. People don't understand, but it worked for us."

In addition to the USO, Mela worked with the state Welfare Department and also conducted visitors on tours through the city's Cristo Rey area. "She put tourists in her convertible and told them about our town," Bob remembers fondly. After marriage, Mela spent more and more time taking care of her ailing mother. Bob joined them for dinner and enjoyed swapping stories. They spoke in their "own Santa Fe language," a mixture of

Robert H. Martin—photo by Fray Angélico Chávez

Mela wearing traditional Spanish mantilla—photo by Robert H. Martin

Mela at family store in Galisteo—photo by Robert H. Martin

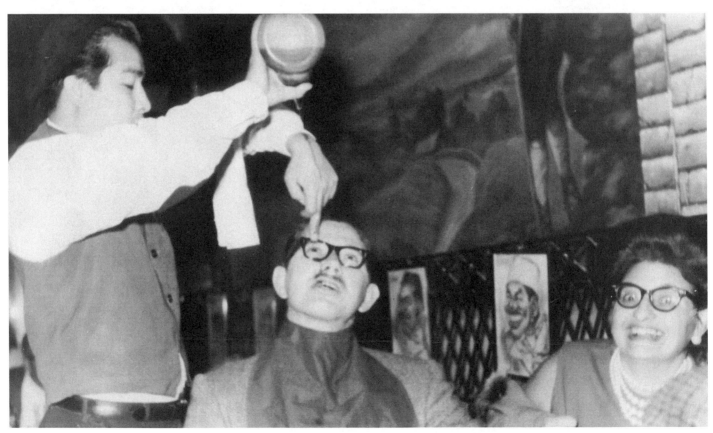

Robert drinking wine from a perón with Mela at the Alcázar in Juárez, Mexico—courtesy Robert H. Martin

The Family

Spanish and English they called "Spanglish"—long before the term came into wide use.

When Pablita died in 1963, Bob and Mela were a long-established Santa Fe couple. She was a featured soloist at St. Francis Cathedral, and enjoyed the role. She was also tapped for other singing roles—such as Gov. Thomas Mabry's inauguration. Mela was also tireless in cultural preservation activities, and was recognized as a civic leader. She and Bob began a tradition, which became famous among their family and friends, for the lovely Christmas cards they produced and sent each year. The cards, a signature item for the Martins, became collector's items for people who received them. Mela and Bob did not have children.

Mela loved life and lived it to the hilt. But in 1955 she fell and broke her kneecap, and was never the same again. Ever after, she was limited in ability and lived in pain. She wore braces, and a fusing operation only made her condition worse. "The doctor told us she got a staph infection in the hospital," Bob says. "It ate away at the cartilage. Her knee became bone rubbing against bone." Mela lost the ability to move her leg, and for years was restricted to a wheelchair. In 1993 she suffered a stroke that left her blind in one eye and damaged her hearing. She died five years later, in 1998. Her years were long—80—but much of her life had been hard due to poor health. Her husband held Mela's hand as she passed away. In her other hand she held a rosary. "We were married 48½ years," Bob says. "I had hoped for 50."

All of Concha's siblings were memorable in their own way, as were her larger-than-life parents, grandparents, great-grandparents, and forebears before them. In the legendary Ortiz y Pino family of New Mexico, every life that enters it becomes a drama in its own right. Members have distinguished themselves in government, the arts, religion, international finance, business, ranching, meteorology, civic service, and many other callings. Oncoming generations can, and do, reflect endlessly upon all the people who came before them, and all the stories they lived. The stories are far too many—far too many—to try to tell them all in this book. Yet one more, with its own special essence, is related below:

When Concha was a litle girl, her favorite uncle was Pedro Ortiz y Pino, her father's younger brother. His life was not long, only from 1882 until 1923, and also had its share of sadness, as two wives died of illness after only a short time with him. But true to the family spirit, Pedro was open to life, and the things that life might bring. One day as he and his third wife, Guadalupe, were walking down a street in Denver, a black woman with two little girls approached them. She was their mother, she said, but could no longer care for them. Could these good people give them a home? Pedro and Guadalupe took the girls back to Galisteo, to join their family. It was like the story of Bluebelle and Alice, the little black girls raised by Capt. Sylvester Davis and Josefa, repeating itself.

Adela, the older of the two girls, took over the role of nanny for Pedro's young son, born to his second wife. Pedro's sister Manuelita (Concha's aunt) gradually assumed the position of foster mother to the girls. As the young son, Pedro Jr., grew up, he thought of Adela as very intelligent, bilingual, and talented in singing and playing the guitar. Looking back, Pedro Jr. says, "My aunt had a lot of faith in her. Time and again she would send my sisters and me with her on trips out of town, with Adela in charge."

THE DIRECTOR
OF THE
INSTITUTE OF SPANISH CULTURE

IN VIEW OF THE QUALIFICATIONS AND
MERITS ACQUIRED BY THE CITED
SRA. DOÑA MELA ORTIZ Y PINO DE MARTIN
IN THE SERVICE OF THOSE IDEALS HELD AS
A COMMON BOND BY THE PEOPLE OF SPANISH
LINEAGE, THERE IS HEREBY CONFERRED ON HER
THE TITLE OF
TITULAR MEMBER
THIS PROPOSED BY THE GOVERNING BODY
OF THIS INSTITUTE.
FOR THAT REASON SHE IS GRANTED
THE USE OF THE INSIGNIA WHICH CORRESPOND
TO THE TITLE, RELYING ON THE QUALITIES
WHICH DISTINGUISH HER, WE ARE AWARE
THAT SHE WILL CONTRIBUTE TO THE GREATER
PRESTIGE OF THE INSTITUTE.

DATED. MADRID, THE 12TH DAY OF
OCTOBER OF THE YEAR 1967.

(SIGNED) THE DIRECTOR
THE SECRETARY GENERAL
GREGORIO MARAÑÓN

Proclamation given to Mela by Spain—courtesy Robert H. Martin

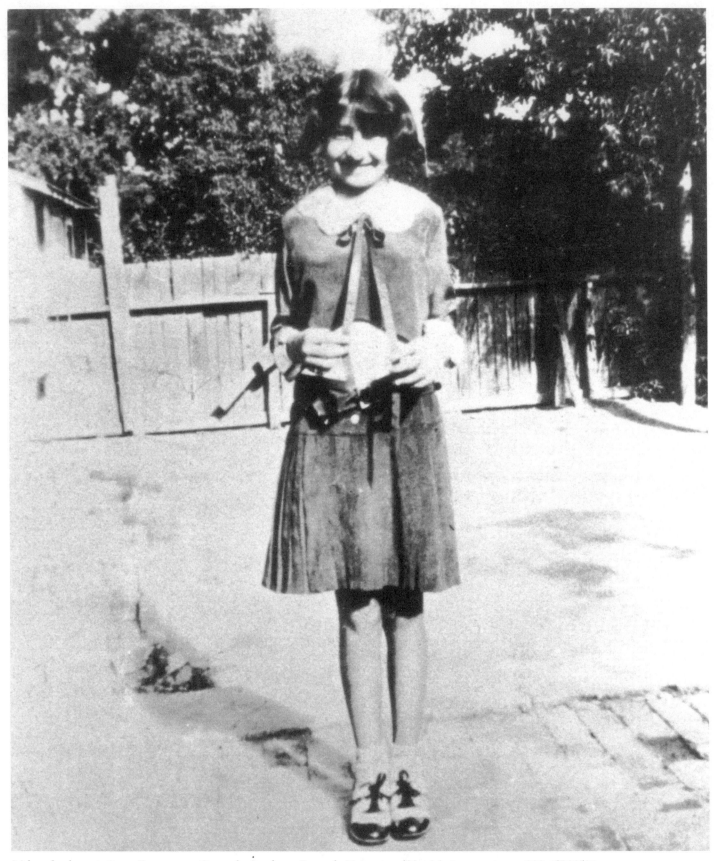

Mela at her home in Santa Fe—courtesy Center for Southwest Research, University of New Mexico, negative no. 000-457-0050.1

The Family

Mela at home in Galisteo—courtesy Center for Southwest Research, University of New Mexico, negative no. 000-457-0051.1

Robert at White Sands, N.M.—photo by Mela Ortiz y Pino de Martin

Mela's mother, Pablita, and Robert at White Sands, N.M.—photo by Mela Ortiz y Pino de Martin

Mela at White Sands, N.M.— photo by Robert H. Martin

Mela poses for photo before going to Governor Mabry's inaugural ball—photo by Robert H. Martin

The Family

A photo of La Conquistadora on a sample of the annual Christmas cards that were Bob and Mela's signature item as a couple—courtesy Robert H. Martin

This year of the Quincentenary we greet you and share with you this Christmas card in honor of the Queen and Patroness of New Mexico and its Villa de Santa Fe,

LA CONQUISTADORA.

Our Lady is robed in special clothing of historical and cultural value and beauty.

Along the path of life You have increased our love for one another, You answered our prayers, You have given us strength and You have blessed us with understanding our Lady of the Holy Rosary.

You have become a symbol of thanksgiving and hope for hundreds of New Mexicans, new found friends and followers. You are indeed a treasured Lady who has earned Her recognition. Bless us with great devotion our treasured Lady.

The Infant in His mother's arms looks so happy being held so tenderly and lovingly by His mother and looking at all of us with that same love, from His mother's embrace.

I'm sure that my mother held her children in the same loving manner that La Conquistadora holds the Infant. My dear mother, there was a glow that radiated from your warmth and kindness when you laid your hand on your children.

La Conquistadora has always been important to Bob and Mela. I have a beautiful story about La Conquistadora. As this story unfolds, 30 years seem like yesterday and again it seems ages ago.

"My mother was seriously ill and not expected to have long to live when I went to visit La Conquistadora on June 11, 1962. I asked Her to give my mother one more year and I would have a special dress made for Her. On June 11 of the following year my mother passed away, the day before my birthday. I followed through with my promise and had the dress for La Conquistadora made by the Carmelites of robin's egg blue velveteen material. When it was finished it was given to Our Lady and She wears it sometimes on my birthday."

Robert photographed Her on the Eugenie Shonnard altar at Rosario Chapel wearing the promised dress.

With loving care La Conquistadora has watched over our lives like the kind and gentle Patroness She is. We ask Her to hold us squarely in the palm of Her hand, to carry us in the warmth of Her love and Her protection.

It is our wish that you have a Merry Christmas and a wonderful, healthy New Year.

Mela & Bob Martin

Above left, Newspaper photo from the Santa Fe New Mexican of Mela and historian Marc Simmons— photo by Robert H. Martin

Above right, Bob and Mela were married for 48½ years— courtesy Robert H. Martin

Right, Mela receives honor from the Spanish government—photo by Robert H. Martin

The Family

One of the last photos with Mela before she died—photo by Robert H. Martin

As years went by, Adela married, and then found a sister and a brother she had not known about. The reunion came when Adela's husband, Camilo Chávez, was working in a mine near Pecos, and started talking with another miner who turned out to be his wife's brother. Later, Camilo took a job with a lumber company in Albuquerque, and could see his family only on weekends. On one such weekend, Adela and her brother and her sons got in a car to drive down to Albuquerque to meet her husband. On the way they stopped to visit Pedro Jr. and his young family in Santa Fe, then pushed on toward Albuquerque on U.S. 85, the road that went down La Bajada, a precipitous, twisting, 500-foot decline. "It was raining cats and dogs," Pedro Jr. recalls. "Going over La Bajada, the road had collapsed. The car slipped off the road, and they were all killed."

The life stories lived and shared by the Ortiz y Pino family teem with pain and joy, tragedy and triumph, abundance and want, love and vengeance, despair and hope, and faith. At this point in the family saga, the stories seem as numerous as the stars. And over the course of her own nine decades, Concha has lived more stories than she can ever tell.

The Family

Mela Ortiz y Pino de Martin—photo by Robert H. Martin

At Mela's funeral service, Santa Fe historian Marc Simmons delivered this eulogy:

Concha Ortiz y Pino de Kleven has asked me to say a few words about her sister and my longtime friend Mela Martin. I think it is especially fitting, on a somber occasion such as this, to reminisce briefly about the person, no longer with us, who is being honored and remembered.

The two things that meant the most to Mela Martin were family and religion. They shaped the configuration of her life. And I think everyone who knew her was aware of that.

Her devotion to La Conquistadora and the enthusiasm she showed annually for the preparation of her famous Christmas cards were manifestations of Mela's deep religious faith.

Growing up in one of New Mexico's most distinguished traditional families, Mela developed a lifelong interest in the remarkable story of her energetic ancestors. From that, it was a logical and easy step into a broad appreciation for New Mexico's history.

During my visits with her over many years, the numerous adventures of the Ortiz y Pino clan inevitably would enter the conversation. Among Mela's favorite subjects was the career of Don Nicolás Pino, one of the three sons of *don* Pedro Bautista Pino, New Mexico's most renowned statesmen of the late colonial period.

Certainly, a high point in Mela's life, as her husband Robert confirms, came in 1967. In that year, the Spanish government awarded Mela Martin membership in the prestigious Instituto de Cultura Hispánica de Madrid. She was the only New Mexico woman ever to receive that honor.

Another thing Mela took pride in was the part she played in the city of Santa Fe receiving a splendid gift from Spain. In 1976, on the occasion of our nation's bicentennial, the Spanish government presented our fair city a beautiful replica of the royal banner that flew over the Palace of the Governors in 1692.

After a perfunctory thank-you, the city officials folded up the banner and put it away in a chest. That was not good enough for Mela Martin!

She went to work and arranged for a special dedication ceremony and placement of the Spanish royal banner on public display. The appropriate observance took place on Friday morning of the Santa Fe Fiesta, with Mela acting as chairperson of the dedication.

Just yesterday, I found a newspaper clipping about the event, with a photo of Mela standing next to the banner hanging in City Hall. The last time I was over there, I looked, and it was still on display.

I would also like to pay tribute, in conclusion, to Mela and Robert's marriage of 48 years. Such a durable union, particularly in this day and age, is highly praiseworthy. In the end, Robert faithfully cared for his beloved wife during the long period of her final illness.

In many ways, Mela Ortiz y Pino de Martin was a memorable person. Mela, I will miss you, especially the sharing of our common love of history.

La cámara fotográfica de Robert Martin

En esta biografía de Concha Ortiz y Pino, este capítulo se refiere al cuñado Robert Martin que figura de relieve como artista fotográfico. Oriundo de Chicago, Robert vino a Los Álamos, N.M., en 1946, donde ocupó el cargo de fotógrafo en el Laboratorio Nacional de Los Álamos, lugar remoto en la meseta Pajarito en las Montañas de Jémez a unas 35 millas de Santa Fe.

Poco después de llegar a Santa Fe, el fotógrafo Bob Martin conoció a la bella Mela Ortiz y Pino, hermana de nuestra biografiada. Bob y Mela se enamoraron y en febrero de 1950 se casaron. La pareja estableció su hogar en Santa Fe y Bob Martin se distinguió en su carrera de fotógrafo no únicamente en el Laboratorio Nacional de Los Álamos sino también por las fotografías que lograba sacar del entorno único y diferente que ofrece esta región de Nuevo México. La vida esponsalicia de Mela y Bob fue una vida feliz. Como esposo de Mela, Bob formaba parte íntima de la distinguida familia Ortiz y Pino. Bob Martin era un hombre feliz en su matrimonio y en su trabajo. Logró recibir varios premios por su talento artístico.

Mela sufrió un accidente en el que se fracturó las dos rodillas y tenía que pasar el resto de su vida en silla de ruedas. Cinco años después, Mela sufrió un infarto antes de pasar a mejor vida en 1998.

Casi a diario, Bob Martin va a visitar a Concha, quien reconoce "como la hermana que nunca tuve yo."

Through the Lens of Robert H. Martin

15

As a young boy growing up in Chicago, Robert H. Martin was given a little box camera as a present from his mother for his 12th birthday. It was the start of something big. That camera led to a career, professional esteem, good pay, worldwide adventures, work that he loved with a passion, and official accolades from many quarters. But ask him, and he will say that the two finest things his camera ever brought him were New Mexico and—by far the most important—the love of his life, his wife Mela Ortiz y Pino.

When he married Mela more than half a century ago, Bob Martin became an integral member of Concha's family, and has remained so ever since. With the vast Ortiz y Pino clan he has shared births and deaths, joys and sorrows, holidays and ordinary days, exotic travels, good times and bad, and everything in between. Yet none of it—none of it—could ever have been predicted by the little Lutheran kid growing up in a poor family in the Upper Midwest in the Great Depression days of the 1930s.

The 1933–34 Chicago World's Fair, celebrating the city's first 100 years of incorporation, opened shortly after young Bob got his camera, so naturally he headed over there with his new toy. He did not have money to pay the admission, but easily compensated for that inconvenience by picking up bottles, newspapers, and other trash and selling them to a junk dealer. Inside the gates he located all the stands where food and Cokes were free, and he earned rides on the giant slide by keeping the site tidy for its operators. Most of all, however, he took pictures. Pictures after pictures after pictures.

To afford the cost of developing them, he bought his own chemicals and built a makeshift darkroom at home. This caused

Self-portrait of Robert H. Martin

some monumental messes, but soon he got the hang of it. Soon he was developing and printing pictures for his friends, and by the time he was 16, he was running his own business, Realistic Photographic Service, complete with stationery and cards. After high school he continued his studies at the Maholy Nagy Institute of Design, the Illinois Institute of Technology and the Winona School of Professional Photography in Indiana. Then World War II broke out.

Bob tried to join the Army, but was declared 4-F for an ironic reason: his peripheral vision was impaired, even though his photographic instincts were superb. So he hired on to do sales promotions at the Zenith Radio Corporation, and usually took his camera with him to company picnics, dances, and other events. At one of them his camera was confiscated by jumpy security guards, because Zenith was also a major defense contractor. Bob handed over the camera without protest, but requested that the images on his film be developed with care. When company officials saw those images, they asked Bob to be the plant's photographer.

In 1946, shortly after the war ended, the Army decided that Bob was qualified for duty after all. After basic training in the infantry, he heard that the top-secret facility in Los Alamos, N.M., that had hastened the war's end by developing an atomic bomb, was

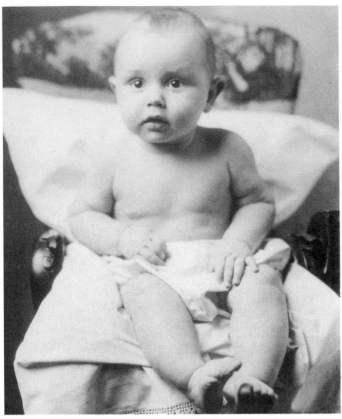

Robert H. Martin was born in Chicago, Ill., in 1921—courtesy Robert H. Martin

Two-year-old Bob Martin with older brother Chester in the back yard of their Chicago home—courtesy Robert H. Martin

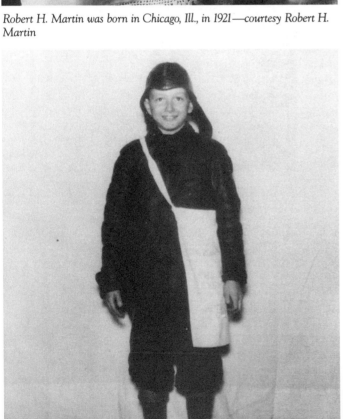

Bob in 1931 selling the Chicago Daily News *and the* Saturday Evening Post*—courtesy Robert H. Martin*

Bob Martin the soldier in 1946—courtesy Robert H. Martin

Through the Lens of Robert H. Martin

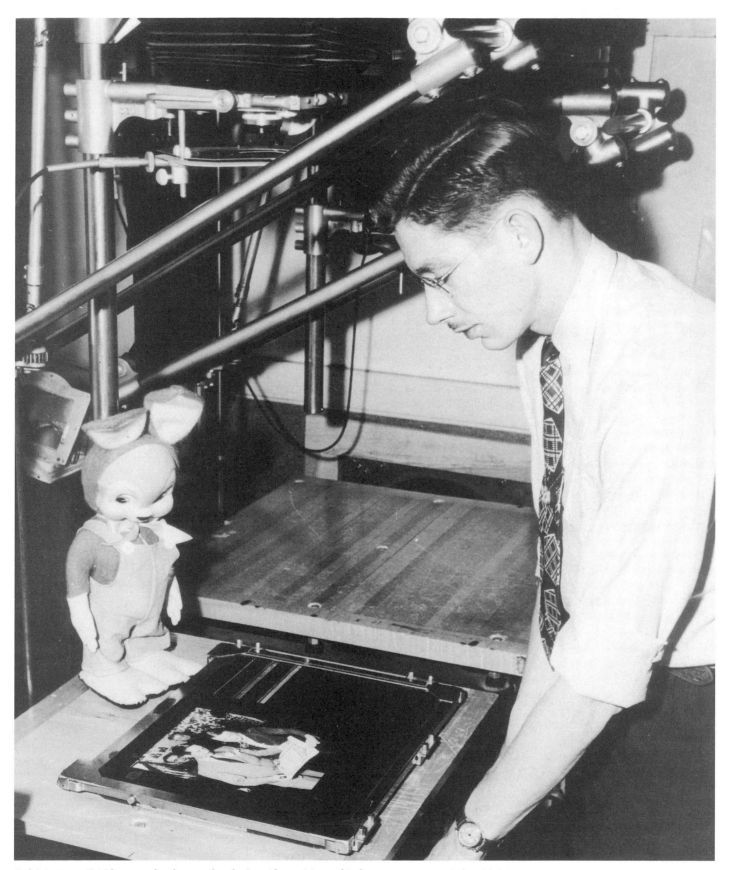

Bob Martin in 1946 becomes the photographer for Los Alamos National Laboratory—courtesy Robert H. Martin

Bob Martin at Eniwetok Atoll in the Pacific Ocean—courtesy Robert H. Martin

seeking a photographer to record the project. He volunteered for the assignment and was accepted. But when he tried to book passage to New Mexico, he found that all the railways and airlines were full. So his parents offered to drive him instead. When their car bumped into Santa Fe on the Old Santa Fe Trail, Bob thought that his directions must be wrong—that the road they were on was just a narrow alley that couldn't possibly be going anywhere. It was a fitting introduction to New Mexico.

His introduction to Los Alamos was just as peculiar. The entire community was still top-secret then, was ringed by security fences, and was patrolled constantly by guards. Bob had an official pass, and so he was let inside. But his parents had to wait for him at the gate. When he came to rejoin them they were very nervous, because the guards had told them that Los Alamos was under a 36-hour alert. As Bob got into the car, the bushes next to it began rustling. Guards carrying pistols, rifles and machine guns swooped down. The moment was tense—until an unconcerned tomcat strolled out from the bush.

The Los Alamos where Bob arrived right after World War II was unlike any other place in America. Located 35 miles northwest of Santa Fe on a mesa in the Jémez Mountains, Los Alamos made the perfect "secret city" when the U.S. government needed a site for the creation of the atomic bomb. It was far distant from any large population. Its difficult mountainous terrain and tranquil lifestyle also made the area attractive. Los Alamos means "the cottonwoods" in Spanish. The Pajarito Plateau, on which Los Alamos is situated, was shaped by a series of volcanic eruptions about 1.2 million years ago. Soft rock formed by the settling volcanic ash enabled ancient native inhabitants to carve out cave homes, now

Through the Lens of Robert H. Martin

Scientists at Bikini Island rescue a giant turtle—photo by Robert H. Martin.

preserved as Bandelier National Monument. Much of the surrounding area is deep evergreen forest of cedar, piñon and pondersoa pine, interspersed with mountain grasslands. Anglo settlers first came to the Pajarito Plateau in the 1880s.

A man named Ashley Pond established the Los Alamos Ranch School in 1917. He thought the facility would help privileged Eastern boys develop into strong educated men. J. Robert Oppenheimer, who grew up to become the University of California physicist chosen by the U.S. government as head of the Manhattan Project, to develop the atomic bomb, knew about the school. He suggested Los Alamos for the site when the the school was closed in 1943 and the Army took over the town. Soon it was populated by many of the greatest scientists in the world. The only houses with bathtubs were the former ranch school teachers' cabins. The scientists received the privilege of using the cabins, and their street was nicknamed Bathtub Row.

Mail and transportation to Los Alamos were convoluted. The only official mailing address for Los Alamos was U.S. Post Office Box 1663 in Santa Fe. Every day a courier picked up the items in the Capital City and took them to Los Alamos for distribution. Several babies born during the Manhattan Project had that box number listed on their birth certificates as their home address. Travel in and out of the city was subject to intense scrutiny, both during the war and after. And the only road connecting Los Alamos to the outside world was treacherous and slow.

Robert Martin, who had no car, recalls hitching rides to Santa Fe that took four or five hours each way. But he had a compelling reason to make that arduous trip: visiting the

Bob Martin, second row, far right, with Los Alamos National Laboratory colleagues conducting nuclear tests at Bikini Island—courtesy Robert H. Martin

young and pretty Mela Ortiz y Pino, program director at the Santa Fe USO Club. Soon their romance was blossoming. When he could not come in person, Bob called her on the telephone, for a quarter per call—a costly sum in those days.

In 1947, the Army turned over control of Los Alamos to the newly created U.S. Atomic Energy Commission, and Bob was faced with a decision. "I was given a choice to stay in the service with a promotion or remain at Los Alamos as a civilian employee," he smiles. "I had already fallen for Mela, so I made up my mind to remain." Making higher pay as the official Los Alamos photographer made his exit from the Army even easier.

In 1949, he volunteered to go to Eniwetok Atoll in the Marshall Islands in the Pacific Ocean, to record the scene of some of the terrible carnage of World War II, and to photograph new nuclear tests. There, amid the blasted hulls of American and Japanese warships rusting in shallow water, he still found some sense of fun, for he sent coconuts to many New Mexico friends who had never seen such a thing before—and were not sure what it was, much less what to do with it. But Bob also was thinking of deeper matters. By mail he and Mela made marriage plans. They were wed in Santa Fe on Feb. 18, 1950.

After his return, the photographer settled down to the daily routine of the Los Alamos commute from his Santa Fe home. Looking back, he has no complaints. "For 30 years, I did jobs I liked. I went through several cars and tires—18,000 miles was good on a set of tires in those days, and I used up about one set a year." To make his drive time more productive, he came up with a novel idea—which literally involved novels.

Eloy Montoya, known as "Monty" at the lab, laughs as he recalls Bob on his way to "the Hill," as employees refer to Los Alamos. "Many times our carpool would pass Robert Martin and see him reading while he was driving!" Faced with this accusation, Bob pleads guilty as charged—with an explanation: "Very few policemen were on duty on the road to Los Alamos. Why should there have been? There were very few accidents. Everyone behaved themselves and cooperated, and there really wasn't much traffic in the beginning, so there wasn't a need for a lot of police." As for reading and driving at the same time, he shrugs and says he could accomplish more that way. "When I told Mela I did that, she thought I was joking. After I retired and several people told her they missed seeing me reading and driving

Through the Lens of Robert H. Martin

The sign reads:

OFFICIAL SCENIC HISTORIC MARKER

GALISTEO

The Galisteo group of the Tanos Indian Nation occupied this area until the latter part of the eighteenth century. Ruins of two important pueblos, San Lazaro and San Cristobal may still be seen. Espejo (1583), and Oñate (1598) were among early Spanish conquistadores to visit these pueblos.

USO SANTA FE N.MEX

Bob Martin working on publicity for the USO in Galisteo—courtesy Robert H. Martin

on the way to Los Alamos, only then did she believe it."

In 1957, the gates surrounding the "Closed City" of Los Alamos finally came down, and the roads into and out of it were opened to the public. The facility is now called Los Alamos National Laboratory (LANL), and for many years has been directed by the University of California and the U.S. Department of Energy, not the Army. In addition to nuclear weapons, which it has continued to develop on a theoretical basis but not on the physical level, the Lab has also pioneered thermonuclear energy, as well as health, chemistry, and biology research. It is a huge economic presence in New Mexico.

In 1980, after 33 years as an employee at the lab, Bob retired. He spent many wonderful years with his wife before the accident in 1955 that broke her knee and left her wheelchair-bound, and then the 1993 stroke that preceded her death in 1998. Bob still lives in the family home he and Mela shared for 48½ years. A chestnut-red poodle, Yvette, bears a longer full name that only Bob uses: Yvette Rouse (red) Ortiz y Pino de Martin. He clearly loves his pet. His surroundings include photos of Mela and other Ortiz y Pinos. The mantle of the fireplace provides a place of honor for an image of Santo Niño (the Holy Infant). Mela's doll collection rests in a place of honor in the house. Key awards line the walls of the home.

The awards have been many. Several came from the Professional Photographers of

Cemetery in Galisteo—photo by Robert H. Martin

Through the Lens of Robert H. Martin

A St. Francis Cathedral winter scene with Fray Angélico Chávez—photo by Robert H. Martin

Fray Angélico Chávez signs his book for John Moody at the USO in 1947—photo by Robert H. Martin

Father Schmidt, Adeline Ortiz and Fray Angélico Chávez in 1947—photo by Robert H. Martin

America, the world's oldest such association, which in 1990 declared Bob a "Master of Photography," its highest distinction. Similar honors have been bestowed on him by the New Mexico Photographers Association, and the Museum of New Mexico gave him a special archival award for recording historic buildings in the state. July 15, 1986, was proclaimed "Robert H. Martin Day" by New Mexico Gov. Toney Anaya. Bob is listed in *Who's Who in the West*, and his work has appeared in the *World Book Encyclopedia* and *National Geographic*. His pictures of Santa Fe have been published in Spain's oldest newspaper, *El Diario* in the city of Cádiz. Several of his individual photographs have been chosen "best in show." One, which he titled *Metal Fatigue*, was of a broken U-joint on his own car. His landscape and abstract photos have won prizes as well.

A special area of concentration has been the Madonna, the Holy Virgin Mary. Each holiday season, he and Mela would fashion another beautiful study of this icon for their Christmas cards, which were treasured by everyone on their list. In addition, he has meticulously recorded the historic progression of Santa Fe's own special Madonna, La Conquistadora, a small wooden statue that accompanied the Spanish troops who reclaimed New Mexico from rebellious Indians in 1692. When Bob arrived in 1946, La Conquistadora was a simple religious figure, but over the years it has gained jewels, fine garments and other accoutrements. His photos show the statue in processions, at the altar, and in other settings. One is in the presence of Archbishop Edwin V. Byrne at a special Papal

Posing for El Baile de las Cascarones *at the USO: Seated: Adeline Ortiz (front center), Father Schmidt, Rosina Muñiz García, Connie Hernández, Fray Angélico Chávez, and John Moody. Standing in back leaning on door is Mrs. Moody. Others unidentified, circa 1947— photo by Robert H. Martin*

La Conquistadora procession: From left to right: Fray Angélico Chávez (with sunglasses), other priest and altar boy, Connie Hernández, Dolores López, and Deanie Ortiz, circa 1948—photo by Robert H. Martin

Through the Lens of Robert H. Martin

Coronation Ceremony in St. Francis Cathedral in 1960.

Fray Angélico Chávez entering the church in Peña Blanca, where he painted the Stations of the Cross depicting the residents of the village—photo by Robert H. Martin

In his spare time, Bob did extensive work for the New Mexico Legislature and the United Press International news service. He has photographed construction projects, such as the building of the Carmelite Monastery in Santa Fe. He has staged comic photos, such as placing a dog next to an outhouse. His friend and Los Alamos colleague Eloy Montoya remembers eating dinner one night at the Rancho de Chimayó restaurant when Bob started staring at a crack in the adobe wall, and eventually took a picture of it. Bob laughs at the memory. "You should have seen the finished product! I enjoyed working with the unusual at times."

Photo albums in his home contain special personal moments and work he considers his favorite subjects. Here, one views the old San Miguel Chapel and the Cuyamungue/Tesuque Mountain with the outline of a thunderbird. Another mountain in the Sangre de Cristo chain shows a horse's head outlined among the greenery. Other striking images, such as Tío Vivo from Taos, a pristine Canyon Road and the now-gone New Mexico Governor's Mansion downtown, by the Santa Fe River, ("its modern-day location is the Inn of the Governors"), all come to life when Bob discusses them. He captured countless Santa Fe scenes: Fiesta queens, San Francisco Street with old cars, the old parochial school, and the old Cross of the Martyrs. Mexico, White Sands, a horse and buggy and the Old Capitol dome also have been subjects. Photos of Archbishop Edwin V.

Fray Angélico Chávez (center), Carmen Anchondo, Pauline Padilla, La Conquistadora, Socorro López and Socorro Anchondo, circa 1948—photo by Robert H. Martin

Byrne capture the long-dead, dignified cleric. Some pictures illustrate Bob's playful side, such as times when he posed the prominent Santa Fe cleric Fray Angélico Chávez in various costumes: the Frank Sinatra look, the gangster look and the archbishop look.

The list of famous people Bob has photographed is long and distinguished. It includes Queen Frederica of Greece; President John F. Kennedy with a button missing from his jacket; President Lyndon Johnson; Dr. Charles Richter, developer of the scale that measures earthquakes; Harold Edgerton, inventor of the strobe light; and, of course, Robert Oppenheimer, plus others too numerous to mention. One of his favorite photos showed the world-famous photographer Edward Steichen with the world-famous writer Carl Sandburg—and the two just happened to be brothers-in-law. That photo is now in the permanent archives of the Museum of Modern Art in New York. A special friend of his was fellow photographer Laura Gilpin, who gained fame for her images of the Navajo people. But Bob's penchant for meeting famous people began early in his life: As an 8-year-old student in Chicago, he once shook hands with inventor Thomas Edison.

A cancer survivor since 1976, Bob stays busy with two other passions: collecting coins and stamps. He also likes to collect cartoons, placing them in plastic covers in a binder, and sending favorites along to friends. On almost a daily basis he visits with Concha, whom he calls "the sister I never had." Quick with a smile and a ready wit, Bob has always maintained a fine sense of humor. But of course he misses Mela a great deal.

Fortunately for him, for the Ortiz y Pino family, and for all the other people who have benefited from his marvelous photographic eye, a vast archive of images keeps the remarkable path of Robert H. Martin's life always vital, frozen in indelible moments.

Fray Angélico Chávez at his 80th birthday party with Bob and Mela's wedding photo— photo by Robert H. Martin

John Moody with Fray Angélico Chávez and unidentified soldier at the Cross of the Martyrs in Santa Fe in 1948—photo by Robert H. Martin

Fray Angélico Chávez, with statue of La Conquistadora that he brought from the Philippines, and John Moody (far right). Others unidentified, circa 1947—photo by Robert H. Martin

La Conquistadora procession on Grant and Palace avenues, circa 1948—photo by Robert H. Martin

Archbishop Byrne, clergy and La Conquistadora in front of the St. Francis Cathedral, circa 1948—photo by Robert H. Martin

Through the Lens of Robert H. Martin

Left to right: (in front) Carmen Anchondo, Socorro Anchondo, (in back) Pauline Padilla, Archbishop Byrne, and Socorro López with La Conquistadora inside Santa Fe Cathedral, circa 1948—photo by Robert H. Martin

The foundation for the Carmelite Monastery being built, circa 1947—photo by Robert H. Martin

Fiesta Candlelight Procession on Washington Avenue, circa 1948—photo by Robert H. Martin

Through the Lens of Robert H. Martin

Making scapulars at the USO, circa 1947 from left to right: unidentified woman, Lorencita Luján standing, unidentified woman, John Moody and Victoria Roybal Sosaya to his left—photo by Robert H. Martin

Santa Fe Fiesta Historical/Hysterical Parade, circa 1947—photo by Robert H. Martin

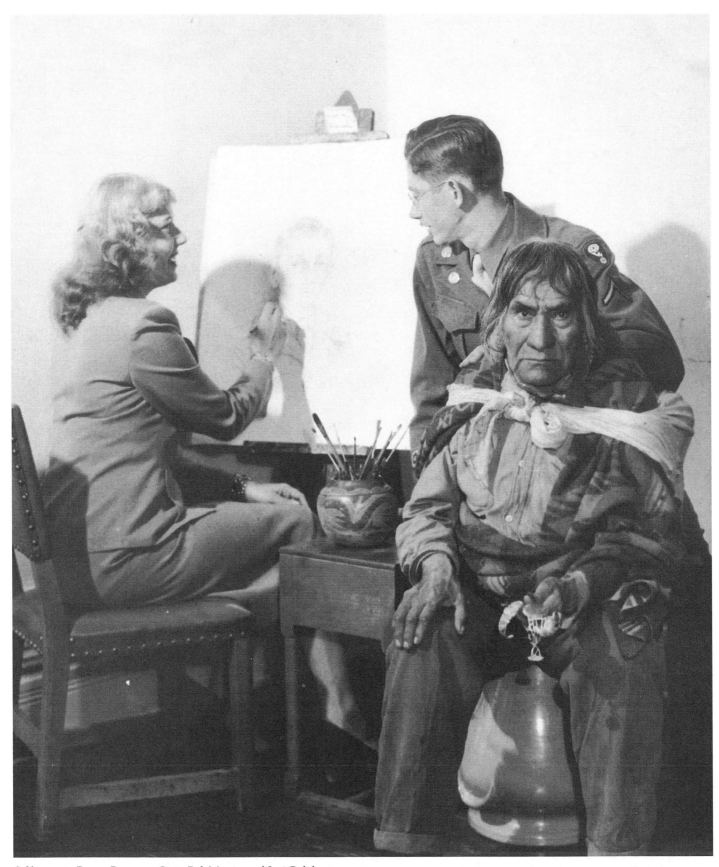

Self-portrait, Ramor Baumann Ortiz, Bob Martin, and José Calabasa

Through the Lens of Robert H. Martin

The Española Rodeo—photo by Robert H. Martin

A pigeon in a shoeshine box when a shine cost 10¢—photo by Robert H. Martin

The artist Pop Chalee and Pansy Stockton in 1948—photo by Robert H. Martin

Through the Lens of Robert H. Martin

Pansy Stockton with her kachina doll collection—photo by Robert H. Martin

Thunderbird image on the Sangre de Cristo Mountains—photo by Robert H. Martin

Horsehead image on the Sangre de Cristo Mountains—photo by Robert H. Martin

Through the Lens of Robert H. Martin

Self-portrait of Robert H. Martin with La Conquistadora

Capítulo 16
Participación en juntas directivas

Pronto después de que su esposo Victor pasó a mejor vida Concha vendió el rancho. Tenía 46 años de edad y tuvo que decidir qué hacer con su vida. Joven, saludable, y económicamente bien puesta, tenía muchas posibilidades. Primero volvió al hogar que ella y Victor habían comprado cerca de la Universidad de Nuevo México en Albuquerque. Ese hogar tenía una biblioteca, espacio adecuado para recibir amistades, varias recámaras, un comedor, muebles de categoría, y un patio de ambiente íntimo.

Ya había desempeñado cargos en el gobierno, y en juntas directivas de organizaciones a las que había prestado servicios, y a la vez le habían brindado mucha satisfacción. Cuando se pasó la voz que estaba interesada en seguir este plan de vida, parecía que el mundo se le echaba encima. Este cuadro sinóptico no nos da suficiente espacio para indicar todas las organizaciones a las que Concha prestó servicio y apoyo. Las actividades a las que se dedicó se agrupan en cuatro clasificaciones: las bellas artes, la historia, apoyo económico a organizaciones en beneficio de personas discapacitadas, y entidades gubernamentales.

Mediante ese tipo de organizaciones ha logrado expresar su amor y cometido a la historia, a distintas organizaciones caritativas, culturales, y a organizaciones que trabajan para socorrer a personas que padecen de minusvalideces. Cinco presidentes de la república nombraron a Concha a juntas directivas al nivel nacional. Con algunos de ellos ha formado amistad.

Después de haber llegado a los 90 años en el año 2000, Concha ha disminuido algunas pero no todas las actividades en las que ha venido activamente participando. Aún hoy día sigue asociada a muchas juntas directivas de distintas organizaciones en pro del bienestar del público.

Choosing to Serve

16

After her husband Victor's sudden death, followed quickly by the sale of Agua Verde, Concha had to decide what next to do in her life. At 46, she was still young and vital, and the proceeds from the ranch sale left her financially secure enough to consider all possibilities. The very first thing she did, however, was to return to the house that she and Victor had bought near the University of New Mexico in Albuquerque. The contrast between her city home and the ramshackle two-room house she had occupied on the ranch was dramatic. In Albuquerque she had a library, an entertainment area, several bedrooms, a separate dining room, fine furniture and a large, enclosed yard. But at 100,000 acres, perhaps her "yard" at the ranch could be called even larger.

"When I moved back to town, it was a different life," Concha says. "I was so hungry for ice cream and sweet rolls and listening to people talk. I would go to the university and listen to lectures, so I could hear people talk about something that was not so mundane as fences and nails." After a period of readjustment to the city, she then reflected upon the different things she had done in her life.

She had been a state legislator. She had earned a college degree. She had been a loving wife to her husband, and a very active faculty wife at the university. She had worked as dean of women at the College of St. Joseph. She had successfully managed a huge ranch, which had seemed headed for bankruptcy before she took charge. Looking back over the years, Concha asked herself what had given her the most satisfaction. The answer was simple: being Victor's wife. But now as his widow, Concha did not want to marry again. "There will never be another Victor," she knew. "He encouraged me to be myself, above all."

In addition to her many official duties, Concha had served on various public-service boards. At the request of Gov. John Miles, she had worked on the Cuarto-Centennial Commission that celebrated the first 400 years of New Mexico's European-linked history. Her fellow members included U.S. Sen. Clinton Anderson and the Vice President of the United States, John Nance Garner. She had been a charter member of the Santa Fe unit of the Women's National Aeronautic Association, which established emergency landing fields around the state. In Albuquerque she had worked for causes as diverse as the Rehabilitation Center, the Cerebral Palsy School, the Camp Fire Girls and the War Fund Campaign during World War II.

Concha had found these positions to be deeply rewarding, for herself personally and for the causes she helped. So she decided to devote her remaining life to similar work. To Concha, such affiliations meant financial support, attendance at meetings, travel when necessary and carrying out the tasks assigned to her. When word went out that she was interested in such service, the world beat a path to her door. In the following years and decades, she served on at least 60 boards, and probably many more. The list stretches on and on, across her eight-page résumé. Space does not allow a full description of all her involvements, but they can be roughly grouped into four major areas of service: the arts, history, aid for people with various handicaps, and government.

Few notable arts organization in New Mexico have attained prominence without Concha's awareness and assistance. Boards on which she has served include: the New Mexico Symphony Orchestra, the Albuquerque Little Theater, UNM Friends of the Arts, the New Mexico Opera Guild, the Taos Center for the Arts, the Santa Fe Desert Chorale, the Orchestra of Santa Fe, and the Festival Foundation, which produces the annual Santa

Concha at the 1940 Cuarto Centennial in Albuquerque, wearing the solid gold necklace mined from the Ortiz Mountains, now worn by La Conquistadora—photo courtesy Robert H. Martin

Concha at the 1940 Cuarto Centennial in Albuquerque, with Edgar Bergen and Charlie McCarthy—courtesy Ron Ortiz Dinkel

Fe Festival for the Arts. There are more, but one organization that compressed her wide-ranging dedication to such causes into one influential position was a state agency, the New Mexico Arts Commission. Created by the Legislature in 1964, the commission had a noble mission: "to preserve, enhance and develop the arts in New Mexico," and "to enrich the quality of life for present and future generations."

As a concerned citizen, Concha pushed hard for passage of the Arts Commission bill. And when it became law she was one of the original members appointed to it by Gov. Jack Campbell. She remained until 1987, a period of 23 years. With substantial sums of money to dispense, the commission quickly became a major mover and shaker on the New Mexico arts scene. In some years the agency gave almost all its allotted funds to large, well-established artistic organizations such as the Santa Fe Opera and the New Mexico Symphony Orchestra. But the philosophy guiding the commission was subject to constant scrutiny, and Concha was one of the foremost scrutinizers.

In 1974, about a dozen arts groups that had received no funding from the commission requested a hearing to express their discontent. Before the official meeting, Concha suggested a pre-session gathering of the commissioners to decide what policies they wished to follow. She raised several key questions: Should the commission fund schools, colleges,

Concha at the 1940 Cuarto Centennial in Albuquerque, standing at right—courtesy Center for Southwest Research, University of New Mexico, negative no. 000-048-0092

museums, and other institutions that were already financed by the state? Should the commission generously fund well-established arts organizations so they could continue to develop? Should the commission fund newcomers, especially ones that did not use people from within the state? Should some previously funded organizations "be on their own by now?" Should projects be funded for educational purposes, or primarily for entertainment value to large audiences? Such provocative questions can never have firm answers set in stone, but because Concha raised these points, they have been part of the arts commission's deliberations ever since.

As a proud and regal member of one of New Mexico's founding Spanish families, with roots stretching back to pre-colonial Spain, Concha was a natural inheritor of a profound sense of history. Many are the organizations through which she has expressed her love of and commitment to history. They include the New Mexico Genealogical Society, the New Mexico Historical Association, the Santa Fe Historical Association, La Cofradía de la Conquistadora (The Confraternity of Our Lady of the Conquest) in Santa Fe, the Wheelwright Museum of the American Indian in Santa Fe, and the Maxwell Museum of Anthropology in Albuquerque. She was a driving force behind the Hispanic wing of the Museum of International Folk Art in Santa Fe, and an active force within the Colonial New Mexico Foundation, which runs the "living museum" in La Ciénega village near Santa Fe, depicting life in Spanish-Colonial times.

Perhaps the most significant of all her historical involvement has been with the Guadalupe Historical Society. This group's reason for existence is the ancient and lovely Santuario de Guadalupe church in downtown Santa Fe. Built by Franciscan missionaries between 1776 and 1798, the sanctuary is recognized by historians as the oldest shrine in the United States dedicated to Our Lady of Guadalupe, patroness saint of the Americas.

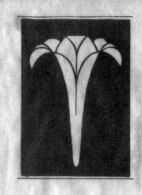

New Mexico Society for Crippled Children & Adults

A TESTIMONIAL

OF A GRATEFUL ORGANIZATION

Presented to

Concha de Fleven

IN RECOGNITION, HONOR AND SINCERE APPRECIATION OF THE DISTINGUISHED
AND UNSELFISH COMMUNITY SERVICE GIVEN TO THE HANDICAPPED, FOR
DEVOTION TO A CAUSE THAT HAS BROUGHT ASSISTANCE AND HAPPINESS TO
MANY THROUGHOUT THE STATE OF NEW MEXICO.

PRESIDENT

EXECUTIVE DIRECTOR

DATE *Oct 15, 1966*

The art in its collection includes a priceless masterpiece by 16th-century Venetian painter Leandro de Ponte Bassano depicting Jesus driving the moneychangers from the temple. Another work, a Baroque oil by José de Alzíbar, one of Colonial Mexico's most renowned painters, portrays Our Lady of Guadalupe as she appeared to a peasant in an apparition in 1531. The church commissioned the 16-foot-by-14-foot image, which was delivered to Santa Fe by mule caravan on El Camino Real from Mexico City.

Parishioners used the church continuously from its construction until 1961. But then the parish needed a larger facility, and one was built. The old church fell vacant for 14 years. Steadily deteriorating, the *santuario* seemed destined for demolition, and its prime downtown site perhaps sold for a large amount of money in Santa Fe's real-estate market.

But in 1974, the Archdiocese of Santa Fe turned over the title of the site to the newly formed Guadalupe Historic Foundation, which was determined to preserve the church. The New Mexico Arts Commission gave the foundation a grant for a feasibility study. In 1975, the American Revolutionary Bicentennial Commission selected the *santuario* as New Mexico's official state project, assisted by a federal grant. The Santa Fe Community Development Commission matched the federal money and added its own grant as well. Private donations poured in, and the ancient church got emergency repairs. The foundation had succeeded in stabilizing one of Santa Fe's most historic sites.

Yet the victory was only temporary, for much still needed to be done. According to a mission statement, "It is the intention of the Guadalupe Historic Foundation that the *santuario* be a 'living' preservation of history. One of the foundation's goals is to enhance community awareness of art, education, history and culture." To achieve this, the church was to become a multi-use facility, still available for religious occasions, but also for

Concha proudly displays a handicap decal for national legislation she was instrumental in passing during the Lyndon B. Johnson presidency—courtesy Concha Ortiz y Pino de Kleven

Choosing to Serve

appropriate musical and theatrical presentations, for arts and crafts shows and for various other community purposes. In order to pass inspection to be licensed for such use, however, the structure required an estimated $200,000 in renovations.

In 1990, Concha converted an honor for herself into assistance for the *santuario*. Friends planning a gala 80th birthday party asked Concha where she would like to hold it. She selected the old church. At her insistence, the invitation read, "It is suggested the contributions to the Santuario de Guadalupe Restoration Fund would be the perfect gift to commemorate her birthday. All gifts will be matched by a generous benefactor. She requests no personal gifts." The party brought in $50,000, which when matched by the benefactor totaled $100,000—fully half of the needed renovation total. The project quickly moved on to a successful conclusion. Foundation officials estimate that at least 120,000 visitors have used the *santuario* since it took on its present role in Santa Fe.

The phrase "handicaps and disabilities" covers a wide range of conditions. And that is the way Concha has approached this area of service. If she sees a problem, she tries to make it better. Organizations whose work she has helped include Lovelace Medical Foundation, Easter Seal Society for Crippled Children and Adults, New Mexico Services for the Blind, Little Haven Center for Emotionally Disturbed Adults, Careers for the Handicapped, UNM Children's Psychiatric Center, Sickle Cell Council of New Mexico, Albuquerque Rehabilitation Center, Bernalillo County District Health Commission, and St. Joseph's Hospital Auxiliary, among others. With the Newgate Project, she helped established a high-school-equivalency program for inmates at the Penitentiary of New Mexico. As rehabilitation chair of the New Mexico chapter of Partners for the Americas, she arranged to send physical therapists to help needy people in the Mexican state of Tabasco, and also arranged to send medical assistance to blind people there.

Sometimes Concha's involvement with assistance programs overlaps with her service on governmental panels. For example, she secured New Mexico Arts Commission funding for art classes at the state prison, and then was gratified when three inmate participants won prizes in a national competition. And sometimes her governmental appointments serve other specific purposes. The mayor of Albuquerque appointed her to the city's zoo advisory board. She has served on Albuquerque's Beautification Committee. She was a member of the State Commission on Streams and Water Pollution. A quasi-governmental position she held was committee member for the New Mexico Governor's Prayer Breakfast. In 1986 she was appointed to the New Mexico Diamond Jubilee and Bicentennial Committee.

Five different U.S. presidents placed Concha on national-level boards. The first was John F. Kennedy, whom Concha met while campaigning for him in New Mexico during the 1960 campaign. In 1961 he named her to the National Council of Upward Bound, under the Office of Economic Opportunity. The Upward Bound program sought to equalize educational opportunities for disadvantaged young people wanting to go to college.

Beyond her official connection with JFK, however, Concha also formed a personal friendship. She recalls that the noted author Erna Fergusson, who came from Albuquerque and knew Concha, expressed interest in meeting Kennedy. So Concha obliged, setting up an introduction. Fergusson presented the president with a copy of her book *New Mexico*. Kennedy responded by giving her a copy of his *Profiles in Courage*, which had won the Pulitzer Prize for non-fiction. "I was happy to arrange the meeting," Concha says modestly.

On another occasion, "President Kennedy told me I could go to Washington and take some friends with me," she says. "He would make certain someone would show us around. I invited everyday people from New Mexico—some of them handicapped, some of them Hispanic. They weren't big shots. Then I called the president and said, 'We're coming.' We went, his people met us, and we saw everything. It was a wonderful present. President Kennedy was so nice. People really liked him."

After Kennedy was assassinated, President Lyndon Johnson named Concha to the National Commission on Architectural Barriers, a board created by Congress. Next, President Richard Nixon placed her on the Advisory Council of the National Institutes of

Concha, Erna Fergusson, President John F. Kennedy, and U.S. Sen. Joseph Montoya— courtesy Center for Southwest Research, University of New Mexico, negative no. 000-457-0013

Health. The next president, Gerald Ford, appointed her to a very influential position, a six-year term with the National Endowment for the Humanities. The post was so important that Concha was not sure at first that she was the person that the Republican president meant to choose. "I asked the person who phoned me: 'Me? Are you sure? Does the president know that I'm a Democrat?' I was assured that my party affiliation was not a problem." Concha was thrilled by the appointment, because, she says, "It meant that now I could *really* help the people." During her term the endowment disbursed millions of dollars to programs nationwide. Finally, in 1977, President Jimmy Carter named her for a second time to the Advisory Council of the National Institutes of Health.

Of all her service on the federal level, the assignment that she cared about most passionately was her appointment by LBJ to the National Commission on Architectural Barriers. She was recommended for the panel by the National Easter Seal Society, which was familiar with her work on behalf of crippled people. Concha was the only female on the 15-member commission, but as always, she was not intimidated.

Choosing to Serve

"Concha was our spirit," says a fellow commission member, Ted Rubin of Colorado, a retired judge. "She had a good attitude and a special friendship with our chairman, a Washington, D.C., architect." The commission existed from 1967 to 1970, and met three or four times a year. On three occasions it took trips to observe firsthand the latest advances in handicapped accessibility. At the University of Illinois branch in Champaign-Urbana, members saw buses with wheelchair lifts, wheelchair basketball in the gym and special elevators for the handicapped at a theater. Later they visited the Rusk Institute in New York City, a pioneering center for rehabilitative surgery. At a glass-engraving factory on Long Island, they watched handicapped employees working at jobs carefully structured to match their disabilities

"We sent staff members to Canada, San Francisco, and other places, to see the beginnings of barge and subway access," Rubin says. "We studied designs to aid the handicapped in multilevel transportation depots. Our responsibility was to provide guidance to the government. All around the country there were barriers to accessibility, not only for the crippled, but also for those with temporary injuries, like a broken foot. We also questioned the roles of ramps. At some point in our lives, we'll all need a ramp. The country was only on the ground floor with the idea of making places accessible."

In the end, the commission developed physical construction standards for buildings that the federal government operated or assisted. "Everything built afterward had to meet the regulations." The breakthrough work done by this panel soon spread out to encompass sidewalks, performance spaces, almost all government buildings, whether local, state or national, and many private establishments as well. After delivering its final report in 1970, the commission disbanded, because its work was done. Concha's connection with fellow member Rubin, however, did not end with the panel.

"During the term of the commission, Concha always referred to me as 'my neighbor,' because New Mexico and Colorado were neighboring states," Rubin says. "I think this created a bond between us. My wife Bunny and I took our children to visit Santa Fe, and Concha and the kids took a real liking to each other. We've continued our friendship through the years. Recently we took our granddaughter to visit Concha. We consider her a role model."

After her time on the commission was completed, Concha continued to advocate for the handicapped. On the local and private level, she worked with Albuquerque restaurants to voluntarily make their premises easier for handicapped people to navigate. She was consulted on the design of the University of Albuquerque's new Fine Arts Center, to make sure it was wheelchair-friendly. When it opened in 1972, a local newspaper took a young wheelchair-bound man through it for a test run. He pronounced the facility "accessible without qualifications."

Concha was interviewed for the same article, and in it she displayed a profound understanding of the obstacles facing disabled people. Most buildings, she said, were "designed for upright people." But the average wheelchair, she pointed out, is 25 inches wide and 41 inches long at its base, and needs a minimum turning radius of 60 inches. "Many people aren't aware of these facts," she told the reporter. "Such things as doorways, drinking fountains, restrooms, steps and washstands are usually taken for granted. But they are not taken for granted by the person in the wheelchair.

"Weatherstripping or a threshold in a doorway—little things—can cause an insurmountable barrier, even when the doorways, otherwise, are ample. Drinking fountains are too high. The trip to the lavatory presents problems ranging from doors that swing inward to towel dispensers that are too high. Furthermore, wheelchairs just don't roll up and down stairs. For every vertical foot of height, a wheelchair needs 12 linear feet of rampway." These powerful and emotional facts were all at Concha's fingertips—and all the readers of the interview with her became informed about these facts, too.

After passing her 90th birthday in 2000, Concha cut back on some, but not all, of her involvements. "I still do board work," she says. "Sometimes other members have to pick me up and take me, but I won't stop. I just keep on going."

Capítulo 17
Momentos sagrados

La religión siempre fue una de las fuerzas principales que motivaba la colonización y las vidas de los españoles que vinieron al Nuevo Mundo.

Así mismo, la religión ha sido una de las fuerzas principales que ha motivado a Concha y a su familia. Para Concha, la religión es un elemento privado que inspira su vida. Ella cree que la persona que tiene un fuerte sentido de la fe deberá hacer bien, particularmente a la patria, los Estados Unidos, patria a la cual Concha le ha prestado servicios y que ama.

Concha manifiesta que aquí en el Suroeste de este país, "nuestra cultura está entrelazada con la religión, y muchas personas no entienden nuestro medio de rendir culto a lo divino o sagrado. Mucha gente piensa que rendimos culto a las imágenes en los retablos y que los retablos son nuestros ídolos." Concha explica que mediante esas imágenes que representan a los santos "a quienes les rogamos que intercedan por nosotros únicamente como intermediarios con Dios."

A los primeros colonizadores los guiaba Juan de Oñate, hombre muy devoto. La devoción de los españoles se refleja en los asentamientos que fundaron en la región que ahora es Nuevo México. La aldea de Galisteo donde ella nació y se crió ha tenido nombres como San Cristóbal, San Lázaro, San Marcos, y San Lucas. El nombre completo de la capital nuevomexicana es La Villa Real de la Santa Fe de San Francisco de Asís.

El enlace de la familia Ortiz y Pino remonta a 1704. Ese año, el Gobernador Interino Páez Hurtado era el presidente de la Cofradía de Nuestra Señora del Rosario, conocida con los nombres La Conquistadora o Nuestra Señora de La Paz. La historia refleja que en 1808, Antonio José Ortiz y su esposa, Rosa Bustamante, construyeron la Capilla del Rosario en el sitio donde La Conquistadora había esperado con la gente a medida que de Vargas y su ejército luchaban para reconquistar la ciudad de Santa Fe.

El rancho Agua Verde no tenía iglesia. Concha mandó que se construyeran tres santuarios: a San José, a María Santísima, y al Santo Niño. Cuando vendió el rancho, trasladó la estatua de la Virgen de Guadalupe a la Gruta en Villanueva.

Gran parte de la fe de doña Concha tiene sus orígenes en los recuerdos que ella tiene de la Navidad. En una entrevista manifestó que la Navidad expresa benevolencia, espíritu servicial, compartir con el prójimo.

Los tres fundamentos de doña Concha y su familia son y han sido la patria, su religión, y la familia.

Sacred Moments

17

When the Spanish came to the New World, religion was a major force in their colonizing quest and in their lives. The religious link was established right from the start. Christopher Columbus, representing Spain, first landed in the Americas on Oct. 12, 1492. Just weeks later in December he was planning Christmas services aboard his flagship, Santa María, so named in honor of the Blessed Virgin Mary. But before the holy day arrived, his ship was wrecked upon a coral reef near what is now Cape Haitien. The native chieftain helped save Columbus and his men. They then built a fortress on the site and named it Navidad—the Spanish word for Christmas.

No force was more powerful than the Catholic religion in shaping Concha and her family—the generations that came before her, her own generation, and the ones that came after. She herself considers her faith the guiding force in her life; but she has her own personal understanding of it. To her, religion is private, not used for sensational purposes, or to impress or brag. And a person with a strong sense of faith must use it properly—particularly in the nation she has served and loved, the United States of America.

"In our country, we believe in the separation of church and state," she says. "This is all good and well and has its time and place. I think we all understand that. The history of our country is based on religious freedom and a ban on persecuting people for their beliefs. Here in the Southwest, our culture is intertwined with religion, and some people don't understand our means of worship. They see the beautiful *retablos* (flat wood with paintings of the images of the saints painted on the surface) and hand-carved *bultos* (free-standing wood carvings of images of a saint) and think we adore idols. But let me explain that in our faith, we ask the saints to intercede for us. They are our intermediaries to God. It's much like a mother asking her son to help someone or an individual making a request of a friend or relative."

Concha's sophisticated comprehension of her religion, entwined with devotion to country and family, is far more complex than the simple Catholic faith imported to the New World in colonial times by the Spanish. In Europe during the Middle Ages, few people knew how to read and write, so folk drama sufficed to spread the word. Performances called *autosacramentales* (acts of faith) served to teach converts and the faithful about religion through action rather than the written word. The *conquistadores* then brought these plays to New Mexico. Three main types of dramas—mystery plays (about the life of Christ), miracle plays (about wonderful, impossible changes from God) and morality plays (the battle between good and evil)—presented the messages the church wanted people to learn. Then in remote outposts in the colonies, the plays became oral tradition.

The early colonists led by Juan de Oñate into New Mexico in 1598 were following a religiously devoted man. As a member of the Hermanos Penitentes (Penitent Brothers), a religious society within the church, Oñate stopped the procession frequently to pray, to place crosses, and to claim the land for God and Spain. Women, often more pious than their husbands, were a major part of the colonial entourage; and another major component consisted of Franciscan friars, who felt that they had much work to do in the name of the Lord—among fellow Spaniards and native inhabitants alike.

Place names throughout New Mexico and the Southwest show evidence of the devotion of the settlers. Río Sacramento (loosely translated, meaning river of the sacrament) received its name because explorers reached this spot on Holy Thursday. Socorro del Cielo (help from

La Conquistadora in 1946—photo by Robert H. Martin

Sacred Moments

A religious service in Israel with Archbishop Michael J. Sheehan—courtesy Concha Ortiz y Pino de Kleven

heaven), now known as Socorro, illustrated aid from above in the form of rain after a severe drought. The *Sangre de Cristo* Mountains (Blood of Christ) are often bathed in bright red color at sunset. The colony's first capital, *San Gabriel,* was named to honor a well-respected saint. Earlier names of Concha's home village of Galisteo were the names of saints: *San Cristóbal, San Lázaro, San Marcos* and *San Lucas.* The full name of New Mexico's capital city is replete with religious reference: *La Villa Real de la Santa Fe de San Francisco de Asís* translates to: the royal village of the holy faith of St. Francis of Assisi. It is, of course, called "Santa Fe." Other New Mexico places with religion-based names are too numerous to list.

Concha's own family has a deep and longstanding connection to historically significant religion, tracing at least to 1704, the year when one of her New Mexico ancestors, Interim Gov. Páez Hurtado, became president of the Confraternity of Our Lady of the Holy Rosary—otherwise known as La Conquistadora, the small statuette of the Virgin that accompanied Gen. *don* Diego de Vargas in his 1692 reconquest of the Indians after their 1680 revolt. Gov. Hurtado and his wife are buried in hallowed ground at La Conquistadora Chapel in St. Francis Cathedral in Santa Fe.

Family papers later credit Concha's ancestors with establishing *La Cofradía de La Conquistadora,* a group dedicated to the statue. In 1769, Comanche Indians killed Lt. Gov. Nicolás Ortiz III in a battle near Abiquiú. His widow, Josefa Bustamante, proposed to the governor that the citizens choose La Conquistadora as the queen of New Mexico and dedicate a confraternity in her honor. When the people of Santa Fe pledged their help, the governor granted *doña* Josefa's request in memory of her husband.

Successive generations carried on the tradition. Concha's family papers note:

> **"In 1808, Antonio José Ortiz (grandson of Páez Hurtado) and his wife, Doña Rosa Bustamante (younger sister of Doña Josefa Bustamante), built the Rosario Chapel on the spot where La Conquistadora had waited with the people as de Vargas and his forces fought for the city of Santa Fe. Antonio José Ortiz served as mayordomo of the Confraternity of La Conquistadora from 1776 to**

Patron saint Remedios—courtesy Concha Ortiz Y Pino de Kleven

```
Photograph of the painting
  NUESTRA SENORA DE LOS REMEDIOS
     from the collection of
  Concha Ortiz y Pino de Kleven,
     Albuquerque, New Mexico

Before this Madonna of the Pino family,
many prayers were offered for the
success of Ambassador, Pedro Bautista
Pino's unique mission.

In 1812, Don Pedro, our great, great
grandfather was chosen by his country-
men to represent them before the King
of Spain and the Spanish Cortes.

The Madonna was painted in the craft's
section of his hacienda in the tradi-
tional style, color and floral decor-
ation of the time.

Originally, it was enshrined in a
gilt frame, Pueblana-stucco style of
Spanish Puebla.
```

1808. He built and enlarged the Conquistadora Chapel at St. Francis Cathedral after it had fallen in ruin in 1798."

Another very tangible indication of the family's religious commitment is a 780-pound, 600-year old bell installed at San Miguel Chapel, the famous "Oldest Church" in downtown Santa Fe. At the Ortiz family's request, the bell was transported by ox cart to Santa Fe in 1812. Concha's papers say: "Nothing in the oldest church in the United States can equal the historic value of the San José bell, which was brought in 1712 to Veracruz, Mexico, by ship from Andalucía, Spain, where it had rung for three centuries."

The devotion continued throughout the generations. Concha's own religious experience began in infancy with her baptism. In childhood she experienced Mamá Fita's role as caretaker of the church in Galisteo, and participated in choir activities and feast-day processions. When Concha left home and lived on her own, she never skipped Mass—not in Santa Fe, not in Washington, D.C., not in Albuquerque.

At Agua Verde Ranch, she missed the presence of a church. Our Lady of Guadalupe Church at the village of Villanueva was the closest facility, but on a 100,000-acre ranch, that location seemed too remote for a person of deep faith. So Concha constructed three scattered religious shrines on ranch property. Built of rock, the shrines enclosed statues of *San José* (St. Joseph), *María Santísima* (the Holy Mother Mary or the Blessed Mother), and *Santo Niño* (the Holy Baby or the Child Jesus). But when Victor died in 1956, Concha decided to sell the ranch. She also decided to relocate a statue of the Virgin of Guadalupe from Agua Verde to the church in Villanueva.

The priest there designed a grotto to display the statue. Church members donated $500 in cash and four months of labor, hauling rocks to the site in an old wagon pulled by horses, and building the shrine. Some 600 invitations were sent out for the dedication ceremonies, which featured an elaborate procession. Little girls in white dresses marched in pairs, tossing flowers and petals in the statue's path. The Sacred Heart Society, proudly displaying its banner, passed by. So did the church choir in a four-wheel-drive vehicle. Some 30 riders on beautifully groomed mounts with shiny saddles added to the parade,

Sacred Moments

A shrine of Our Lady of Guadalupe, funded by Concha in Villanueva, N.M.—courtesy Concha Ortiz y Pino de Kleven

led by the grotto committee chairman on his beautiful white horse. *Padrino* (sponsor) couples carried the statue of Our Lady. Every few steps, the *padrinos* turned over the duty to other eager participants. Priests and servers walked at the end of the line. One mile from the starting point, the parade arrived at the grotto. The priest blessed the statue and celebrated a Mass. The procession was followed by dinner at the parish.

A year later, a Catholic missionary placed *La Cruz Misionera* (the missionary cross) at the grotto. The church priest then decided to install the Stations of the Cross on a pathway rising to an outside mesa. He enlisted volunteer carpenters to make wooden crosses for each Station. Parishioners voted to light the Stations with electricity, and sponsored the project with raffles and a dance. Just before Christmas in 1959, Sister Rosela of the Order of the Sorrowful Mother switched on the lights.

A few years later, the parish decided to build a stairway to the grotto. Fifty students spent two weeks working on the project. But although they cut steps, they did not use cement, so the stairs remained somewhat similar to a cow trail. In the summer of 1969, a dozen or so men from the parish followed up with 219 solid, cemented steps. The workers could not drive a truck into the work area, so they hauled 60 sacks of mixed cement in 5-gallon cans. Three years later, the grotto committee added St. Joseph to the tableau. Concha paid for it. Her religious tribute had grown into a monument.

But in 1972, vandals struck. They destroyed the statue of the Virgin, other images and the

Concha, an ardent fundraiser for religious causes—photo by Robert H. Martin

Concha's 80th birthday party at the Santuario de Guadalupe in Santa Fe, where she raised $100,000 for the restoration of the church—photo by Robert H. Martin

Concha walks in a procession in Santa Fe as a member of the Knights and Ladies of the Holy Sepulchre—courtesy Mary Ryland

grotto. Because of the vicious manner in which the statues' faces were destroyed, the church's 91- year-old caretaker believed that people "fighting with the saints" committed the act. "The grotto was built with a donation from Concha Ortiz y Pino de Kleven," said an article in *The Albuquerque Journal*. And then Concha resolved to rebuild it, with a $10,000 donation. The newspaper announcement reporting her gift called Concha "the matriarch of preservation of New Mexico's Hispanic arts." After the re-dedication of the restored shrine, the editor of *The Albuquerque Tribune* wrote: "The wonderful world of yesterday is not completely dead in New Mexico." The people of Villanueva, he said, still believed in God and were unashamed to show the world.

As Concha says, "Archbishop Sheehan says that I never do what he tells me, and he's right!"—photo courtesy Concha Ortiz y Pino de Kleven

One year later, the church wanted to add one more statue, *Santo Niño* (the Baby Jesus), to complete the Holy Family in the grotto. "Again we went to see Mrs. Concha," the committee chairman said. "She told us that the most wonderful thing that could happen in Villanueva was to have the Holy Family together in this most scenic place." In May 1974, a new ceremony was held for the expanded grotto, which by then measured 12 feet high, 14 feet wide and 30 feet long. Countless visitors since then have left flowers, rosaries, and candles for the Holy Family.

Much of Concha's faith is rooted in her Christmas memories. In a published interview she declared Christmas a religious celebration, and used words such as "humanitarianism, helpfulness, and sharing" to describe it. During her formative years, Concha's holiday season started each year on Dec. 12, with *La Fiesta de Nuestra Señora de Guadalupe* (the feast of Our Lady of Guadalupe). Food always featured heavily on that day, and Mamá Fita made certain that all the poor villagers of Galisteo received plenty from her kitchen.

Concha, Pedro, Mela, and Reynalda with Archbishop Robert Sánchez—photo by Robert H. Martin

Concha especially loved the celebration of *Las Posadas* (the search for shelter). Starting nine days before Christmas, residents re-enacted Mary and Joseph's search for shelter because there was no room at the inn. The drama also featured Lucifer, with his red uniform and long pitchfork. Each night, a procession headed by Mary riding on a burro led by Joseph went to a different home, singing a request for shelter. Lucifer and the occupants of the house stayed inside and replied by sending them away. Lucifer also warned village children to behave or they wouldn't get a gift when Baby Jesus came. After each night's episode, hosts invited guests in for refreshments and for singing Spanish carols such as *"Noche de Paz"* ("Silent Night") and *"Vamos Todos a Belén"* ("Let's All Go to Bethlehem"), accompanied by guitars and violins. Before Midnight Mass (*La Misa del Gallo*) on Christmas Eve, Concha's parents invited guests to their home for a big party, always attended by the priest. Festivities continued after church.

In 1995 during a pilgrimage to the Holy Land, Archbishop Michael J. Sheehan presented 17 members of the Archdiocese of Santa Fe with the title Knight/Lady of the Holy Sepulchre. The designation was made to His

A statue of San José, patron
saint of Galisteo, that has been
in Concha's family for five
generations—courtesy Concha
Ortiz y Pino de Kleven

Sacred Moments

The grotto in Villanueva, N.M., 1957—courtesy Concha Ortiz y Pino de Kleven

Beatitude Michael Sabbah, Latin Patriarch of Jerusalem, who bestowed the symbolic pilgrim shell upon the Knights and Ladies. Concha was one of the honored 17. Recipients earn the award by remaining a knight or lady in good standing and making a pilgrimage to Jerusalem to pray at the Holy Sepulchre of the Risen Christ. In addition, they must help maintain the living presence of the church in the land where Jesus lived and died. The scallop shell in oxidized silver includes red, fired enamel bordered with gold. In its center, the Cross of the Order represents the five wounds of Christ. It is an extremely distinguished honor.

A church service at the restored grotto in Villanueva, N.M.—courtesy Concha Oriz y Pino de Kleven

Today Concha's home includes a section displaying the beautiful *bultos* of the Hispanic culture, including San José and the Blessed Mother. Arrayed in front of the carved wooden statues are flowers, small wreaths, and other items of beauty to complete the arrangement. The bedrock ideals—country, religion, and family—invoked long ago as the credo of the Ortiz y Pino family have guided Concha all her life. But first among these three, as a passage of scripture might say, has been religion.

Capítulo 18
Las amistades de Concha

Entre sus amistades, Concha cuenta con personas de todas edades. Han aprendido lecciones valiosas, entre ellas: "Vivir siempre en un entorno bello y exponer a la prole a ese tipo de entorno. Gozar de una fe fuerte. Y sobre todo, a medida que vas entrando en edad, formar amistades con personas jóvenes."

Una de las amistades que tipifica la mencionada filosofía es María Elena Álvarez, redactora de Prime Time, publicación dedicada a personas ya entradas en edad. María Elena, mucho más joven, conoció a Concha hace algunos años y desde entonces han disfrutado de una una íntima amistad. El amor que ambas tienen a la herencia española ha fortalecido la amistad entre las dos.

Otra íntima amistad de Concha es Andrés Segura, administrador de Servicios Humanos del Departamento de Salud de Nuevo México. El abuelo de Segura fue vecino del Agua Verde y tuvo relaciones comerciales con el padre de Concha, José Ortiz y Pino. Segura la ha acompañado en viajes a distintos países y a distintas ciudades interesantes en este país. Los dos han asistido a conferencias, el teatro, y conciertos, ensanchando el lazo mutuo de crianza y tradiciones. Segura cuenta que Concha es una mujer muy inteligente que siempre está al día respecto a lo que está ocurriendo en el mundo y en la política al nivel local, nacional, e internacional.

Pese a que Concha se mudó de Albuquerque a Santa Fe hace algunos años, Segura sigue en contacto con ella. Dice Segura, "Una vez formas amistad con Concha, esa amistad no se pierde."

Friends Along the Way

18

María Elena Álvarez, editor of *Prime Time*, a New Mexico-based journal for seniors, says she has learned many important life lessons from Concha. "Always live in a beautiful environment, and expose your daughters to it" is one. "Have strong faith" is another. "And above all, befriend younger people as you age."

Álvarez is a perfect example of that third adage. She and Concha met some years ago when Álvarez was arts editor of the *Albuquerque Journal*. They struck an instant rapport, which quickly grew into a deep friendship, despite the fact that Concha is 40 years older than Álvarez. Right from the start, Álvarez says, Concha told her "we were *parientes*—family members." Then for years, until Concha moved to Santa Fe from Albuquerque, the two socialized at least once a month.

Their outings were varied: lunches, Hispanic cultural functions, black-tie dinners. And patrolling secondhand stores, looking for bargains. "Concha had an eye for quality," Álvarez smiles. "It wasn't uncommon for her to find Gucci or Chanel at Thrift Town. She bought coats, skirts, purses, and scarves for her exquisite collection." The women also frequently dined with Gerald Crawford, editor of the *Journal*. "She loved going out to dinner, and she also had a great appreciation of the male person." Álvarez says she considered herself a member of Concha's "cultural retinue." "Entertaining her took more than one person," she explains. "It took a whole army. Concha led a very rich life."

As a journalist as well as a friend, Álvarez found Concha fascinating. Some of her fondest memories, she says, are of sitting for hours in Concha's home,

Concha in Latin America—courtesy Concha Ortiz y Pino de Kleven

listening to tales. Along the way, she was learning Concha's life story. Eventually she assigned a writer from *Prime Time* to profile Concha. A playful and revealing remark that Concha made in the article was: "Santa Fe is the cultural appendage of my hometown, Galisteo."

Two bonds between Concha and Álvarez have been their shared pride in their Hispanic heritage and their shared enjoyment of being female. "I always loved my people," Concha once said in an interview, reflecting on her Spanish roots. "Especially the little ones, not just the important ones." As for female identity, Álvarez adds: "Concha has helped me and many other women in Santa Fe and Albuquerque. She invited me places, encouraged me and supported me. I'm from the baby boomer generation, but despite the age difference,

Concha at the Pyramids in Giza outside Cairo, Egypt— courtesy Concha Ortiz y Pino de Kleven

Concha made the connection. Concha mentored a lot of us who were part of her entourage." Among other things Concha taught by example, Álvarez says, were "etiquette, finishing-school touches."

Several times Álvarez has taken her daughters, Carmen Elizabeth and Magdalena, to visit Concha, occasions that were a pleasure for everyone. A key piece of advice that Concha gives to little girls is to "be feminine." Álvarez feels that Concha has been a "surrogate mother" to her. And indeed, Concha, who had no children of her own, has noted that she does consider some of her friends "my children." Álvarez sums up by saying, "Concha has

Friends Along the Way

In Bogotá, Colombia, in 1973, Concha represents the United States as a goodwill ambassador—courtesy Concha Ortiz y Pino de Kleven

Concha poses at the Leaning Tower of Pisa in Italy—courtesy Concha Ortiz y Pino de Kleven

projected unconditional love. She's been with me for different stages of my life. She will always be with me."

"Some people call Concha a 'grande dame,'" muses Andrés Segura, the human resources administrator of the state Health Department. "Others call her 'the most powerful woman in New Mexico.' I just call her 'my best friend.'" The two met in 1972 at a reception at the University of New Mexico. At once they discovered a bond: Segura's rancher-grandfather

Friends Along the Way

was a neighbor to Agua Verde, and also had conducted business with José Ortiz y Pino, Concha's father. Segura and Concha had lots to talk about. Soon they were meeting frequently. "She used to say to me: 'Of the three close men in my life—my father, Victor, and you—not a damn one of you could ever use a hammer.' She thought she could, but the truth is, she couldn't either. Speaking of Victor, everybody just loved him. I didn't know him, but Concha often made that statement."

Segura continues: "I was fascinated by her. We became partners in crime. We'd have dinner once a week, and shop on weekends—I spent many a Saturday at Dillard's with her. We'd go on Sunday drives. Sometimes we'd travel." One of Concha's great loves has been travel, he points out. She usually went abroad twice a year, often to Europe. Then there was the photo safari to Africa, the trip to Egypt, music tours, package deals arranged by the Albuquerque Museum to visit the Metropolitan Museum of Art in New York. "She has led a hard, beautiful, romantic life," Segura says.

In addition to faraway places, Concha has loved visiting Mexico, California, Arizona and local fiestas all over New Mexico. "We went to Mexico City and Puebla on a tour sponsored by Archbishop Robert Sánchez," Segura remembers. If a historical or social organization was sponsoring an interesting event, Concha would attend. For their mother's health, Concha and her sister Mela took Pablita to California several times a year. "Concha was always serving on boards that sponsored big functions, and of course she would always be there," Segura says. "She went wherever she was invited. She never turned anyone down. If anyone ever enjoyed life, Concha did. She was quite a part of the social scene." Other experiences that he shared with her included lectures, plays and concerts at Popejoy Hall in Albuquerque, where Concha always got season tickets.

"There was much love between a younger man and an older woman," Segura says. "Our age difference was 39 years, so I felt she was sort of a mother figure. My own mom died of cancer at age 70, and Concha attended the funeral. At the time, she said, 'Your mom left me in charge of you. God help us!' But our real bond was our *crianza* (upbringing), our traditional ways. In our conversations we'd always let loose. It was wonderful!"

Segura describes Concha as "an extremely bright woman," and adds: "She was well-read and up-to-date with political and world affairs. Concha got involved in mayoral races, district court races, everything. She was very civic-minded. She kept current by watching television programs, reading newspaper and magazine articles, talking with knowledgeable individuals. She also loved going to the movies." He recalls that one of Concha's favorites was *Selena*, about the life and death of the Mexican-American superstar Tejano singer by that name, who was murdered by an associate in 1995.

"Her house was always ready for company," Segura says. "It was just perfect, a showcase. She always sat in high heels and slacks, with her legs crossed. Concha always sat in the same place when she entertained. She and her guests sat near the fireplace, between her books and the tea service. Everyone sat in large overstuffed chairs with bear claws." Someone else impressed by Concha's house was *Albuquerque Tribune* writer Charlotte Black, who described it as "a good place to chat." Black also reported: "Tables and a mantelpiece hold family mementos, and the plain white walls are covered with family pictures and framed souvenirs of her many careers—careers in helping others."

The *Tribune* writer was also impressed by Concha herself. "And she's still trim, still beautifully groomed, still wearing the distinctive bouffant hairstyle she adopted many years ago. Her lipstick is bright and freshly applied, and she has dressed up her black jumpsuit with a silvery brooch, worn off-center at the waistline." Many times Concha has seen such references to her "elegance." Her response? "I am shocked when people talk about it. I never think about it. It's the spontaneity of living and acting that makes one elegant, not any prescribed manner of dressing and acting. I think if one has good breeding and a joy of life, you can't help but be elegant."

Although Concha moved to Santa Fe a few years ago, Segura stays in close contact with telephone calls and visits. "Once you're Concha's friend," he says, "you remain that way. It can't be helped. It's a wonderful role to play."

La vida social

Concha y su hermana Mela siguieron la costumbre de la familia Ortiz mediante su participación en actividades sociales en Galisteo tanto como en Santa Fe. Así las dos, tanto como sus esposos, fueron partícipes en fiestas y reuniones de tipo social. En un artículo publicado en 1933 consta que en Galisteo, en una fiesta dedicada a Nuestra Señora de los Remedios, Concha decidió revivir la Corrida de Gallos, costumbre que remonta a siglos pasados en el territorio español del Nuevo Mundo. En esta fiesta en Galisteo participaron jinetes indios de los pueblos de Santo Domingo y San Felipe. Después de la Corrida de Gallos, los padres de Concha fueron los anfitriones de un banquete en el que deleitaron a sus huéspedes con comidas típicas de la cocina nuevomexicana. Las canciones folclóricas que Concha había reunido en su colección deleitaban a la gente de la región. El renacimiento de la canción folclórica sirvió también para perpetuar otro tipo de entretenimiento hispánico. Por este medio, Concha logró facilitarle al pueblo el orgullo de un placer inherente en el pueblo hispánico. Mela, que había estudiado música, con mucho entusiasmo dirigía las canciones que cantaba la gente que se reunía en la Plaza de Santa Fe.

A las fiestas particulares de la familia Ortiz y Pino asistían muchos políticos y sus esposas, que en esa época pertenecían o al partido demócrata y o al partido republicano. Muchos de los invitados a fiestas particulares de la familia eran dignatarios de gobiernos de otros países.

En todo lugar donde se presentaba doña Concha, siempre con su gran presencia, la gente se acercaba a saludarla y así mismo saludaba ella a todo el público que estaba presente.

Mixing and Mingling

Concha, Paul Vasallo, UNM Library director, and William "Bud" Davis, UNM president—courtesy Center for Southwest Research, University of New Mexico, negative no. 000-457-0021

As members of one of New Mexico's most prominent families—the Ortiz y Pino clan—Concha and Mela and their husbands moved easily through any circles of society they wished to, and often set the social scene. In doing so, however, Concha and Mela were only following a family custom in which they grew up, and which they loved.

The *New Mexico Magazine* of December 1933—10 years before Concha's wedding and 17 before Mela's—features a grand social occasion in Galisteo. Under the title "La Corrida del Gallo at Galisteo" and the subtitle "Fiesta Days Are Revived in the Spanish Village Near Santa Fe," the article describes the celebration of Oct. 22, 1933. The centerpiece was a traditional Spanish event called a "rooster pull"—"*corrida del gallo.*" Before 1933, the last time such an event had been held in Galisteo was 1876, but Concha decided to revive it. (In contemporary times, rooster pulls have fallen out of favor and are seldom held, because

Mela's bridal portrait. Photo by John J. Michnovicz—courtesy Robert H. Martin

the rooster suffers. But in 1933, such considerations had not been raised, and Concha's party was given in a spirit of traditional, old-fashioned fun.)

The Galisteo fiesta was dedicated to the village patroness, *Nuestra Señora de los Remedios* (Our Lady of Help), and was a fund-raiser for the Galisteo vocational school established to assist residents during the Depression. For the rooster pull, Concha arranged for members of the San Felipe and Santo Domingo Indian pueblos to oppose young men from Galisteo in a frantic horseback competition to capture the chicken. The furious action lasted for about an hour and a half. At one point, Miguel Anaya of Galisteo made a successful grab, but then the pueblo riders took the bird away from him. More mounted jousting followed, until finally José María Leyba rode away with the trophy for Galisteo. The green-shirted referee was Sheriff Jesús Baca, on a beautiful pinto horse.

Mamá Fita made her rambling home, with its thick adobe walls, high ceilings, and antiques brought into the area by wagon trains, ready for any guests who wished to stay. Old *santos* and family portraits provided a homey touch. Her carpeted floors and many beds lent a welcoming air for visitors. Smells from the kitchen revealed a ready supply of *chile con carne* (chile with meat), *chiles rellenos* (stuffed green chile), *posole* (hominy dish), barbecued lamb ribs, *buñuelos* (fry bread), and black coffee, lest any visitors go away hungry. The large enclosing adobe wall, big corral, and cottonwoods and poplars provided a serene, secure area. After the *corrida* and before the rosary at the San José church, Concha's parents hosted a dinner at their home. Musicians provided entertainment. Then the all-day fiesta was capped by a *gran baile*—a grand ball.

The big party in Galisteo was just one of many times when Concha brought music and fun into the dreary days of the Depression. In her personal journal, Concha wrote: "During the 1930s, I made use of my collection of folk songs by leading thousands of persons on the Santa Fe Plaza in singing these folk songs with the accompaniment of the Santa Fe Band. This was free entertainment, and persons from all over the county joined the singing. From this, renewed interest in New Mexico folklore grew, and subsequently I organized weekly folk-dancing sessions in a donated hall with musicians paid by city businessmen. From the revival of folk dances and folklore, the 'Sociedad Folklórica' emerged (to revive and perpetuate traditional

Mixing and Mingling

Fray Angélico Chávez
marrying Robert and Mela
with Concha as maid of
honor—courtesy Robert H.
Martin

Hispanic entertainment), which brought about a renewed pride in something that was an inherent pleasure." Mela, a music student, participated enthusiastically and frequently led the singing on the Plaza.

The 1940s and 1950s were a time of much home entertaining, with lots of guests and food and drink. After Concha and Victor married in 1943, their large home on Las Lomas in Albuquerque became a center of social activity, with professors, doctors, lawyers, government officials, and other professional people in their circle. In turn, they constantly received invitations to parties at other people's homes. But in 1951, their social whirl stopped abruptly, when Concha left Albuquerque to run Agua Verde. She always assumed that the partying would resume when she returned. But with Victor's sudden death, that phase of her life ended.

Meanwhile, in Santa Fe, younger sister Mela and her suitor, Robert Martin, embarked upon their own romance, which began in 1946 and culminated in their wedding on Feb. 18, 1950. Without a doubt, the wedding was the social event of the season in Santa Fe. José Ortiz y Pino, in a wheelchair, gave his daughter in marriage. Concha served as her sister's matron of honor. Bridegroom Bob and his brother, Chester, the best man, met Concha and the rest of the wedding party at a chapel adjacent to the main altar at St. Francis Cathedral. Because Bob was a Lutheran, the couple could not wed at the Catholic cathedral's main altar. When the bride entered, she wore white velvet.

Mela performs at La Fonda Hotel in Santa Fe with Jimmy Palermo on accordion and Billy Palou with maracas in 1948—photo by Robert H. Martin

During the ceremony, Bob presented Mela with *las aras* (the financial offering), a Spanish custom that represented the husband's first money for the marriage, a symbol of acceptance of his financial responsibility. The offering included 14 Spanish *reales*, or approximately $1.75 in modern money. Mela then gave this money to the church, as the first donation from her new family. Some 500 people joined the newlyweds for a gala reception at La Fonda, Santa Fe's premier hotel. Guests included Archbishop Edwin V. Byrne, New Mexico Gov. Tom Mabry, two former governors, the editor of *New Mexico Magazine*, and friends and relatives from many walks and all stations of life.

The wedding ceremony was conducted by a special friend of Bob and Mela, Fray Angélico Chávez. A prominent cleric in Santa Fe, Fray Angélico first met the couple when they were working together on a USO photo exhibit on Los Alamos. Chávez admired Bob's work, and asked him to take pictures for a church pamphlet. The shots included Fray Chávez in front of the cathedral, and poses of the cleric with a group of young women—with the La Conquistadora icon, or in the cathedral's bell tower. That project led to many other collaborations between the photographer and the priest, and Chávez often

Mixing and Mingling

Bob and Mela dancing the night away at La Fonda Hotel during the Sante Fe Fiesta—courtesy Robert H. Martin

Queen Frederica of Greece with her daughter Princess Sofía, the current queen of Spain, circa 1958—photo by Robert H. Martin

Mixing and Mingling

Concha wearing her signature Spanish attire during festive occasions—courtesy Concha Ortiz y Pino de Kleven

Concha with Ann Knighman, writer Willa Cather's close friend—photo by Robert H. Martin

accompanied Bob and Mela on photo shoots. "Fray Angélico and I were great friends," Bob reports. "He often blamed me for his developing a taste for Cutty Sark. Whenever I gave him a gift, it would usually be a bottle of scotch and some cigars."

As a married couple, Bob and Mela enjoyed entertaining in their Camino Cacto home. Bob says that often 50 or 60 people came to their parties. "We invited *políticos* from both the Democratic and Republican parties. Della and Joe Montoya (Joseph M. Montoya, a Democratic state legislator who became a U.S. senator) would arrive, and then Lorencita and Manuel (Santa Fe Mayor Manuel Luján Sr., a Republican) would enter arm-in-arm. The Lujáns were a very attractive, distinguished and devoted couple. Plus, a lot of doctors came. We lived in a mostly medical neighborhood."

Sometimes parties at the Martin house transcended local and state guest lists to go national and even international in scope. A November 1967 article in *The New Mexican* told of one. "Visitors from Spain Bestow Honors and, In Turn, Are Honored by Officials," said the headline. The story related that the New Mexico State Police had escorted two important Spanish dignitaries—Professor José María Otero de Navacués, President of the Committee of Nuclear Energy and Francisco Pascual Martínez, *Secretaría General*

Mixing and Mingling

Técnica (Executive Secretary) of Spain's Atomic Energy Commission)—on an official New Mexico visit.

Their first stop was the State Capitol, where Secretary of State Ernestine Evans bestowed upon them the honorary title of *Hidalgo* ("nobleman"), of New Mexico. Then they toured Santa Fe, stopping at the San Miguel Mission to greet Brother Luis, a native of Castile, Spain, and two other churches—Cristo Rey and St. Francis Cathedral—as well as Canyon Road and some art galleries. Bob and Mela accompanied the visitors, and then hosted them at a grand dinner party at their home.

The glittering guest list included Santa Fe Mayor Pat Hollis, architect John Gaw Meem, former ambassador to Switzerland Robert McKinney, U.S. Court of Appeals Judge Oliver Seth, and several doctors, lawyers, writers, government officials, educators and military officers. Condolences were sent by U.S. Sen. Joseph Montoya, U.S. Rep. Johnny Walker, and U.S. President Lyndon Johnson, who were unable to leave their duties in Washington to attend.

Very special guests that evening, said the newspaper article, were "members of old Santa Fe families of Spanish descent, and Santa Feans who have traveled in Spain recently." From the Ortiz y Pino family alone, more than a dozen members attended. In hosting the party, Mela set out to honor the visitors from Spain. And they reciprocated, by bestowing upon her a titular award, a parchment diploma from *El Instituto de Cultura Hispánica de Madrid, España*, which saluted her efforts in preserving the legacy of her Spanish ancestors in North America. Few people who attended ever forgot that party.

But many other events took place in less-formal circumstances and places. Looking back on those days, Bob Martin lists several favorite memories. *La Baile de Cascarones* (Dance of

Ulric Musel, Fred White, Ansel Adams and Concha— courtesy Center for Southwest Research, University of New Mexico, negative no. 000-457-0014

Concha was a regular on the party circuit. Photo by Barbara Allen Coch—courtesy of Center for Southwest Research, University of New Mexico, negative no. 000-457-0021

the Eggshells), sponsored annually by *La Sociedad Folklórica*, was always a highlight, wherever it was held. The big moment came when the partygoers cracked open eggshells filled with confetti. Many events were held at the Lensic Theater. A popular daytime meeting place was over cherry Cokes at the soda fountain of Zook's Pharmacy on the Plaza, in the site now occupied by a Haagen-Däzs ice cream outlet.

For dinner, Bob says, "El Nido in Tesuque was the melting pot of the people. The owners at the time, Mimi and Charlie, then opened the Palace Restaurant downtown, and many of us started to frequent it instead of making the drive." Located on Don Gaspar Avenue downtown across from the De Vargas Hotel, Bob recalls, was a tiny restaurant called "Tony's U&I," which served choice Kansas City steaks. "Government and political figures and anybody who was anybody lined up in their finery outside this little hole in the wall, waiting for a chance to get in. Tony, the owner, cooked, ran the cash register, did everything." La Fonda was another hot spot. "We'd go there and dance. Late at night the bar was packed with friendly people. We knew at least half of them at any given time. Now, if you know one person, hang on to him or her."

In 1958, Bob brushed up against royalty. Queen Frederica of Greece and her daughter Princess Sophia were visiting New Mexico, and Bob was asked to photograph them. Mela accompanied him. In 1987 the grown-up princess became Queen Sofía of Spain—and the sharp-eyed Bob noted: "When she was a princess, she spelled her name with a 'ph,' and now that she's a queen, she spells it with an 'f.'" But of course, the letter "f" is the Spanish version of the name. In any event, when Queen Sofía of Spain visited Santa Fe decades later, Bob sent to her hotel a copy of his long-ago photographic study of her as a princess. The queen responded with a telegram of thanks.

Mixing and Mingling

During Concha's time as a faculty wife at UNM, her social life was centered in Albuquerque. Then from 1951 to 1956, when she ran Agua Verde, she removed herself from the scene. After Victor's totally unexpected death, Concha carefully chose ways to get involved again. One of the avenues she found was through the young Santa Fe Opera, started in 1957 by a brash young man named John Crosby. Concha attended some early performances, and because of her love of the arts, she became one of the venture's steadfast supporters. With the opera's 20th anniversary drawing near in 1976, the upscale magazine *Town and Country* ran a big spread on Santa Fe's "glitterati."

"Enchanting Santa Fe" was the article's title, and in a portfolio of 19 photographs it showcased the city's movers and shakers. Santa Fe Opera President Mrs. Walter "Peach" Mayer sat at the open-air theater with founder Crosby. Renowned photographer Eliot Porter stood with his wife Aline in the doorway of their Tesuque home. Gov. Jerry Apodaca and his wife Clara played tennis at the governor's mansion. Famed World War II cartoonist Bill Mauldin stood next to his private airplane. Movie actress Greer Garson wore Western garb outside the theater named for her at the College of Santa Fe. Taos Ski Valley

Mela and Concha with Beatrice Chauvenet, author of John Gaw Meem: A Pioneer in Historical Preservation—*photo by Robert H. Martin*

founder Ernie Blake rode a ski lift. Former U.S. Interior Secretary Stewart Udall dined with his wife, Lee, on an outdoor patio. It was a *Who's Who* gallery of Santa Fe.

There among them was Concha, in a traditional Spanish costume of mantilla, shawl and fan, in the village cemetery at Galisteo. The article noted that the huge Oritz Land Grant, once New Mexico's largest, had been dissipated, sold off, and broken up. Remnants of Concha's past now included her grandmother's house, a little land, and a local museum with furniture, silver, and old vestments from the chapel. And one other memento: Concha was proud that Hispanic residents of the Santa Fe area still used some of the old Spanish words brought to New Mexico by conquistadors in the 16th century.

In 1979 a young woman named María Albritton was hired to work the front desk at La Fonda in Santa Fe. One day a regal-looking woman came into the hotel for lunch, Albritton recalls. "At once I noticed the buzz around her. People were running around saying 'She's here.' And I was wondering, 'Who's she?'" The woman looked very Hispanic to Albritton. She was wearing turquoise jewelry and fancy earrings, and her hair was pulled back into a bun. "I thought she must be a celebrity or a model—so Santa Fe-ish. Actually, I thought she resembled a Spanish princess. She walked around the room and talked to everyone. And the owner of La Fonda, Sam Ballen, rushed out to greet her. Later, I found out she was Concha Ortiz y Pino de Kleven."

CAPÍTULO 20
Las recompensas

Desde niña Concha inició carrera en la que prestaba servicio al prójimo sin pensar en homenajes ni recompensas. Sencillamente estaba perpetuando una tradición de la familia Ortiz y Pino. Sus abuelos y sus padres habían sentado el ejemplo que así es la vida, dice doña Concha. Dedicación al trabajo y realizar metas era cosa muy natural que ella realizaba, a medida que aportaba su ayuda en beneficio del prójimo. Mucha gente y grupos de gente que se han beneficiado de su generosidad han manifestado su agradecimiento de maneras extraordinarias.

En varias ocasiones le han brindado recepciones, banquetes, celebraciones de todo tipo. Con el fin de reconocer sus bienestares, le han brindado su retrato y esculturas de su semejanza. Personas distinguidas de altos niveles le han rendido homenajes con pergaminos de honor y reconociendo su generosidad y actos benéficos. Un día especial en la historia de Nuevo México fue dedicado a Concha Ortiz y Pino de Kleven. Agradecida siempre y contenta con un sencillo "Dios te bendiga," la perspectiva de doña Concha es que la mejor recompensa son los resultados que su obras benéficas han logrado. Es una tradición que heredó de su abuelita Mamá Fita y su madre, cuando la mandaban que hiciera mandados con el fin de socorrer a sus vecinos aldeanos en Galisteo.

Esa tradición ha seguido durante toda su vida, sea cuando participaba en campañas para elegir candidatos, de legisladora, durante su vida de esposa del profesor Kleven en la Universidad de Nuevo México, cuando se encargó del Agua Verde que estaba en crisis económica, y en las postrimerías de su vida que ella continuamente ha dedicado con el fin de servir a la humanidad.

Entre muchísimos títulos honorarios otorgados a doña Concha, la Universidad de Albuquerque le otorgó el doctorado honorario en humanidades, la Ciudad de Cádiz le otorgó ciudadanía honoraria a ella y a su prima Reynalda Ortiz y Pino de Dinkel, los concejales de la Municipalidad de Albuquerque la nombraron una de las distinguidas damas al reconocer su trabajo en pro de las personas discapacitadas, la Junta de Regentes de la Universidad de Nuevo México le presentó la Medalla de Reconocimiento por una vida dedicada al mejoramiento del prójimo. El historiador Marc Simmons ha manifestado que "la aportación de Concha a fin de promover el bienestar de la humanidad no tiene igual." El finado Sabine Ulibarrí, profesor eméritus de la Universidad de Nuevo México, una vez manifestó, "En su jornada en esta vida, Concha ha beneficiado las bellas artes y la sociedad de Nuevo México con dignidad, encanto, y autoridad...durante su vida ha logrado hacer cambios con gracia y así ha mejorado la vida del ser humano." Muchos honores más constan en detalle en esta biografía en inglés en la que figuran los honores y reconocimientos otorgados a doña Concha, objeto de esta biografía.

Cuando le preguntan a nuestra biografiada qué en resumen cuente respecto a su vida durante la cual ha logrado mucho reconocimiento oficial y del pueblo en general, ella con total modestia, atribuye su gran éxito a sus ancestros, particularmente Mamá Fita, "todos quienes inculcaron con ahínco en mi persona que siempre socorriera al prójimo y que me esforzara aportar lo mejor a todo el mundo." Agrega doña Concha, "Aparentemente, he logrado cumplir lo que mis antecedentes me inculcaron."

Honors Come

20

When Concha, as a little girl, embarked on her long life of service to others, it was without a thought of accolades or rewards. She was just following the family traditions and ideals of those who came before her: *don* Pedro Bautista Pino and his sons, Mamá Fita and Capt. Sylvester Davis, her own parents. "My role models taught me: 'This is the way life is,'" she says. Hard work and accomplishing goals were things that were expected of her, and those are things she delivered. Nothing special about it. But many of the countless people and causes she helped have thanked her in extraordinary ways.

On several occasions she has been honored with receptions, dinners, and celebrations of various kinds. The walls of her home are lined with official certificates of recognition and appreciation. Portraits and sculptures have been created to salute her. Some of the most powerful and important people in New Mexico and the nation have sent her personal letters of commendation. An entire day in the history of New Mexico was dedicated in her honor. And sometimes the tribute came in spoken words only, simple words like: "Bless you." Concha has appreciated all of it, but keeps her own perspective: "A thank-you was wonderful, but my true reward was the end result—seeing the world become a better place because I was able to do something about it."

This sense of feeling good by doing good first came to her when Mamá Fita and her mother would send Concha out on childhood errands, delivering assistance to the villagers of Galisteo. It continued

In 1949 Concha was named the best-dressed woman in Albuquerque

when she campaigned politically to elect candidates who could lead the country out of the Great Depression. She took this feeling with her when she was elected to the New Mexico Legislature in her own right. As a faculty wife at the University of New Mexico, she was constantly assisting students, faculty members and spouses, the university itself— and, of course, her husband. At Agua Verde, the challenge became completely different, but once again she delivered, bringing an important part of her family heritage back to financial well-being. And after she found herself widowed, she decided to devote the rest of her life to service.

Perhaps her first official reward came in 1939, when the Santa Fe Chamber of Commerce voted to give the young legislator an honorary membership in the group. She had to think it over, because her father had instructed her not to take gifts for political duty. But in the end, she accepted graciously, because no money was involved, and the accompanying citation spelled that the tribute was "in recognition of services rendered to Santa Fe and the State of New Mexico." A year later, an organization called the Quivira Society saluted

Concha addresses a University of New Mexico commencement —courtesy Concha Ortiz y Pino de Kleven

Concha and other members of her family upon the publication of *Three New Mexico Chronicles*, written by her great-great-grandfather Pedro Bautista Pino, after his history-making 1812 voyage to Spain to represent New Mexico in the Spanish *Cortes*.

When she lived in Albuquerque, while married to Victor, Concha gained two different types of distinction—one of them official, and one of them not-so-official. In a 1949 poll, she was selected The Best-Dressed Woman in Albuquerque. During this same period, her longtime friend Andrés Segura reports slyly, "She was also known as having the most beautiful legs in Albuquerque, because she looked so terrific in high heels. She always looked so elegant in a dress and high heels, dancing at one of the nightclubs."

An exemplary honor came in 1970, when the Albuquerque Museum Foundation commissioned the internationally distinguished Santa Fe sculptor Una Hanbury to immortalize Concha's likeness in a bronze bust. Now one of 20 bronzes in the museum's permanent collection, the piece was ordered for multiple reasons. Concha had served on the museum board for several years. Her cumulative body of work made her a splendid representative of the contributions made by leading New Mexico families, starting with the Spanish era. And the bronze bust was a different type of art than other items at the museum. In a newspaper interview at the time of the unveiling, Concha said: "I see the bronze as a symbol of the Ortiz y Pino family, as well as other colonial families: C de Baca, Bustamante, Gallegos, Coronado and others."

The kudos kept coming. In 1971, New Mexico Gov. Bruce King named Concha a Colonel Aide-de-Camp, an honorary title recognizing her contributions to the state. That distinction was embellished in 1975 when Secretary of State Ernestine Evans proclaimed Concha a *Hildago de calificada nobleza en servicio del Estado de Nuevo México*—a person of

Honors Come

nobility in the service of New Mexico. The honor was presented in conjunction with a trip Concha made to Cádiz, Spain, that year with her cousin Reynalda Ortiz y Pino de Dinkel to honor their ancestor *don* Pedro. The women were named honorary citizens of Cádiz and given membership in a Spanish cultural society. In return, the mayor of Cádiz was made an honorary citizen of Santa Fe. Concha arranged the designation.

Concha receives an honorary degree from the sisters at St. Joseph's College in Albuquerque—courtesy Concha Ortiz y Pino de Kleven

The year 1975 saw Concha receive an Honorary Doctor of Humanities degree from the University of Albuquerque, where she had been dean of women several years earlier, when the institution was called St. Joseph's College. The next year, 1976, which was the 200th anniversary of America as a nation, brought Concha three awards. The Albuquerque City Council named her one of that city's outstanding women, for her work for the handicapped. The American Association of University Women went one better by choosing her as one of the "ten outstanding women in New Mexico since 1850." And the Museum of Albuquerque honored her for "bettering the life of the state."

In 1977, the Rotary Club recognized Concha's service to the handicapped, and the state Cultural Properties Review Committee saluted her preservation efforts. In 1981 the Maxwell Museum at UNM thanked Concha for years of assistance. And in 1982, the state gave her another certificate of nobility and a separate certificate of appreciation. That same year also brought the first annual Santa Fe Festival of the Arts, which stated in its official program: "Concha Ortiz y Pino de Kleven, sometimes referred to as 'the most powerful woman in New Mexico,' is recognized by most New Mexicans—if not in person then by her reputation of dedicated service to her state. Although Concha's activities extend to almost all possible fields of endeavor, the festival would like to honor her especially for her outstanding contributions to the arts and humanities."

A bronze bust of Concha, by Santa Fe sculptor Ana Hanbury, is on permanent display at the Albuquerque Museum—courtesy Center for Southwest Research, University of New Mexico, negative no. 000-457-0025

Honors Come

In 1985 the University of New Mexico board of regents bestowed upon Concha a Medal of Recognition for "a lifetime of service." In 1987 the New Mexico Commission on the Status of Women put her in the state Women's Hall of Fame. The year 1990 brought a place in Albuquerque's Senior Hall of Fame. Praise of her on that occasion was effusive: "The activities of her life are legendary," said Carole Kinney, a former first lady of the city. "Señora Kleven has had a lifelong love affair with the culture, language, and land of New Mexico's diverse people. She is a formidable force of talents, energy, and foresightedness, which is unequaled," said Josie Luján of the village of Chimayó. The Archbishop of Santa Fe, Robert Sánchez, said, "Literally, every field of concern and endeavor has received her input, her assistance, and been blessed by her presence." Said historian Marc Simmons: "Concha's long record of public service is without peer." And Dr. Sabine Ulibarrí, a professor emeritus at UNM, added, "Concha has walked through the history, the arts and the society of New Mexico with dignity, charm, and authority…in the process she has changed and influenced the world she has graced for the better."

Sculptor Una Hanbury with her bust of Concha in 1982— courtesy Concha Ortiz y Pino de Kleven

In 1992 a publication titled *Hispanic Heroes— Portraits of New Mexicans Who Have Made a Difference* spotlighted 18 people who had left an indelible mark

Artist Helen Mitchem with her portrait of Concha—courtesy Concha Ortiz y Pino de Kleven

on the state. The list was nothing if not diverse. It included U.S. Sen. Dennis Chávez, one of two New Mexico historical figures immortalized in the Hall of Statuary in the nation's Capitol in Washington, D.C. But also listed was Reies López Tijerina, who went to federal prison for leading a land-grant rebellion in northern New Mexico in the 1960s. Two 18th-century Spanish explorers—Anastasio Domínguez and Silvestre Vélez de Escalante—were honored for their 1776 expedition at the same time as the American Revolution. The first Hispanic archbishop of Santa Fe, Robert Sánchez, was selected.

Unforgettable women were equally represented on the colorful list. One was Gertrudes Barcelo, also known as "Doña Tules," a notorious Santa Fe bordello madam who was a generous supporter of charity and the fledgling American government in the Territorial period. Another was Nancy López-Knight, a top-ranked female professional golfer in the modern era. Another was Nina Otero-Warren, a leader in the suffragette cause bringing women the right to vote in 1919. And right there with them was Concha. In 1992 Concha was also featured in the book *Nuestras Mujueres–Hispanas of New Mexico—Their Images and Their Lives, 1582–1982*. In 1999, *Vista Magazine* named Concha Ortiz y Pino de Kleven a Latina of the Century.

Concha visits with Archbishop Robert Sánchez, and the King and Queen of Spain at St. Francis Cathedral in the 1980s—photo by Robert H. Martin

Concha receives a lifetime achievement award from the National Hispanic Cultural Foundation, with historian Marc Simmons, and U.S. Senators Pete Domenici and Jeff Bingaman officiating—courtesy Concha Ortiz y Pino de Kleven

A 2004 picture of Concha Ortiz y Pino next to her photo on permanent display at the New Mexico Legislature—photo by Ana Pacheco

In 1992 the Albuquerque Hispanic Quincentennial Committee added another accolade in selecting Concha for its Lifetime Achievement Award, along with two men. The *Albuquerque Journal* said of her: "Concha Ortiz y Pino de Kleven represents the charm of an era which historians might say ended 50 to 75 years ago. She walks with an air of dignity, she has a distinctive style, which exudes confidence, she speaks softly but with authority— yet is feminine and charming. She is a study in sophistication."

When the state's Hispanic Culture Foundation gave Concha its highest honor in 1996 and named her a Trustee Emeritus, New Mexico Gov. Gary Johnson took the opportunity to officially declare Oct. 11 of that year "Concha Ortiz y Pino de Kleven Day" throughout the state. At an Oct. 12 banquet, 550 people came to pay tribute. An accolade presented there was a letter from an official in Madrid, Spain, who described Concha as a "daughter who has known how to preserve and devote herself to the most important values of the mother country."

A letter from U.S. President Bill Clinton added: "Through almost eight decades of challenge and change, you have devoted your time, energy, and extraordinary talents to the well-being of the people of New Mexico and of our nation. You have witnessed a lot of history in your lifetime, and you have made your own distinctive mark on that history, both in public service and as a private citizen. With vision and determination, you have worked to empower those who historically have been denied access to the American Dream, and you have done much to enrich the social, political, and artistic life of New Mexico. The Hispanic people and culture have made profound and far-reaching contributions to the growth, development and character of our nation, and you can take pride in the vital part that you have played in advancing that legacy." Three years later, when 89-year-old Concha

Honors Come

CONCHA ORTIZ y PINO BUILDING

embarked upon the "Save America's Treasures Tour of the American Southwest," first lady Hillary Rodham Clinton sent more words of tribute.

On July 16, 2004, the permanent, metal lettering on a state-government structure in the Capitol Complex in central Santa Fe was unveiled. The words said: "Concha Ortiz y Pino Building." An article in the next day's *Santa Fe New Mexican* reported: "The woman that Gov. Bill Richardson called a treasure and a 'crown jewel of New Mexico' looked every inch worthy of any and all honors as she sat, back erect despite her 94 years, her makeup flawless despite the heat, as friends, family and admirers turned out to see another state building named after a New Mexico legend."

An earlier story in the *Albuquerque Journal* had stated: "When talking with Concha Ortiz y Pino de Kleven, it quickly becomes clear that in her mind, her greatest accomplishments aren't necessarily reflected in the myriad certificates and awards covering her walls. It's in the memories of friendships formed and the people she helped along the way." The article then quotes Concha: "Life is so interesting, if you don't sit on it. The worst thing, to me, is the accumulation of goods that don't help anyone. I see so many people like that. It's sickening. It's stinginess of the heart."

When Concha is asked to sum up the life she has led, which has resulted in so much official recognition, she is unfailingly modest. And she always—*always*—traces everything back to her roots. "My family, especially Mamá Fita, taught me to help others and do my best," she says. "Apparently I succeeded in that."

Summer 2004 ceremony for a building named for Concha: left to right are Stuart Ashman, Director of the N.M. Office of Cultural Affairs, N.M. Cabinet Secretary of General Services Edward López Jr., Concha, and Gov. Bill Richardson—photo by Ana Pacheco

Epílogo: El porvenir

La tradición de la familia de los Ortiz y Pino tiene sus raíces en una época muy remota antes de que doña Josefa diera a luz a su nieta Concha, nuestra biografiada. Esa tradición sigue hasta hoy día y seguirá pese a que la familia se encuentra esparcida en muchos estados de los Estados Unidos, América Central, y en otros lugares distantes. Los familiares desempeñan sus talentos en profesiones y oficios muy variados. Muchos familiares han permanecido en Nuevo México y siguen aportando servicio al estado en distintos cargos, como ser comisionados de condado, legisladores y otros cargos públicos, y así mismo en la empresa privada.

Entre ellos hay quienes no olvidan las palabras de Nicolás Pino, que hizo votos de servir a la patria tanto como al estado de Nuevo México. Tampoco olvidan los orígenes de sus antepasados en Galisteo, donde muchos de ellos se han dedicado a conservar la iglesia, a renovar el camposanto, y a dirigir el museo local. Pese a que muchos de los Ortiz y Pino se han ido a vivir a otros lugares jamás olvidan sus raíces ancestrales, indelebles, enclavadas en Nuevo México, Tierra Encantadora.

Epilogue: Into the Future

The Ortiz y Pino family tradition began long before Concha, it continues now, and it will continue on. It stretches back endlessly into the past, and reaches far ahead into the future. On New Mexican soil alone, the family traces its roots back through nine generations that preceded Concha. And even earlier, before the bold colonists came to settle in the New World, the family bloodline spanned previous epochs in the mother country, Spain. Concha's own long life passed the nine-decade mark in the year 2000, and during her lifetime she has seen three more generations born into her family.

Members who entered the family in the years after Concha have lived many places and done many things. Their diverse geography includes California, Arizona, Colorado, Pennsylvania, Massachusetts, Nicaragua, and other distant locales. It includes cities as large as Boston and Philadelphia and places as small as nameless villages in Central America. Their work has been even more varied. It includes military service to America, in World War II, in Vietnam and other conflicts. It encompasses college teaching and elementary and high-school teaching and running a nursery school, veterinary medicine and medicine for humans, physical therapy, automobile sales, restaurant management, weaving, real estate, writing books, furniture making, ranching, accounting, the law, governmental agencies, Girl Scouts administration, being a painter or an emergency medical technician, and owning a stable and teaching horseback riding.

Sen. Jerry Ortiz y Pino, is Pedro's son and current member of the New Mexico State Legislature—courtesy Ortiz y Pino family

While some members of the Ortiz y Pino family relocated to other places, many others stayed close to their origins in New Mexico, where, true to tradition, they have contributed to the state in several ways: as county commissioners, as state legislators, as head of the New Mexico Parks Commission, and in other public offices. It all started with an ancestor, *don* Nicolás Pino, who vowed: "I will serve America and New Mexico, and members of my family will serve after me." Nor has the family ever forgotten its rural base, the village of Galisteo, where members of the clan have maintained the church, renovated the cemetery, and directed a local museum.

One member, Dr. Loretta Ortiz y Pino, is a pediatrician at the Taos Clinic for Children and Youth in northern New Mexico. She earned a medical degree at Stanford University, completed her residency in Denver, served in the National Health Service Corps, worked at the Navajo reservation hospital in Shiprock, N.M., for 14 years, and joined a University of New Mexico medical project in Nicaragua. When she returned, she felt the need for some rest and recuperation, so she arranged for a sabbatical, but also agreed to volunteer her services at the Villa Theresa Clinic in Santa Fe. During this time she went to Concha's 80th birthday party in 1990. She recalls it well. "Concha asked me, 'Now, Loretta, what are you doing?' When I told her I was on sabbatical, she wagged her finger at me and told me firmly, 'You need to get back to work as soon as possible!'"

The family of Pedro and Vangie Ortiz y Pino pose for a 50th wedding anniversary. In the back row, left to right: Michaela Bruzzese, Donna Bruzzese, Carlos Ortiz y Pino, Jana Ortiz y Pino, Jacob Ortiz Y Pino, Vernon White, Heather White, Kristen García, Kim García, David Ortiz y Pino, and Jessica Ortiz y Pino. Pedro and Vangie's children are seated with them in the middle row from left to right: Jerry, Loretta, Paul, Vangie and Pedro Ortiz y Pino, Roberta, Louise, and Mike. In the front row: Miriam Ortiz y Pino, Luke Ortiz y Pino, Ben Ortiz y Pino, Chris Ortiz y Pino, Nicholas Ortiz y Pino, and Stephanie White—courtesy Jerry Ortiz y Pino

José Ortiz y Pino III (Frank Ortiz y Davis' son) with his wife, Yolanda, at the family compound in Galisteo—courtesy María Ortiz y Pino

Descendants of Josefita and Ramón Gómez are, back row left to right Scott Victor, Jude, Raul, Pablo, Manolo, Frank Gómez, Jeff Miles, and Clay Willard. In the middle row: Mike Varela, Tonya, Zach, Teresa, Pauline Gómez, Carla, Francie, Rose Willard, and Sharon, holding Kara. Bottom: Steve Gómez, Max, Alice Gómez, and Susan Varela—courtesy Susan Varela

José Ortiz y Pino IV, Yolanda, José III, and María Ortiz y Pino—courtesy María Ortiz y Pino

A family reunion in the summer of 2004, descendants of Pedro Ortiz y Pino, and Reynalda Ortiz y Pino. At left, standing: Judy Hasted, Roberta White, next row Loretta Ortiz y Pino, Pedro Ortiz y Pino, and Louise Stevenson. Seated left: Paul Ortiz y Pino, Jerry Ortiz y Pino, and Ron Ortiz Dinkel. In the front row: Michael Ortiz y Pino—courtesy Judy Hasted

Margo Ortiz y Davis (Frank Ortiz y Davis' daughter) and her husband, Charles Truscott—courtesy Margo Ortiz y Davis

Epilogue: Into the Future

María Ortiz y Davis Catanach (Frank Ortiz y Davis' daughter) second from left, with her children Thomas, Anthony Jr., and Angela Catanach—courtesy María Catanach

The children of Reynalda Ortiz y Pino de Dinkel, Judith Dinkel Brito Hasted and her brother Ron Ortiz Dinkel—courtesy Ron Ortiz Dinkel

Chart 1: Pino Family Ancestors

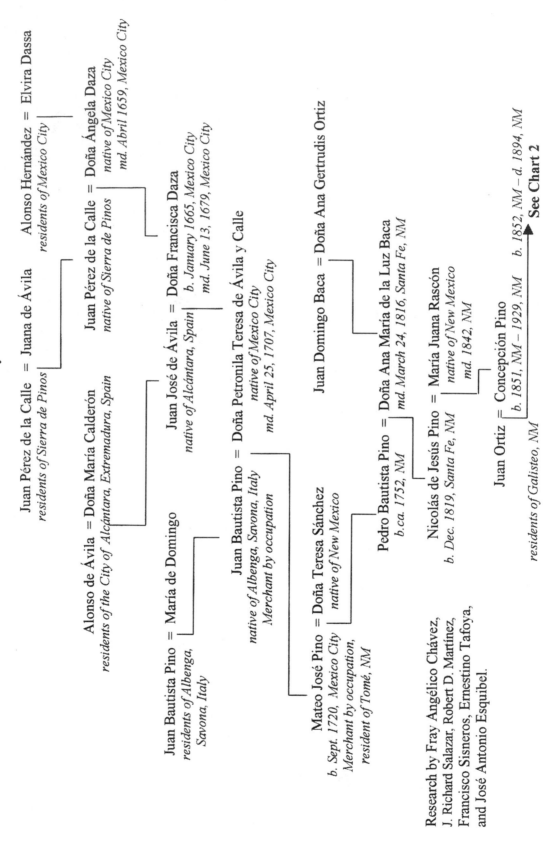

Juan Pérez de la Calle = Juana de Ávila
residents of Sierra de Pinos

Alonso Hernández = Elvira Dassa
residents of Mexico City

Juan Pérez de la Calle = Doña Ángela Daza
native of Sierra de Pinos *native of Mexico City*
md. Abril 1659, Mexico City

Alonso de Ávila = Doña María Calderón
residents of the City of Alcántara, Extremadura, Spain

Juan José de Ávila = Doña Francisca Daza
native of Alcántara, Spain *b. January 1665, Mexico City*
md. June 13, 1679, Mexico City

Juan Bautista Pino = María de Domingo
residents of Albenga,
Savona, Italy

Juan Bautista Pino = Doña Petronila Teresa de Ávila y Calle
native of Albenga, Savona, Italy *native of Mexico City*
Merchant by occupation *md. April 25, 1707, Mexico City*

Juan Domingo Baca = Doña Ana Gertrudis Ortiz

Mateo José Pino = Doña Teresa Sánchez
b. Sept. 1720, Mexico City *native of New Mexico*
Merchant by occupation,
resident of Tomé, NM

Pedro Bautista Pino = Doña Ana María de la Luz Baca
b.ca. 1752, NM *md. March 24, 1816, Santa Fe, NM*

Nicolás de Jesús Pino = María Juana Rascón
b. Dec. 1819, Santa Fe, NM *native of New Mexico*
md. 1842, NM

Juan Ortiz = Concepción Pino
b. 1851, NM – 1929, NM *b. 1852, NM – d. 1894, NM*
See Chart 2
residents of Galisteo, NM

Research by Fray Angélico Chávez,
J. Richard Salazar, Robert D. Martínez,
Francisco Sisneros, Ernestino Tafoya,
and José Antonio Esquibel.

Epilogue: Into the Future

Genealogy of the Ortiz y Pino Family
Chart 2: Ortiz y Pino Descendants

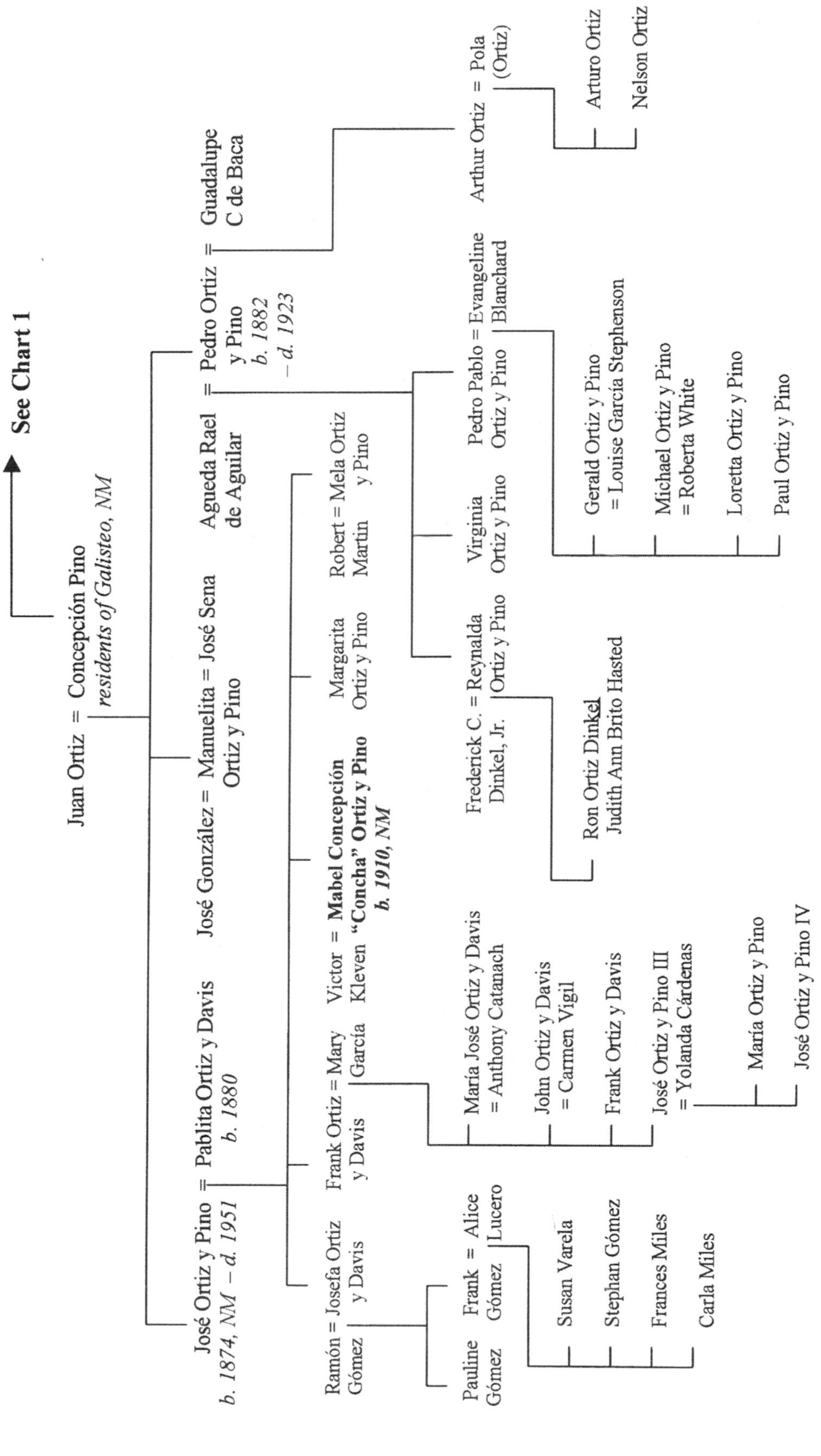

→ **See Chart 1**

Juan Ortiz = Concepción Pino
residents of Galisteo, NM

José González = Manuelita
Ortiz y Pino

Agueda Rael
de Aguilar

Pedro Ortiz = Guadalupe
y Pino   C de Baca
b. 1882
– d. 1923

Arthur Ortiz = Pola
                        (Ortiz)

Arturo Ortiz

Nelson Ortiz

José Ortiz y Pino = Pablita Ortiz y Davis
b. 1874, NM – d. 1951   *b. 1880*

Frank Ortiz = Mary   Victor = **Mabel Concepción**
y Davis   García   Kleven   **"Concha" Ortiz y Pino**
                                            b. 1910, NM

Margarita
Ortiz y Pino

Robert = Mela Ortiz
Martin   y Pino

Frederick C. = Reynalda
Dinkel, Jr.   Ortiz y Pino

Ron Ortiz Dinkel
Judith Ann Brito Hasted

Virginia
Ortiz y Pino

Pedro Pablo = Evangeline
Ortiz y Pino   Blanchard

Gerald Ortiz y Pino
= Louise García Stephenson

Michael Ortiz y Pino
= Roberta White

Loretta Ortiz y Pino

Paul Ortiz y Pino

Ramón = Josefa Ortiz
Gómez   y Davis

Maria José Ortiz y Davis
= Anthony Catanach

John Ortiz y Davis
= Carmen Vigil

Frank Ortiz y Davis

José Ortiz y Pino III
= Yolanda Cárdenas

María Ortiz y Pino

José Ortiz y Pino IV

Pauline   Frank = Alice
Gómez   Gómez   Lucero

Susan Varela

Stephan Gómez

Frances Miles

Carla Miles

Three New Generations of the Ortiz y Pino Family not included on this chart.

Bibliography

Albuquerque Journal (Author Not Listed, November 19, 1972). "New U of A Fine Arts Center Accessible to Handicapped"

Álvarez, María Elena (August 16, 2004). Telephone Interview. Albuquerque, New Mexico

Anonymous Author (Undated). "Mela Martin, Steward of Spanish Culture, Dies." *The New Mexican*

Anonymous Author (September 13, 1946). "Mela Ortiz y Pino Program Director for USO to Open Soon." *The New Mexican*

Anonymous Author (October 30, 1980). "Thanks, Mrs. Martin." *The New Mexican*

Anonymous Author (May 1, 1977). "Martin Photos Displayed." *The New Mexican*

Anonymous Author (June 7, 1991). "A Gift of Photographic History." *The New Mexican/Pasatiempo*

Anonymous Author (May 20, 1990). "Birthday Party to Honor Longtime Patron of the Arts." *Albuquerque Journal*

Anonymous Author (November 9, 1967). "Visitors from Spain Bestow Honors and, in Turn, are Honored by Officials." *The New Mexican*

Anonymous Source (August 17, 2004). Telephone Interview. Albuquerque, New Mexico

Antón, Waldo (July 12, 2004). Written Questionnaire. Santa Fe, New Mexico

Aragón, Alfred A. (September 26-October 24, 1996). "Great Records Managers in History: Concha Ortiz y Pino de Kleven." *Round the Roundhouse*

Archdiocese of Santa Fe (April/May 1996). "Archbishop and Others Receive Pilgrim Shell in Jerusalem." Archdiocese of Santa Fe Publication

Arellano, Anselmo (Fall 1995). "Springer's Faye Lucero Shared a Political First," *La Herencia* Magazine

Barela, Margaret (January 1993). "High Ideals Motivate Galisteo's Grand Dame." *New Mexico Magazine*

Bauman, John F., and Coode, Thomas H. (1988). *In the Eyes of the Great Depression—New Deal Reporters and The Agony of the American People.* Northern Illinois University Press

Billington, Monroe Lee (1991). *New Mexico's Buffalo Soldiers 1866–1900.* University Press of Colorado

Black, Charlotte (June 6, 1983). "Grand Dame Marks Milestones." Albuquerque Tribune

Brown, Cathi (July 14, 2004). Written Questionnaire. Albuquerque, New Mexico.

Burg, David F. (1996). *The Great Depression—An Eyewitness History.* Facts on File, Inc.

Bursey, Joseph A. (January 1940). "Baa, Baa Black Sheep." *New Mexico Magazine*

Castellano, Virginia (July 14, 2004). Written Questionnaire.

Santa Fe, New Mexico

Carmack, George (June 3, 1972). "A Letter From the Editor: Villanueva Visited—A Grotto and a Way of Life." Albuquerque Tribune

Chávez, Gabriel (August 25, 2004). Telephone Interview. Taos, New Mexico

Clinton, Bill (October 11, 1996). Personal Letter to Concha Ortiz y Pino de Kleven. White House; Washington, D.C.

Coan, Mary W. (December 1933). "La Corrida del Gallo at Galisteo." *New Mexico Magazine*

Conkin, Paul K. (1967, 1975). *The New Deal, 2nd edition.* AHM Publishing.

Córdova, Josephine M. (1976). *No Lloro Pero Me Acuerdo.* Taylor Publishing Company

Córdova, Kathryn M. (Summer 1996). "The Range Wars Sought to Change the West." *La Herencia*

Córdova, Kathryn M. (December 17, 18 and 28, 1988). Program for Dramatic Production *And Then There Were Shepherds.* Taos Community Auditorium (Taos, New Mexico); San José de Gracia Church (Trampas, New Mexico); and Sangre de Cristo Church (San Luis, Colorado)

Córdova, Kathryn M. (December 1992). "Christmas in 1942: A Columbus Adventure." *Christmas in Taos*

Córdova, Kathryn M. (Spring 1998). "New World Women." *La Herencia* Magazine

Córdova, Kathryn M. (Spring 1998). "Oñate Center Showcasing History." *La Herencia* Magazine

Córdova, Kathryn M. (August 29-30, 1998). "Cuartocentenario Taos Proud." *Taos Cuartocentenario*

Córdova, Kathryn M. (Fall 2002). "Confessions of a Fiesta Queen." *La Herencia; Journal North* (August 30, 2002)

DeFleur, Dennis (2002). *Understanding Mass Communication—A Liberal Arts Perspective, 7th edition.* Houghton Mifflin Company

Del Castillo, Richard Griswold (1990). *The Treaty of Guadalupe Hidalgo, A Legacy of Conflict.* University of Oklahoma Press

Díaz, Rose and Barnhart, Jan Dodson, editors, (1992). *Hispanic Heroes—Portraits of New Mexicans Who Have Made a Difference.* Starlight Publishing, Inc.

Dios, John (Date Unknown). "Faculty Facets." *University of New Mexico Faculty Newsletter*

Fergusson, Erna (1964). *New Mexico.* Alfred A. Knopf

Flexner, Eleanor (1959). *Century of Struggle—The Women's Rights Movement in the United States.* The Belknap Press of Harvard University Press

Forrest, Earle R. (1929). *Missions and Pueblos of the Southwest.* The Arthur H. Clark Company

Gallegos, Pete V. (March 26, 1988). "The Grotto of Our Lady

of Guadalupe in Villanueva." *Las Vegas Victorian Gazette*

Grant, Blanche (1963). *When Old Trails Were New*. The Rio Grande Press

Guadalupe Historic Foundation (Undated). *Noticias del Santuario de Guadalupe*

Hanlon, Ferroll Clark (1995). *Life on the Range and Other Memories—The Early Years in the Estancia Valley and Taos*. C&M Enterprises

Harbert, Nancy (1992). *New Mexico*. Compass American Guides, Fodor's Travel Publications, Inc.

Hay, Calla (December 12, 1943). "Kleven-Ortiz y Pino Wedding." *The New Mexican*

Hoffman, Will (Undated). "Arts Commission Grant Policies to Face Challenges at Meeting," *Albuquerque Journal*

Jaramillo, Cleofas (1983). *Romance of a Little Village Girl*. UNM Press, Pasó Por Aquí Series

Jensen, Joan and Miller, Darlis A. (1986). *New Mexico Women—Intercultural Perspectives*. University of New Mexico Press

Johnson, Jeannie (August 1, 1998). "Woman Had Long History in Santa Fe." *Journal North*

Johnson, Paul (August 16, 2004). Telephone Interview. Taos, New Mexico

Julyan, Robert (1996). *The Place Names of New Mexico*. University of New Mexico Press

Kinney, Carol N. (August 15, 1990). Personal Letter to Senior Foundation, Inc. Albuquerque, New Mexico

Larson, Robert W. (1968). *New Mexico's Quest for Statehood, 1846-1912*. University of New Mexico Press

Leckie, William H. (1967). *The Buffalo Soldiers—A Narrative of the Negro Cavalry in the West*. University of Oklahoma Press

Ligon de Ita, Nancy (July 29, 1998). "Mela Ortiz y Pino de Martin." Faxed Notes

Los Alamos Meeting and Visitor Bureau (2004). *The Los Alamos Visitors' Guide*. Los Alamos, New Mexico

Louchheim, Katie, editor (1983). *The Making of the New Deal—The Insiders Speak*. Harvard University Press

Love, Marian F. (June 1988). "Vignette...Mela Ortiz y Pino de Martin—Popular Songstress Lauded for Efforts to Preserve Spanish Culture." *The Santa Fean*

Luchetti, Cathy and Olwell, Carol (1982). *Women of the West*. Crown Trade Paperbacks

Luján, Josie E. (August 6, 1990). Personal Letter to Senior Foundation, Inc. Chimayo, New Mexico

Martin, Robert (April 9, 2004 and August 11, 2004). Personal Interviews. Santa Fe, New Mexico

Martin, Robert (December/January 1975). "La Conquistadora." Photos with text by Anonymous Author. *The Santa Fean*

Maxwell, Grant (September, 1935, Vol. XIII, no. 9). "Schools of New Mexico." *New Mexico Magazine*

McCoach, Randall (September 21, 2003). "Interview with Pedro Ortiz y Pino." Albuquerque, New Mexico

Mc Elvaine, Robert S. (2000). *The Depression and the New Deal—A History in Documents*. Oxford University Press

Merriam-Webster, *Webster's Collegiate Dictionary, Fifth Edition*. G. and C. Merriam Co., Publishers

Montoya, Eloy (August 11, 2004). Personal Interview. Santa Fe, New Mexico

Montoya, Stella (August 11, 2004). Personal Interview. Santa Fe, New Mexico.

Myres, Sandra L. (1982). *Westering Women and the Frontier Experience, 1800-1915*. University of New Mexico Press

New Mexico Legislative Council Services, *The New Mexico State Legislature*. State of New Mexico

Ortiz y Pino, Jerry (August 24, 2004). Telephone Interview. Albuquerque, New Mexico

Ortiz y Pino, Jerry (May 21, 2004). Personal Interview. Albuquerque, New Mexico

Ortiz y Pino, José III (1981). *Don José, the Last Patrón*. Sunstone Press

Ortiz y Pino, José III (August 11, 2004). Personal Interview. Galisteo, New Mexico

Ortiz y Pino, Dr. Loretta (July 31, 2004). Personal Interview. Taos, New Mexico

Ortiz y Pino, María (August 11, 2004). Personal Interview. Galisteo, New Mexico

Ortiz y Pino, María (August 25, 2004). Telephone Interview. Galisteo, New Mexico

Ortiz y Pino de Kleven, Concha (Undated). Family papers and notes. Located at the Center for Southwest Research in the University of New Mexico Zimmerman Library and in possession of Concha Ortiz y Pino de Kleven

Ortiz y Pino de Kleven, Interviews on the following dates: March 18 and 25, 2004; April 9, 14 and 28, 2004; May 5, 9 and 23, 2004; and June 7 and 14, 2004. Santa Fe, New Mexico

Ortiz y Pino de Kleven, Concha (Undated). Personal Written Résumé. Santa Fe, New Mexico

Penrose, Steve (Undated). "New Mexico's Aristocratic Lady." *Albuquerque Journal*

Propp, Wren (August 3, 1998). "Martin a Tribute to N.M., Her Family." ("The Insider Column"). *Albuquerque Journal*

Propp, Wren (Undated). "Mending Our Lady's Shrine." *Albuquerque Journal*

Rebolledo, Tey Diana, editor (1992). *Nuestras Mujeres— Hispanas of New Mexico, Their Images and Their Lives, 1582–1992*. El Norte Publications/Academia

Rubin, H. Ted (August 15, 2004). Telephone Interview. Boulder, Colorado

Russell, Inez (July 17, 2004). "Woman Pioneer—Concha Ortiz y Pino de Kleven Honored at Ceremony Gracing a South Capitol Building With her Name." *The New Mexican*

Sálaz, Rubén, (1999). *New Mexico—A Brief Multi-History*. Cosmic House

Sánchez, Robert, Archbishop, (August 1, 1990). Personal Letter to Senior Foundation, Inc., Albuquerque, New Mexico

Sando, Joe (1992). *Pueblo Nations*. Clear Light Publishers

Santillanes, Millie, (November 21, 1992). "Local Celebration Met Quincentennial Expectations." *Albuquerque Journal*

Schissel, Lillian; Ruiz, Vickie L.; and Monk, Janice, editors (1988). *Western Women—Their Land, Their Lives*.

University of New Mexico Press

Segura, Andrés (August 7, 2004). Personal Interview. Albuquerque, New Mexico

Seidman, Carrie (October 1996). "The Grand Dame of New Mexico." *Sage Magazine.* (*Albuquerque Journal*)

Simmons, Marc (Undated). "Trail Dust—An Old Book in a New Time." *Santa Fe Reporter*

Simmons, Marc (August 2–8, 2000). "Trail Dust: Concha." *Santa Fe Reporter*

Simmons, Marc (August 3, 1998). "Eulogy for Mela Martin"

Simmons, Marc (September 9-15, 1998). "Trail Dust: The Royal Spanish Banner." *Santa Fe Reporter*

Simmons, Marc (July 27, 1990). Personal Letter to Senior Foundation, Inc. Cerrillos, New Mexico

Snow, Patricia Gabbett (October 22, 1999). "Pride and Joy— City Honors Lifelong Contributions with Living Treasure Awards." *Albuquerque Journal*

Stanley, F. (June 1995). *The Galisteo (New Mexico) Story.* Pep, Texas Publishing

Stein, Marjorie Shapiro (Undated). "Elegant Concha Ortiz y Pino." *Prime Time*

Steinberg, David (May 15, 1994). "Sculpture Honors Lifetime of Service." *Albuquerque Journal*

The United Educators, Inc. (1966). *American Educator*, Lake Bluff, Illinois

Twitchell, Ralph Emerson, Esq. (1963). *Leading Facts of New Mexico History, Volume II.* Horn and Wallace Publishing

Ulibarrí, Sabine R., Dr. ((August 15, 1990). Personal Letter to Senior Foundation Inc., Albuquerque, New Mexico

Watkins, T.H. (1991). *The Hungry Years—A Narrative History of the Great Depression In America.* Henry Holt and Co.

Weber, David J. (1992). *The Spanish Frontier in North America.* Yale University Press

Weigle, Marta, editor (1993). *Women of New Mexico— Depression Era Images.* Ancient City Press

Wilks, Flo (Undated). *Albuquerque Journal,* "Long Cultural Heritage Backs Her Interest in Fine Arts"

Page numbers in italics refer to photographs and illustrations

Adams, Ansel: 57, *169*
Adela: 95
Adoption: 95; child reclaimed by birth-mother: 71, 75
Advisory Council of the National Institutes of Health: 141–42
African Americans in New Mexico: *see* Black communities in New Mexico
Agua Verde Ranch: 71, 76–87; debt: 84, 86; employees: 85–86; improvements: 86; ranch house: 85
Albritton, Maria: 171
Albuquerque Hispanic Quincentennial Committee: 180
Albuquerque Journal: 155
Albuquerque Little Theatre: 135
Albuquerque Museum Foundation: 174
Alvarez, Carmen Elizabeth: 156
Alvarez, Magdalena: 156
Alvarez, Maria Elena: 154–59
American Association of University Women: 175
Anaya, Miguel: 162
Anchondo, Carmen: *120, 125*
Anchondo, Socorro: *120, 125*
Anderson, Clinton P.: 135
Apodaca, Clara: 171
Apodaca, Jerry: 171
Artists: 57
Ashman, Stuart: *181*

Baca, Ana María: 7
Baca, Frank: *55*
Baca, Jesús: 162
Ballen, Sam: 171
Barela, Patrocino: 57
Bars: i, 83, 84, 85–86
Baumann Ortiz, Ramor: *128*
Bent, Charles: 47
Bergen, Edgar: *137*
Best Dressed Woman in Albuquerque: 174
Bikini Island: *112*
Billy the Kid: 35
Bingaman, Jeff: *179*

Black communities in New Mexico: history: 34–35
Blake, Ernie: 171
Bluebelle: *see* Jackson, Braulia (nickname: Bluebelle)
Brown, Loren: 57
Buffalo Soldiers: *34*, 34–35
Bustamante, Josefa: 147
Byrne, Bishop Edwin V.: *vi, 74*, 119, *124, 125*, 164

Calabasa, José: *128*
Camp Fire Girls: 135
Careers for the handicapped: 141
Carter, Jimmy: 142
Cassidy, Ina Sizer: 57
Cattle: 17, 77; certificate of brand: *78, 79*
Cerebral Palsy School: 135
Chalee, Pop: *130*
Chauvenet, Beatrice: *171*
Chávez, Antonio: *38*
Chávez, Dennis: *54*, 62
Chávez, Fray Angelico: *115, 116, 117, 118, 119, 120, 121*, 121, *122, 123, 163*, 164, 168
Christmas: 17, 151
Christmas cards: *101*
Church and state: 145
Civil War, 1860-1864: 9, 21, 34
Clinton, Bill: 180
Clinton, Hillary Rodham: 181
Cofradía de la Conquistadora, La: 138, 147–48
College of St. Joseph: 45, 69
Colonial Hispanic Crafts Society of Galisteo: 55
Colonial Hispanic Crafts Society of New Mexico: *corrido de gallo*: *56*; invitation to dinner and dance: *56*
Concha Ortiz y Pino Building: xi, 181
Concha Ortiz y Pino de Kleven Day: 180
Córdova, Kathryn M.: x
Cortes of Cádiz: 4–5, 7
Crosby, John: 171
Cuatro-Centennial Commission: 135
Cutting, Bronson: 62

Davis, Sylvester: 9, 11, 23, 33, 35, 77
de Vargas, Diego: 3, 16–17, 147
Depression: see Great Depression
Depression livestock policy: 77–78
Dinkel, Ron: *181*
Domenici, Pete: *179*
Don Pedro Mine: 17

Easter Seal Society: 141
Education in New Mexico: 61–62; history: 43–45
Elkins, Stephen B.: 21–22
Ellison, Samuel: 92
Eniwetok Atoll: *111*, 112
Española, N. Mex.: *129*
Espinosa, Aurelio: 62; correspondence: *61*
Evans, Ernestine: 169
Exposición sucinta y sencilla de la provincia del Nuevo México, La: 4–5, 7

Ferdinand VII (king of Spain): 7
Fergusson, Erna: 141, *142*
Festival Foundation: 135
Folklore: 57
Ford, Gerald: 142
Franklin D. Roosevelt Caravan: *53*
Frederica, Queen (of Greece): *166*, 170

Gable, Clark: correspondence: 67, *68*
Galisteo, N. Mex.: xi, 11–18, 24–31, 36;
    cemetery: *114*; churches: 16; fiestas and
    entertainments: 17, 161–62; livestock: 77
Galisteo, N.Mex.: 9
García, María: 92
Garner, John Nance: 135
Garson, Greer: 171
Genealogy: Ortiz y Pino family: 188-89
George Washington University: 45
Geronimo: 35
Gilpin, Laura: 121
Gómez, Frank: 91
Gómez, Pauline: *30*, 69, 91
Gómez, Ramón: *90*, 91
Gonzales, Cleofas: 23
Grant, Blanche: 57
Great Depression: 52–57

Hanbury, Una: *177*; bronze bust: 174
Hasted, Judy: *181*
Hernández, Connie: *117, 118*
Hidalgo de Calificada Nobleza a Servicio del Estado de Nuevo México: 174–75
Hispanic Culture Foundation: 180
Hispanic Heroes: 177–78
Hollis, Pat: 169
Homestead Act: 11, 17, 77
Homesteaders: 13, 25, 77
Hurtado, Páez: 147

Instituto de Cultura Hispánica de Madrid: 95, 169
Irving, Irene: *31*

Jackson, Alice: 22, 33, *33*; marriage: 39
Jackson, Braulia (nickname: Bluebelle): 23,
    32–39, *33, 37, 38*, 44; childhood chores: 28,
    35; childhood mischief: 36–44; marriage and
    children: 39
Jaramillo, Cleofas: *44*
Jerusalem, Israel: 153
Johnson, Frank: *31*
Johnson, Gary: 180
Johnson, Lyndon B.: 141
Juan Carlos, King (of Spain): *179*

Kennedy, John F.: 141, *142*
King, Bruce: 174
Kinney, Carol: 177
Kleven, Victor: *69, 70, 71, 72, 73, 74, 75*, 135;
    death: 75, 87; early education: 68; marriage to
    Concha Ortiz y Pino: 64–75; ranch life: 86–87;
    Rhodes Scholar: 68; wedding: 69–70; World
    War I, 1914-1918 and League of Nations: 68
Knighman, Ann: *168*

La Ciénega Museum: 138
La Cofradía de la Conquistadora: see Cofradía de
    la Conquistadora, La
La Conquistadora: 17, *101*, 117, *118*, 119, *123*,
    125, 127, 133, 146, 147, 164
*La exposición sucinta y sencilla de la provincia
    del Nuevo Méexico, La: see Exposición sucinta
    y sencilla de la provincia del Nuevo México, La*

La Fonda Hotel: 164
Lamy, Jean Baptiste: 43
Las Posadas: 151
League of Nations: 68
League of United Latin-American Citizens: 61
Lee, Floyd: 84
Leyba, José María: 162
Livestock: 77–78; branding and castrating: 83
López, Dolores: *118*
López, Edward, Jr.: *181*
López, Socorro: *120, 125*
Loretto Academy: 41, *41*, 43
Los Alamos, N. Mex.: 110–13
Los Alamos National Laboratory: 107, 110
Los Alamos Ranch School: 111
Lovelace Medical Foundation: 141
Lucero, Felipa: 23, 28, *29*
Lucero-White, Aurora: 57
Luján, Josie: 177
Luján, Lorencita: *127*
Luján, Lorenzita: 168
Luján, Manuel: 168

Mabry, Tom: 164
Mamá Fita: *see* Ortiz y Davis, Josefa "Mamá Fita"
Manuel: *84*
Martin, Robert H.: *75*, 92, *93, 94*, 95, *98, 99, 102, 108, 109, 110, 113, 128, 133, 163, 165*; early education: 107; hospitality: 168–69; marriage to Mela Ortiz y Pino: 112, 163–64; photographic career: 106–33; retirement: 113
Martínez, Antonio José: 43
Martínez, Ben: 57
Martínez, Francisco Pascual: 169
Martínez, Manuela: *25*
Martínez, Reyes: 57
Mauldin, Bill: 171
Maxwell Museum of Anthropology: 138, 175
Mayer, Mrs. Walter "Peach": 171
Mayer, Rev. Theo: 69
McGrath, Marie: 69
McKinney, Robert: 169
Meem, John Gaw: 169
Mercantile store: 9, 25, *28*, 84
Mexican American War, 1846-1848: 19, 47
Miera y Pacheco Map: 57, *57*

Miles, John D.: 135
Miles, John E.: 55, *60*, 60–61
Mitchell, Albert: 84
Mitchem, Helen: *178*
Montoya, Della: 168
Montoya, Eloy: 112, 119
Montoya, Joseph: *142*, 168
Moody, John: *116, 117, 122, 123, 127*
Moody, Mrs.: *117*
Muñíz García, Rosina: *117*
Musel, Ulnin: *169*
Museum of International Folk Art: 138

National Commission on Architectural Barriers: 141–43
National Council for Upward Bound: 141
National Endowment for the Humanities: 142
New Deal: 57
New Mexico: Constitutional Convention: 19, 22, 49, 51; religious place names: 145, 147; statehood: 18–23; territorial government: 19, 21–22
New Mexico Arts Commission: 137–38
New Mexico District Court decree: 84
New Mexico Genealogical Society: 138
New Mexico Governor's Prayer Breakfast: 141
New Mexico Historical Association: 138
New Mexico Legislature: 43–45; majority whip: 59
New Mexico Opera Guild: 135
New Mexico Services for the Blind: 141
New Mexico State Highway Department: 86
New Mexico Symphony Orchestra: 135, 137
New Mexico Territorial Legislature: 47–48
Newgate Project: 141
Nixon, Richard: 141
Nuestra Señora de Guadalupe: 151
Nuestra Señora de los Remedios: *148*, 162
Nuns: 43

Oppenheimer, J. Robert: 111, 121
Orchestra of Santa Fe: 135
Ortiz, Adeline: *116, 117*
Ortiz, Antonio José: 147
Ortiz, Deanie: *118*
Ortiz, Juan: 9, 13, *30, 48*, 77

Ortiz Land Grant: 17
Ortiz, Manuelita: *25, 26*
Ortiz, Nicolás: 3, 7, 147
Ortiz y Alarid, Gaspar: *12*
Ortiz y Davis, Frank: 22, *26, 27, 30, 33,* 41, 69, 83, 84, *84, 85, 89,* 91, 92; descendants: *185, 187*
Ortiz y Davis, Josefa "Mamá Fita": 7, 9, 11–13, *12,* 23, *26,* 27–28, *31,* 35–36, 77, 162; advisor to politicians: 51; gravestone: *29;* hospitality: 12, 27
Ortiz y Davis, Manuela: *10*
Ortiz y Davis, Pablita: *10, 13,* 13, *26, 30, 31, 75, 81, 89, 99;* death: 95; immediate family: 22, 25–27, 91, 92
Ortiz y Davis, Pedro: *10*
Ortiz y Pino, Concha: xi, *26, 27, 30, 31, 33, 37, 41, 42, 53, 55, 60, 72, 75, 84, 85, 87, 89, 91, 103, 136, 137, 138, 140, 142, 150, 151, 155, 156, 157, 158, 163, 167, 168, 169, 170, 171, 173, 175, 176, 177, 178, 180, 181;* Agua Verde Ranch: 76–87, *82;* ancestors: 3–7, 8–13; attitude toward Women's Liberation Movement: 51; baptism: *20, 21,* 22–23; birth: 18–23; campaign literature: *63;* childhood: 24–31; childhood chores: 28, 35; childhood mischief: 36–38, 43; Depression and the Franklin D. Roosevelt Caravan: 52–57; early romances: 65–67; education: 38, 40–45, 63; faculty wife: 70–71; friends: 154–59; friendship with Bluebell: 32–39; giving political speeches: 57; graduation from Loretto Academy: 45; honorary doctorate from the University of Albuquerque: 45; honors: 172–81; immediate family: 88–105, 121; legislative career: 58–63; majority whip, New Mexico House of Representatives: 59; marriage to Victor Kleven: 64–75; Ortiz y Pino family in the 21st century: 183; philosophy: 181; place of birth: 14–17; political roots: 46–51; public-service boards: 134–53; ranch management: 84; recreations: 154–59; religion: 144–53; social events: 160–72; wedding: 69–70; widowhood: 135
Ortiz y Pino family: in the 21st century: 182–87; genealogy: 188–89
Ortiz y Pino, Jerry: *183*
Ortiz y Pino, José: *13, 25, 26,* 29, *30, 31, 80, 81, 89;* Concha Ortiz y Pino's education: 38, 45; homesteaders: 77; immediate family: 22, 26–27, 91; land and property: 17, 25; legislative career: 49, 59; marriage to Pablita Ortiz y Davis: 13; named Concha Ortiz y Pino manager of Agua Verde Ranch: 83–84; New Mexico Legislature: 43, 49; Parkinson's disease: 83; ranch management: 83; sponsor of Concha Ortiz y Pino's political work: 55–56, 57
Ortiz y Pino, José, III: *184, 185*
Ortiz y Pino, José, IV: *185*
Ortiz y Pino, Josefita: 22, 30, *89, 90,* 91
Ortiz y Pino, Loretta: 183
Ortiz y Pino, Manuelita: 10, 95
Ortiz y Pino, Margaret: *30;* death: 39
Ortiz y Pino, Margarita: *186*
Ortiz y Pino, María: *185*
Ortiz y Pino, Mela: *30, 31, 37,* 69, *75, 89, 91,* 91, 92, *94,* 95, *96, 97,* 99, *100, 102, 103, 104,* 121, *151,* 161, *162, 163, 164, 165, 171;* death: 113; eulogy: *105;* hospitality: 168–69; marriage to Robert H. Martin: 112, 163–64
Ortiz y Pino, Pedro: *25,* 95, *184;* descendants: *186*
Ortiz y Pino, Pedro, Jr.: 95, *151*
Ortiz y Pino, Vangie: *184*
Ortiz y Pino, Yolanda: *184, 185*
Ortiz y Pino de Dinkel, Reynalda: *26, 33, 151,* 175
Ortiz y Pino family: in the 21st century: 182–87; genealogy: 188–89
Otero de Navacués, José María: 168
Otero-Warren, Nina: 49, *50,* 51

Padilla, Pauline: *120, 125*
Palermo, Jimmy: *164*
Palmer, Friend: 12, 22–23, 33
Palou, Billy: *164*
Partido system: 77
Partners for the Americas: 141
Paulhan, Rev. E.: 23
Pecos, N. Mex.: churches: *20*
Pino, Concepción: 9
Pino de Ortiz, Margarita: *25*

Pino, Facundo: 47
Pino, Germán: 23
Pino, Mateo José: 3
Pino, Miguel: 48
Pino, Narciso: *6*
Pino, Nicolás de Jesús: 7, 9, 47, *48*
Pino, Pedro Bautista: *3*, 3–5, 7, 47, 77, 174
Pino de Ortiz, Margarita: *25*
Pond, Ashley: 111
Popejoy, Tom: 63
Porter, Elliot: 171
Pueblo Indians: 7; revolt, 1680: 16

Quivira Society: 174–75

Railroad: 17
Ranch management: 78
Ranching: 9, 11
Reginalda, B. A.: *74*
Religion: 86–87
Religious place names: New Mexico: 145, 147
Richardson, Bill: ix, *181*
Roosevelt, Franklin D.: presidential campaign:
    52–57, 59
Rotary Club: 175
Roybal Sosaya, Victoria: *127*
Rubin, Ted: 143
Ryan, Helen Chandler: 57

Sabbah, Michael: 151
San Antonio Church: *20*
San Cristóbal Mission: 15
San Felipe Pueblo: 162
San José: *152*
San José bell: San Miguel Chapel: 148
San Miguel Chapel: San José bell: 148
Sánchez, Archbishop Robert: *151, 179*
Sánchez de Pino, Maria: 3
Sánchez, Juan: 57
Sandburg, Carl: 121
Sangre de Cristo Mountains, N. Mex.: *132*
Santa Fe Chamber of Commerce: 173
Santa Fe Desert Chorale: 135
Santa Fe Festival of the Arts: 175
Santa Fe Fiesta: *127*
Santa Fe Historical Association: 138

Santa Fe, N. Mex.: 41, 43, 110–13, 119, *126*;
    restaurants: 170; songs and dances: 162–63
Santa Fe Opera: 137, 171
Santa Fe Trail: 19, 35
Santo Domingo Pueblo: 162
Santuario de Guadalupe: 138–39, 141
Schmidt, Father: *116, 117*
Sedillo, Juan A. A.: *62*
Segura, Andrés: 158–59, 174
Seth, Oliver: 169
Sewell, Bruce: 55
Sheehan, Michael J.: *147*, 151, *151*
Sheep: 13, 17, 77; certificate of mark: 25, *79*;
    Karakul breed: 83; lambing season: 80;
    shearing: 80, 83
Shepherds: Basque: 77
Simmons, Marc: *102, 105*, 177, *179*
Sitting Bull: 35
Slavery: 21
Sociedad Folklórica: 163
Sophia, Queen (of Spain): *166*, 170, *179*
Sosaya, Angela: 44
Spanish language: 22, 43, 61–62
St. Francis Cathedral: 69, *115, 124*
St. Joseph's College: 69, *74*, 175
St. Michael's College: 41, 43
Stockton, Pansy: *130, 131*

Taos Center for the Arts: 135
Taos, N. Mex.: rebellion against the U.S.
    Territorial government: 47
Tía Vicenta: *29*
Tingley, Clyde: *53*, 55
Torrance County, N. Mex.: 9, 11
Treaty of Guadalupe Hidalgo: 17, 19
Truscott, Charles: *186*
Turro, Mr.: *89*

Udall, Stewart: 171
Ulibarrí, Sabine: 177
United Nations: 71
University of Albuquerque: 45, 175
University of New Mexico: *174*; Board of
    Regents: 177; Friends of the Arts: 135; School
    of Inter-American Affairs: 45, 63, 67–68
USO (United Service Organizations): 92

Victorio: 35
Villa, Pancho: 35
Villanueva, Juanita: *25*
Villanueva, N. Mex.: *153*; church: 148–49, 151

War Fund Campaign: 135
Wheelwright Museum of the American Indian:
    138
White, Fred: *169*
Women's National Aeronautic Association: 135
Women's rights: 49, 60
Women's suffrage: 49, 51
World War I, 1914-1918: 17, 68
World War II, 1914-1918: 92, 107, 111
World War II, 1941-1945: 69
Writers: 57

Zimmerman, James: 63

About the Author

Kathryn M. Córdova lives in El Prado, N. M., with her husband, Arsenio, with whom she raised three children. A retired public-school teacher, she continues instructing part-time in Taos and Los Alamos, at the University of New Mexico branches where she helped establish an associate program in communications and journalism. Active in community affairs, she also free-lances for newspapers and magazines, contributes to books, and edits the Taos County Historical Society publication.

Córdova has written four books, and has received several awards: Teacher of the Year, New Mexico Law-Related Education; Walk the Talk Education Advocacy Award, New Mexico Hispano Round Table; Governor's Award for Outstanding New Mexico Women; Communicator of Achievement, New Mexico Press Women; and Woman of the Year, American Biographical Institute. She has held several positions in the New Mexico Press Women and the National Federation of Press Women. She currently is working toward a doctorate in education.